The
Guattari Reader

"Readers who are unfamiliar with the work of Guattari will find that Genosko's collection contains fluid translations that are a point of departure for understanding schizo-analysis. *The Guattari Reader* contains many previously untranslated works and offers both supporters and detractors of the anti-psychiatry movement the much-needed occasion to (re)assess the scope and direction of Guattari's psycho-political trajectory."

Deborah Cook, University of Windsor

"Guattari's important place in contemporary social theory has yet to be fully acknowledged. Genosko's selection of significant writings from Guattari's eclectic range of interests – schizo-analysis, psychotherapy critique, queer theory, left politics, semiotics – provides an excellent introduction to Pierre-Félix Guattari's life and work. This book should be read by anyone searching for new critical perspectives on power, subjectivity, and social institutions."

Timothy W. Luke, Virginia Polytechnic Institute
and State University

D1526659

BLACKWELL READERS

In a number of disciplines, across a number of decades, and in a number of languages, writers and texts have emerged which require the attention of students and scholars around the world. United only by a concern with radical ideas, *Blackwell Readers* collect and introduce the works of preeminent theorists. Often translating works for the first time (Levinas, Irigaray, Lyotard, Blanchot, Kristeva) or presenting material previously inaccessible (CLR James, Fanon, Elias) each volume in the series introduces and represents work which is now fundamental to study in the humanities and social sciences. (See also *Blackwell Critical Readers*)

Already Published
The Lyotard Reader
Edited by Andrew Benjamin

The Irigaray Reader
Edited by Margaret Whitford

The Kristeva Reader
Edited by Toril Moi

The Levinas Reader
Edited by Sean Hand

The CLR James Reader
Edited by Anna Grimshaw

The Wittgenstein Reader
Edited by Sir Anthony Kenny

The Blanchot Reader
Edited by Michael Holland

The Guattari Reader
Edited by Gary Genosko

The Cavell Reader
Edited by Stephen Mulhall

Forthcoming:
The Benjamin Reader
Edited by Drew Milne

The Fanon Reader
Edited by Homi Bhabha

The Lukács Reader
Edited by Arpad Kadarkay

The Guattari Reader

Pierre-Félix Guattari

Edited by

Gary Genosko

BLACKWELL
Publishers

Copyright © Blackwell Publishers Ltd, 1996

First published 1996

2 4 6 8 10 9 7 5 3 1

Blackwell Publishers Ltd
108 Cowley Road
Oxford OX4 1JF
UK

Blackwell Publishers Inc
238 Main Street
Cambridge, Massachusetts 02142
USA

British Library Cataloguing in Publication Data

A CIP catalogue record for this book is available from the British Library.

Library of Congress Cataloging-in-Publication Data
Guattari, Félix.
[Selections. English. 1996]
A Guattari reader / Pierre-Félix Guattari; edited by Gary Genosko.
p. cm. – (Blackwell readers)
ISBN 0–631–19707–9. – ISBN 0–631–19708–7
1. Criticism – History – 20 century. 2. Criticism – Psychological aspects. 3. Psychoanalysis
and literature. I. Genosko, Gary. II. Title. III. Series.
PN94.G83 1996   95-42828
194 – dc20   CIP

Typeset in 10 on 12pt Plantin
by Pure Tech India Limited, Pondicherry, India
Printed in Great Britain by Hartnolls Limited, Bodmin, Cornwall
This book is printed on acid-free paper

Contents

Acknowledgments

I am indebted to the advice and service so generously offered by the following people: Brian Massumi, Jean-François Côté, Peter Van Wyck, John O'Neill, and Nicholas Zurbrugg. Paul Bouissac, Jacques Pain, Mike Gane, Michael Hardt, Judith Squires, Tim Murphy, and Charles Stivale pointed me in the right directions. Special notice needs to be given to the translators who worked with me on this project: Sophie Thomas, John Caruana, Lang Baker, Charles Dudas, Peter Trnka, Ben Freedman, Todd Dufresne, and Fadi Abou-Rihan. Samir Gandesha and Amresh Sinha provided moral support. In addition, many people facilitated the permissions process in the UK, France, and the US. Rachel Ariss provided warm support and incisive comments, and our daughter Hannah kept me on schedule.

This project was conceived during a very convivial lunch with my editor Simon Prosser in a café in New Cross near Goldsmiths' College in London where I was a Visiting Research Fellow in Sociology in 1993–94. Special thanks to Chris Jenks for his invitation, and to Les Back for his encouragement.

For permission to reprint and/or translate material, the author and the publisher are grateful to the following:

"The Divided Laing" ["Laing divisé", *QL* 132 (1972)], "Franco Basaglia: Guerrilla Psychiatrist" ["La contestation psychiatrique", *QL* 94 (1970)], "The Postmodern Impasse" ["L'impasse post-moderne", *QL* 456 (1986)] and "The Left as Processual Passion" ["La Gauche comme passion processuelle", *QL* 422 (194)] are all used with the kind permission of *La Quinzaine littéraire*.

"Mary Barnes' 'Trip' " ["Le voyage de Mary Barnes", copyright © *Le Nouvel Observateur* (28 mai 1973)]. Used with the kind permission of the publisher.

"The First Positive Task of Schizoanalysis", reprinted from G. Deleuze and F. Guattari, *Anti-Oedipus*, trans. by H. Lane, M. Seem, R. Hurley, translation copyright © 1977 by Viking Penguin, a division of Penguin Books USA Inc. Used with the kind permission of the publisher.

"Regimes, Pathways, Subjects", reprinted from Zone 6: *Incorporations*, eds. Jonathan Crary and Sanford Kwinter (New York: Zone Books, 1992). Copyright © Urzone, Inc. Used with the kind permission of the publisher.

"Postmodernism and Ethical Abdication", reprinted from *Photofile* 39 (July 1993). Used with the kind permission of Nicholas Zurbrugg.

"Institutional Practice and Politics" ["Entretiens 1985: Félix Guattari", from *Pratique de l'institutionnel et politique* (Vigneux: Editions Matrice, 1985). Used with the kind permission of the publisher.

"Semiological subjection, semiotic enslavement" ["Assujettissement sémiologique, asservissement sémiotique"], from F. Guattari, *L'Inconscient machinique* (Fontenay-Sous-Bois: Editions Recherches, 1979); "The Place of the Signifier in the Institution" ["La place du signifiant dans l'institution"] and "Three Billion Perverts on the Stand" ["Trois milliards de pervers à la barre"], from *La Révolution moléculaire* (Fontenay-sous-Bois: Editions Recherches, 1977)]. Copyright © Editions Recherches. Used with the kind permission of the publisher.

"Ritornellos and Existential Affects", reprinted from *Discourse* 12.2 (1990). Used with the kind permission of the publisher.

"Subjectivities, for better or for worse" ["*Subjectivités, pour le meilleur et pour le pire*"], *Chimères* 8 (1990)]. Used with the kind permission of the publisher.

"A Liberation of Desire: An Interview [by George Stambolian]", reprinted from *Homosexualities and French Literature: Cultural Contexts / Critical Texts*, eds. G. Stambolian and E. Marks. Copyright © 1979 by Cornell University Press. Used with the kind permission of the publisher.

"Towards a New Perspective on Identity: An Interview with Félix Guattari", reprinted from *Angelaki* 1/1 (Sept. 1993). Used with the kind permission of the publisher.

"Capitalistic Systems, Structures and Processes", by F. Guattari and Eric Alliez, reprinted from *Molecular Revolution* trans. Brian Darling (Penguin Books Ltd., 1984), translation copyright © Brian Darling, 1984. Used with the kind permission of the publisher.

"Communist Propositions", reprinted from *Communists Like Us*, by F. Guattari and Antonio Negri, trans. Michael Ryan (New York: Semiotext(e), 1990). Translation copyright © 1990 Semiotext(e). Used with the kind permission of the publisher.

"Remaking Social Practices" ["Pour une refondation des pratiques sociales"], *Le Monde diplomatique* (Octobre 1992). Used with the kind permission of the publisher.

"The Four Truths of Psychiatry" ["Les quatre vérités de la psychiatrie"] and "Psychoanalysis Should Get a Grip on Life" ["La psychanalyse doit être en prise directe avec la vie"] and "The Microphysics of Power and Microphysics of Desire" ["Microphysique des pouvoirs et micropolitiques des désirs", from F. Guattari, *Les Années d'hiver* 1980–1985 (Paris: copyright © Bernard Barrault, 1986).

"The Transference" ["Le transfert"], from F. Guattari, *psychanalyse et transversalité* (Paris: copyright © François Maspero, 1972).

"Genet Regained", trans. Brian Massumi, reprinted from *Journal: A Contemporary Arts Magazine* 47/5 (1987).

Every effort has been made to obtain the necessary permissions with reference to material under copyright. Should there be, however, any omissions in this respect, we apologize and will be pleased to make the appropriate acknowledgments.

Introduction

En bref, toujours et plus que jamais: la révolution moléculaire. [In short, always and more than ever: the molecular revolution.] Félix Guattari, 'La révolution moléculaire', *Le Monde* (7 déc. 1990): 2.

All *Readers* tell the story of their editors' reading and *The Guattari Reader* is no exception. The articles and interviews in this volume are assembled around five themes: "The Vicissitudes of Therapy", "From Schizo Bypasses to Postmodern Impasses"; "Discursive Interlude" [a long interview on a variety of topics]; "Polysemiosis"; "Queer/Subjectivities", and "Red and Green Micropolitical Ecologies". In other words, this *Reader* addresses the issues of anti-psychiatry and anti-psychoanalysis; the schizo process and the promise of a post-media era set against the dead end of postmodern theory; a wild and woolly polysemiotics based on creative extrapolations from the glossematics of Louis Hjelmslev and the semiotics of C.S. Peirce; the queering – that is, the polyphonic potentialization – of subjectivity; a theory of capitalism and how, and why, to resist it. These do not by any means cover the entire field of Guattari's work, nor are the individual pieces meant to neatly tie up the five arrangements. None of the arrangements are solid blocks; they are all porous, internally diverse, and crossed by multiple thematics.

We are on the verge of a long-delayed and for some, long-awaited, explosion of interest in and publishing – in English, at least – on Guattari as his work emerges from the shadow of Gilles Deleuze *The Guattari Reader* will find itself in good company. Still, how many of you have been to a Deleuze and Guattari conference and not heard more than a few words on Guattari? Too many? Yet I have not attempted to separate Guattari from his co-authors. Such an attempt would be completely wrongheaded in Guattari's own terms. Still, I am sorely tempted – merely as a provocation – to frame the problem sociologically in terms of a generational (perhaps even a departmental) divide among readers, but this, too, would distort the important lessons Deleuze *and* Guattari have taught about the conjunction – among others – between their names. I have included Guattari and Deleuze and Alliez and Negri . . . because it was not by accident that they all ended up writing together and between one another.

I will not enter here into a detailed justification of my selections. There is too much to say about them, none of which could satisfy all of the possible objections to them. Which is not to say that I'm not inviting second guesses. I did, however, want to avoid an imbalance between material already available in English and previously untranslated material (the situation is always, in this regard, fluid; a few retranslations of material are included), as well as using both short and long pieces, and have included journalistic articles as punctuation for the longer technical bits. I also wanted to make use of as many statements of position as muddy explorations (although, personally, I enjoy wading through the latter).

Instead, in this introduction I want to provide some background and critical material drawn from a variety of sources which support the themes that run through this *Reader*, without, I hope strangling any of the sections, and choking out the reader's own de-and reterritorializations. The first two introductory essays situate Guattari in terms of significant events, places, and debates in the European anti-psychiatry movement. The key concept under discussion is the 'sector', and the key site is La Borde clinic. The third section is organized around the concept of the therapeutic bestiary, and uses the 'animal' as a device for revealing tendencies in Freudian analysis against which Guattari theorized and also inherited and adapted to his own needs. Guattari, too, has a bestiary. The goal of the section on schizoanalysis is to explicate elements central to Guattari's "pragmatics of the unconscious" and provide an example of how a difficult concept such as the machine may be put to work on a text from pop culture. The final introductory section is devoted to Guattari's theory of Integrated World Capitalism and the emergence of his alternative brands of communistic and ecosophical thinking. The introduction ends by taking note of some of the particular political projects in which Guattari was involved before his death on August 29, 1992. Choose, then, as you like, and make connections as your reading progresses; treat this *Reader* like a rhizome. Or make a diagram. There is no need to match the following introductory sections to particular arrangements of material. This is supposed to be a user-friendly collection rather than a stodgy manual!

1 Anti-Psychiatry and the Sector

Throughout its various manifestations in literature, media, and even cinema, the anti-psychiatry movement of the early 1970s discovered the close relationship between psychiatric and other forms of repression. In Guattari's view this decisive discovery led to a variety of developments in different European countries, some examples of which are reviewed in his essay, cobbled together from previously published short articles, "Alternative à la psychiatrie".[1] For example, Le Réseau was established in Brussels in 1975. The Belgian project centered on developing an "alternative to the sector", and many radical psychiatrists from France, Italy, and elsewhere contributed to a colloquium held in January of that year. This colloquium blossomed into the European Network for Alternatives to Psychiatry. The phenomenon of *sectorisation* refers to psychiatric facilities outside hospitals (including day hospitals, dispensaries, home visits, drug rehab programs, etc.) which, in France, are divided into sectors or districts serving the mental health needs of as many as 60–70,000 people.[2] The sector, let us say, brought psychiatry to the "community". The figure of 70,000 (mentioned by Guattari, among many others) acquired a life of its own and a relevance far beyond its initial importance. This was considered to be the smallest district and thus was not, in relation to super-sectors of over 200,000 inhabitants, normative. But unfortunately it became so. The rigid formula of three beds per thousand, based on the ideal figure of 70,000 people per sector, very quickly bore no relation to the reality for many doctors in the fast-growing surburban satellite cities around Paris.

The question of the sector had an enormous impact on French, and European, mainstream and radical psychiatry. For what was at issue was nothing less than whether the *hors l'hôpital* could succeed in something other than reproducing the psychiatry *dans l'hôpital*. *Sectorisation* became the official doctrine of the French Ministry of Health in 1960, the year the famous Circulaire du 15 mars was issued by Ministère Aujaleu, long-serving Directeur général de la santé (1956–64), a military doctor and close ally of De Gaulle. A community mental health pilot project was launched in the XIIIth *arrondissement* of Paris. It was only after the events of May 1968 and in the early 1970s, that this experiment in *sectorisation* became the model for actual changes in the delivery of a national mental health care system. But the XIIIth, too, acquired a mythic dimension, despite the questions raised about whether it was transposable to other fully socialized sectors since it was, among other things, semi-private, without a hospital infrastructure, or an asylum. It needs to be kept in mind that *sectorisation* had a silent period from 1964 to 68 after Aujaleu was replaced.

Initially, the "policy of the sector" was considered by many activists to be socially progressive, given the need to reform the French asylum system. But by the time the policy was put into place, it was considered to be reactionary.[3] Members of Le Réseau with personal experience of this policy, and whose political views at first allowed them to cooperate with it in good will, "came to realize", as Guattari put it, "that no fundamental problem will be solved in this domain as long as we do not have the goal of what they call a *depsychiatrization of madness*".[4] This understanding of the condition of the psychiatrized is reached through the recognition that psychiatric repression functions by other means in the absence of hospitals: to use Guattari's imagery, a neuroleptic or chemical straightjacket replaces a physical straightjacket. In developing his perspective on "popular alternatives to psychiatry", Guattari emphasized that mental illness was irreducible to social alienation and the critique of capitalism. As Guattari explains, it is not so much a matter of "politicizing madness" as of opening the eyes of traditional political organizations to the hitherto misunderstood relationships between a series of problems concerning the condition of the mentally ill, immigrants, women, children, etc. Indeed, Guattari's own practice aimed at overcoming the reduction to social alienation, which denies and suppresses the specificity of madness, and evading the trap of familialism, which in its turn denies, by excluding, extra-familial or social factors.

Although Guattari came to criticize the elitist and largely theoretical aspects of what is called the second wave of anti-psychiatry – to which I will return momentarily – for him it was still in many ways superior to the first phase of the movement. In the first phase, doctors such as Thomas Szasz maintained, in his influential *The Myth of Mental Illness*,[5] that mental illness was a *myth* that needed to be debunked so that a non-medical model of social dis-ease, existential and ethical problems of living (interpersonal and moral conflicts), could emerge and provide for a radical critique and renewed understanding of existing practices. Szasz would later, in another *myth* book, this time *The Myth of Psychotherapy*,[6] suggest that psychotherapy be renamed *iatrologic*, belonging to rhetoric and logic, as an art of healing souls without medical, professional, and institutional pretensions. His paradigm was hysteria – a diagnosis he demythologized by using a game-conflict model to reveal that it was a longstanding term of evasion referring to a condition arising from a person's inability to forget old rules and relinquish playing old games, often marked by the refusal to play any games at all. By the same token, transference-neurosis arose from the projection of old goals on new games; likewise, disappointment-reactions of varying degrees resulted from the recognition that there were no transcendentally valid games. Guattari would not, however, play Szasz's game of social alienation.

Despite his differences with Franco Basaglia, the Italian anti-psychiatrist of the second wave, Guattari claimed that Basaglia's work challenged both anti-psychiatric elitism, marginality, and did not flirt with the "convenient myth" hypothesis. In Guattari's review of Basaglia's

L'institution en négation,[7] he defends Basaglia's critical approach to the ideas of British reformers such as Maxwell Jones and applauds his ability to refuse the reformist politics of the sector. Basaglia's group *Psichiatria Democratica* was a mental health employees' association and lobby group whose task was to influence change in psychiatric practices and to politically educate its members on matters such as refusing to become "functionaries of consent", refusing to use "medical alibis", while admitting the reality of psychiatric problems, learning to deal with psychopathological problems related to conditions at work, at home, in the city, in the university, etc.

The documentary film *Fous à délier* was created by the group at the hospital in Parma gathered around Mario Tomasini (Marco Bellochio, Sylvano Agnosti, Sandro Petraglia, Stefano Rulli). This film was, for Guattari, "the illustration of the politics adopted by the mental health workers in Italy united around Basaglia, Giovanni Jervis and the militants of the movement Psichiatria Democratica".[8] In *Fous à délier*, psychiatric survivors face the camera and recount their experiences. But it is not only a record of ordeals. Some of the most poignant stories, Guattari notes, are those told by children who were "caught in the machinery of medico-pedagogical sectorization"; the many women who relate the horrors of their lives in the hospital retain their dignity and display resilience in dealing with the daily challenges and fears of life outside the hospital. To these examples are added the testimonies of labor activists who recount their efforts at integrating so-called "profoundly mentally deficient" persons into the workplace, transforming themselves, their new comrades, and the atmosphere on the shop floor, in the process.

Guattari's praise for this film was high indeed. He wrote: "In my view this film does not call for debate: it closes it. The time has come to close the files, the files of the psychiatric hospital – archaic or modernist versions –, the files of sectorization, those of medico-pedagogical institutions, those of psychoanalysis, etc. What is on the agenda is no longer grand theoretical demonstrations, vehement denunciations and programs of all kinds, but genuine *passages à l'acte* (actings out)".[9] What is called for, then, is the genuine revelation of hithero suppressed (and even repressed) experiences and events in the psycho-pharmaceutical complex, with political militantism focusing on everyday life and the transformation of public opinion, rather than on the creation of utopian communities with few social effects. Forget guruism, *le lacanism*, psychoanalytical silence, and all miniaturizations of repression, all shrinking. But don't forget them altogether since the confessions of a star of madness like Mary Barnes can reveal the inner-workings – pressures, contradictions, absurdities, failures, successes – of English anti-psychiatric projects such as Kingsley Hall.[10] Men and women in documentary films such as *Fous à délier* do not always produce truths, Guattari admits, even if, ultimately, everything concerning the psychiatric hospital must be, with a view to both balance and urgency, brought into direct contact with the "minimum good sense of people directly concerned" such as those who found their voices in the film and those who watched it. Roger Gentis, too, praised *Fous à délier* and the work of Psichiatria Democratica, but wondered whether it was a difference in the political situation in Italy that made this progressive change possible. To this question he answered no: provincial communist administrations were not "naturally open and receptive" to problems and solutions [pro]posed by anti-psychiatric activists.[11] For his part, Guattari believed (circa 1970) that national conditions needed to be taken into account since in Italy "the state of the hospitals and the legislation is undoubtedly one of the most archaic in Europe".[12] Circa 1989, Guattari would again turn to the Italian example, this time pointing to the work of Franco Rotelli in the psychiatric hospital in Trieste. Rotelli's group transformed the hospital into an international cultural centre whose political goal was the transformation of traditional psychiatry and other psychiatric hospitals in Italy.[13]

More recently, Guattari praised the revelatory aesthetic of *film-verité* in the cause of making visible the interfaces between patient-doctor-institution in Raymond Depardon's film *Urgences*.[14] The twenty-odd sequences in the documentary, shot at the psychiatric *service des urgences* of the Hôtel-Dieu in Paris, powerfully reveal that "it is our own subjectivity which finds itself encircled in this nightmarish carousel" of alcoholics, depressives, compulsives, etc. While *film-verité* can access the "interiority of madness and dereliction", Guattari emphasized that "the spectacle of all these existential ruptures work directly upon our own lines of fragility". Depardon's film brings the viewer into contact with a phenomenon to which one is close, even if one is content to treat this proximity as a sufficient distance.

In terms of institutional politics, Guattari stated that the staff psychiatrists in general "are totally deprived of the means of organizing a humane reception worthy of the name". Whether or not there is a demand for a humane reception is a question that they need to ask themselves. Guattari was, however, unequivocal: a reception facility must distinguish between new arrivals whose stays will be long and who therefore may be admitted in a relaxed manner, and those new arrivals who will have much shorter stays. Having made this distinction, however, Guattari maintained that with regard to the latter: "The expeditious interviews dispensed one after another by the psychiatrists would not even suffice in such cases, especially if the people who turned up are to remain there for only a few hours".[15] Since this problem is well known to specialists in institutional therapy, Guattari could ask: "Why, then, is it there today in the heart of Paris?"

If, on the one hand, English anti-psychiatry distinguished itself brilliantly on the theoretical level but held confused political goals, then, on the other hand, in Germany the SPK (Sozialistiches Patientenkollectiv), despite being burdened with an "ossified Hegelianism", created an "unambiguous political cleavage".[16] For Guattari, the "affaire de Heidelberg" of 1971 marked "the first time psychiatric combat was taken to the street, to the quarter, to the entire city. Like the 22nd of March at Nanterre, the SPK was mobilized around a real struggle. . . ."[17]

In the Polyclinic at the University of Heidelberg, a group of forty patients and their doctor (Hubert) developed a critique of the institution in which psychiatry was shown to function as an instrument of repression. The director of the clinic considered this group to be "a collective of hate and aggression". Guattari remarks that what began as a "little intra-hospital experiment became a mass struggle", largely in virtue of the fact that as institutional opposition to the collective increased, so did state resistance. Guattari relates that when administrative and legal means failed to dissolve the group, a vote was taken behind closed doors in the University Senate mandating a public show of force. Using an unrelated event in suburban Heidelberg involving an exchange of gunfire as an excuse, 300 riot cops, helicopters, and special brigades were mobilized with the goal of crushing the SPK. Patients and doctors were arrested, Dr. Huber's children were kidnapped, and many of the persons arrested were drugged into submission in order to make it appear that they were cooperating with the invading force. Dr. Huber and his wife languished in prison for years on trumped-up charges that, first of all, they themselves were insane, and second, that they were terrorists. No end of legal irregularities and police dirty tricks surrounded the case. It needs to be kept in mind that on several occasions in the 1970s Guattari, too, was harassed by the French police who searched his apartment in Paris and La Borde on the trail of, as they say, "suspected" militants and "pornographic" publications. In Chapter 5, "Queer/Subjectivities", the first entry "Three Billion Perverts On The Stand" is the collection of notes Guattari used in his legal defense against the charge of "affronting public decency" brought about by the publication of an issue on homosexuality of the journal he edited, *Recherches*.

Far beyond reformist politics of all sorts, the example of the SPK posed for Guattari a new kind of practice in which the patients themselves, having repudiated reformism and the seductions of modernization, established an inextricable link between political struggle and mental illness, making madness the concern of everyone. And they did this despite the reticence of the left to enter into new kinds of alliances with groups that normally did not march through the streets, attend meetings, and tow the party line. Guattari could thus state: "To put it in a somewhat excessive manner, the SPK is in a way the equivalent of the Commune de Paris on the level of proletarian struggles".[18] The German example also needs to be contrasted with Basaglia's experiments in Gorizia. The latter ended, Guattari thinks, not by falling into theoretical dogmatism, but by turning the "rightfully violent" negation of repressive institutions into institutional change based upon social alienation rather than on an understanding of the "unconscious signifying assemblage [where] madness dwells, [and] which predetermines the structural field in which political options, drives, and revolutionary inhibitions are deployed, beside and beyond social and economic determinisms".[19]

Turning briefly, then, to Spain circa 1975 and the activities of the Psychiatrists Against Francoism of the Hospital of Conxo, in Saint-Jacques-de-Compostelle, in Galicia, Guattari describes some effects of the process of modernization (loss of beds, shrinking of the hospitalized population, deterioration of the staff–patient ratio, the recruitment of young doctors – at first for full-time positions but, later, in a standard union- and unity-busting measure, reducing these to part-time). The hospital was, however, transformed through the implementation of an open door policy, patient self-determination, meetings between staff and patients, and community contact. These changes were met with a "violent fascist reaction" in which, ultimately, the government installed a new director and used the occasion of the national strike of the MIR (Les Médecins Internes Résidents) to gut the staff and replace them with their own appointees.

This anti-psychiatric episode was inseparable, Guattari believed, from the anti-fascist struggle in Galicia against the Franco government's non-recognition of Galician cultural and political heritage and aspirations. "Under these conditions", Guattari wrote, "it is impossible to envisage a partial amelioration of the fate of the psychiatric inmates at the hospital without gradually raising all the other problems of the emancipation of the Galician people."[20] The issues raised by modernization point in several directions in this case: the loss of traditional rural community organizations dealing with the mentally ill, coupled with the will to improve the conditions of the hospitalized, and give staff better salaries. Guattari concludes that the lesson of the Galician response to modernization is that the anti-psychiatric struggle must hold onto the goal of separating madness from its administration and evaluation by specialists and groups of experts.

II La Borde

Before co-founding La Borde with Guattari, the psychiatrist Jean Oury practised at the clinics of St. Alban (1947–49) and Saumery (1949–53).

For him "Saumery represented a kind of concrete initiation period into the technical and medical problems posed by psychopathology, but equally an initiation into a collective life with all its misadventures".[21] Guattari, Oury recalls, visited him for long periods at Saumery. Saumery was also Guattari's initiation into psychiatry. Oury convinced him to abandon his study of pharmacy for a politically committed psychiatry.[22] While at St. Alban, Oury met François Tosquelles, whose criticisms of psychiatry, psychoanalysis, and phenomenology, which he developed during his wartime psychiatric work in Catalonia, would have a decisive influence on St. Alban, and later, on La Borde.

Oury downplays any suggestion that a group at Saumery made a "bid for power" by leaving the clinic in order to found La Borde. Rather, the case was less dramatic. Saumery was a small clinic that had already expanded from 12 to 50 beds. The absence of a psychiatric hospital in the department of Loir-et-Cher presented the opportunity to build something original from the ground up.

Jean-Claude Pollack, co-author with Danièle Sabourin of *La Borde ou le droit à la folie*, for which Guattari wrote the introduction "La Borde, un lieu-dit", remarks of the Lacanian beginnings of the clinic: "When I first arrived at La Borde one didn't have the right to speak if one had not gone over Lacan with a fine tooth comb."[23] Despite the fact that Guattari was analyzed by Lacan and neither abandoned his seminar nor renounced l'Ecole freudienne – well, except to the extent that he came to see Lacan's brand of structuralized psychoanalysis as as religion devoted to the cultivation and initiation of followers – the "duo of Oury-Guattari" never required, we are told, the same degree of blind followership. Not everyone shares this opinion. Lacan's breakway school had many connections with the GTPSI (Groupe de travail de psychothérapie institutionnelle), founded at St. Alban in 1960, and a fixture at La Borde. Guattari mentions in passing the "Caro affair" in his review of several books by R. D. Laing in "Laing divisé."[24] He keeps his distance from this affair by using it as an example of the French public's sensitivity to the problems of madness after the events of 1968, and as an instance of the need to scrutinize every event which considers itself to be in some way exemplary, an operation which he does not perform. Guy Caro was the medical director of the Clinique Burloud in Rennes. In September 1971, he was fired from his post after initiating liberal reforms that had the support of the community, the patients (primarily students) and staff. Sherry Turkle implicates Guattari in the "Lacanian anti-psychiatric clique" whose denigration of Caro's reforms, on the grounds that they were under-theorized and insufficiently politicized, led to his firing. She likens the weekend seminars at La Borde (Saturday at 6 p.m.) to Lacan's Wednesday seminars in Paris as places for star-gazing. She quotes Robert

Castel's sarcastic remarks to the effect that: "Poor Dr. Caro who is only a progressive psychiatrist and a political militant from the provinces and who had frequented neither Lacan's Wednesdays nor Cour-Cheverny weekends."[25] Of course, for every bone Turkle has to pick with the dynamic duo of Oury-Guattari and their followers, there is a positive counterexample.

For his part, Oury was, according to Pollack, "often perceived [by l'Ecole freudienne] as an irregular of a dangerous heterodoxy". Even so, Pollack thinks that Oury's seminar at La Borde was "probably the most often followed exegesis, and the most 'pedagogic' of the work on Lacan."[26] Guattari considered Pollack and Sabourin's book to be much more than a work *on* La Borde: it was written *from* La Borde and *belonged* there.[27] La Borde was a "black hole: the result of a semiotic collapse which rises again, you don't know when! Sometimes fluxes of sign-particles are released, some of which settle in the form of texts, like this one".[28]

It was the treatment of psychotics that set La Borde apart from most public hospitals in France; it was also at first a private clinic, until *la sécurité sociale* stepped in. Guattari and Oury wrote La Borde's constitution called "Constitution de l'An 1" the year the clinic opened in 1953. While Guattari was there at the beginning, his involvement increased after 1955. The myth of La Borde was propagated, Oury laments, not by those who worked there, but by the intellectuals who for a time spent their winter vacations there, at the place – a chateau, after all – that became known as the "St. Trop de la Sologne!". For Oury, there were too many people full of their own degrees visiting the hospital in order to admire the spectacle of *les Labordiens*; worst of all, these intellectual hordes were impossible to "civilize".[29] It seemed that one of the elementary accomplishments of the first wave of psychiatric reform – that physicians speak to their patients – had been forgotten. The mythmaking continues unabated, even by those who have worked there for decades, like Marie Depussé: "the mad cried when Oury told them of Félix's death, the following day in the great hall. 'Thank you for telling us in this way,' they responded. In exchange, despite a great deal of wandering during the night, for lack of sleep, they were polite, tender, making no noise".[30] It was the private status of La Borde, Oury laments, that helped to propagate its mysteries and myths. While he regrets that it was not a public institution, primarily for economic reasons (an opinion that Guattari did not share), he also wants to discount the myth that its private status gave the doctors the freedom to experiment in ways that would not have been permitted in a hospital setting.[31] The mythic dimension of St. Alban is much the same. During the Second World War, with Paris occupied, the director Lucien Bonnafé would provide "asylum" for the poet Paul Eluard in the fall of 1943; much has been written about this episode.[32] Still, this much of the myth is true: the rescue of Tosquelles from a French refugee camp, after the latter had fled the war in Spain, and passed through the Pyrénées on foot. First Eluard, then, the Dadaist Tzara, the "red psychiatrist" Tosquelles, the arrival of the new director Bonnafé, refugees of all sorts, resistance fighters, a hiding place for many doctors, all nestled away at a 1,000 metres altitude deep in Lozère.[33]

In general, the politics of the sector turned the attention of psychiatrists away from the hospital and its structures into the community. But the community at issue was difficult to define, for it was not only geographic and demographic in nature, but had juridical, economic, theoretical, sociological, and organizational features and consequences. The extra-hospital focus of the sector served the interests of a variant of anti-psychiatry as a geo-psychiatry of an active, peripetatic sectorial type. As Bonnafé and Tosquelles explain, *géo-psychiatrie* is a "species of migrant work", of the sort that was common at St. Alban with its outside consultations, medico-pedagogical relations, and even its intra-hospital therapeutic groups; that is, with its deterritorializations.[34] Psychiatry is embedded in geography, *le cru*. Local human geography is the milieu of *géo-psychiatrie*. And to the extent that it may be called geophilosophical, this psychiatry "affirms the power of a milieu".[35]

As recently as June 1992, two months before his death, Guattari was still referring to the lessons in human, particularly, workers' "understanding of human relations" in the film *Fous à délier*. Although the "heroic epoque" of anti-psychiatry may have ended, Guattari did not refer to such examples with cynicism, but in the context of his theorization of the formation of new alliances between the worker's movement, feminist and ecological movements. The formation of a "new progressive axis" must, Guattari believed, be substituted for the old left-right split.[36]

The thinkers of the second wave of anti-psychiatry – that infelicitous label coined by David Cooper – have mostly passed away: Laing, Cooper, Basaglia; Guattari and, most recently, Tosquelles. Gentis is still writing, and Oury remains at La Borde. Szasz, from the first wave, soldiers on. Developments in the delivery of mental health services during the 1980s in France did not encourage Guattari. Although he did not predict the privatization of psychiatry, he found a sort of "collusion between a certain corporatism (psychiatrists, health care groups) and the cumbersome state structures which administer French psychiatry". With little room for social innovation and collective experimentation to provide examples, Guattari witnessed a tendency towards a "generalized colourlessness".[37] Even the most "lively and interesting" experiments of the sector cannot correct the "institutional conditions that make *life*, social life, impossible." For Guattari, "the true scandal is the existence of

incarcerative structures which literally exterminate the mentally ill and
the personnel who work there, in the place of creating living systems."[38]

III A Therapeutic Bestiary

Of the many sophisticated critical insights into psychoanalysis made by
Guattari in his own writings as well as in his collaborations with Deleuze,
the idea of becoming-animal presents a particularly rewarding way into
the concept of the assemblage and how one connects with it through
unnatural participation.

Does psychoanalysis have a zoological vision? In a brilliant essay written with Deleuze, "1914: One Or Several Wolves?" in *A Thousand
Plateaus*, Guattari answers in the negative and shifts his loyalty behind
the Wolf-Man who, it is said, took revenge upon Freud in a letter to
Muriel Gardiner in 1945, by pointing out Herr Doktor's irreversible
blindness to animals.[39] Deleuze and Guattari fail to mention that the
letter in question was directed at Gardiner's daughter, whose interest in
animals the Wolf-Man wanted to encourage, perhaps even cultivate:
"Nothing . . . can be of greater value to a young person than a love of
nature and understanding of natural science, particularly of animals".
Deleuze and Guattari end their essay on this note, but omit the tail end
of the quote: "Animals played a large part in my childhood also. In my
case they were wolves."[40] Despite what Freud thought, I know a few
things about animals, the Wolf-Man seems to be saying. In "One Or
Several Wolves?" the Wolf-Man gets off the couch and runs with his
pack. The only kind of animals that psychoanalysis understands are
"individuated animals, family pets, sentimental, Oedpial animals each
with its own petty history, 'my' cat, 'my' dog."[41] Freud would not allow
his patient to become wolf, to join the pack with which he was already in
communication. In becoming-animal one neither imagines taking on the
features of a given creature nor actually becomes one. Instead, and thus
becoming is neither totemic nor biological (hence, unnatural), one connects up with some elements of a wolf, or something closely related, to
compose a molecular wolf, perhaps even by bumping against your friends
as you run for together for the bus. Becoming is always molecular.
Assemblages are composed, and decomposed, and recomposed without
a molar unity informing them.[42] This is what Freud abandoned for the
sake of his fable of phobic animals, thus blinkering his zoological vision.
And such a vision for Deleuze and Guattari enables one to see that "every
animal is fundamentally a band, a pack".[43] Psychoanalysis couldn't see
that what was real was the becoming, because it always pointed elsewhere.

There are many reasons for this restricted field of vision.[44] Until Anna's dog entered the scene circa 1925, Freud had little or no close contact with animals. Indeed, the socio-semiotic significance of Anna's German shepherd named Wolfi was never acknowledged by Freud; that is, it came to be one of the many visible vehicles of the persecution of Jews and a potent sign of National Socialism. Martha Freud knew better. The status of dogs in the culture of the *shetl* also pointed in the direction of the brutish guard dog patrolling its borders. Strangely enough, Freud's dogs would patrol his office. Freud's emotional investment in his dogs overrode these cultural codes as well as his wife's annoyance at his habit of feeding Wolfi and his succession of chows from the table.[45] Freud's vision was further limited by his sociocultural milieu: horses, dogs, cats, certain birds (pigeons), even the animals of the medical establishment, would have been commonplace. Freud was familiar with animal hallucinations and a small selection of domesticates, pets and otherwise. Freud may even have learned a few lessons about animals from the "sexual research" carried out at the zoo at Schönbrunn on the outskirts of Vienna by his young patient Little Hans. Most important, however, was Freud's love of dogs. Elsewhere I have shown that the psychoanalytic bestiary is rife with dogs.[46] Suffice to say that it is no mere rhetorical taunt to say that every time Freud heard wolf he thought dog. The "analyst's bow-wow" circulated around Freud's theory, practice, and personal relations.

As far as large animals and male children are concerned, phobic animals, thought Freud, are substitutes for the father. Sandor Ferenczi's young patient Little Arpad, as well as Little Hans, were trapped in Freud's bestiary by the single apologue under which their becomings-animal were subsumed. Chickens, horses, even wolves: it doesn't matter, it's really daddy. There is more. As Deleuze and Guattari show, Freud was quite incapable of seeing wolves. They were quickly transformed into sheep dogs or goats. Moreover, Freud would not let the Wolf-Man look into the riveting gazes of his dream wolves. He preferred the more reassuring reversal that they were looked at as if they were unseeing objects for our inspection, tortured zoo animals in a bad dream of the domination of the wild. Freud didn't even admit that the Wolf-Man had the same name as his daughter's dog!

Deleuze and Guattari do not substitute something for Freud's substitution. Daddy is not replaced by a molecular assemblage. A molar Daddy could deterritorialize himself and take a place on the body-without-organs of the pack. But he will take a different position with new and varying interrelations with other changing elements every time he joins an organless body in composition. As Deleuze and Guattari specify, multiplicity "was created precisely in order to escape the abstract

opposition between the multiple and the one . . . ."[47] In the history of
philosophy one finds many different kinds of multiplicities: some macro-,
some micro-. Opposition, interpenetration, overlapping, provocative extensions, mutually modifying disturbances: there is no dualism at work
here! Just "multiplicities of mulitiplicites forming a single *assemblage*,
operating in the same *assemblage*"[48] in which we are caught up at one time
or another. Or so they say, despite the occasional slip back – which they
don't deny – into hierarchized abstract distinctions favoring the *wild*
multiplicity over the *domesticated* individual. Christopher L. Miller has
catalogued an impressive array of elements foreign to Deleuze and Guattari's project; there are sanitizations for the sake of their rhizomorphic
and nomadic "happy talk", a few corpses stuffed into the footnotes, too
strong a claim of immunity from factual error, exoticism, uncritical
citations, stereotypes, elements of colonization (rhizome in its botanical
sense).[49]

If Freud tried to reduce the Wolf-Man's pack to his father, and Deleuze and Guattari, in spite of themselves, privilege the wild pack-multi-
plicity, we should pay special attention to those packs trained to hunt
together (wolfhounds), not so much to level the dualism, but to provide
an occasion for the combination of wild and domesticated packs. The
Wolf-Man, it needs to be recognized, had a long standing interest in
wolves because of his experiences on his father's estate in White Russia.
This was wolf country. Wolf-hunts were commonplace.[50] This memory
is both evidence of the Wolf-Man's experience of the pack, and Freud's
lack of interest in his patient's origins, but also an instance of the meeting
of wild and domesticated packs (wolfhounds preparing for the wolf
hunt). Sheep dogs, it might be mentioned, often have to fight off wolves
when flock-and pack-multiplicities collide. In addition, Deleuze and
Guattari set up a straw-dog as a sign of all of Freud's canine bestiary (his
chows and pekinese, Anna's German Shepherd, Marie Bonaparte's
chows, Dorothy Burlingham's dogs, etc.), further debasing the domesticated side of the dualism. Surely they would appreciate a mixed pack, a
loose assemblage of wolves banished from their packs, lone hunters and
solitary pairs becoming pack-like during the mating season, de-domesti-
cated "feral" dogs, lost bow-wows, wolves, diamond dogs, Kristevan
packs, and the rest.

Every therapeutics has its bestiary. These considerations on becoming-
animal make it abundantly clear that the psychoanalytic bestiary is one of
the critical objects of schizoanalysis. Schizoanalysis does not simply
throw open the cages of the psychoanalytic zoo! The thematic of the
bestiary is a way into the schizoanalytic project. Consider a classic like
Guattari's essay "Transversalité". Transversality does nothing less than
schizophrenize the transference. The transference is the libidinal tie

between the analyst and the analysand that is subject to analysis. At first Freud thought it could be enlisted as a therapeutic ally, but later realized it could be a form of resistance, a powerfully seductive, even dangerous, bond. The transference, then, must be dismantled piece by piece and completely resolved in order for an analysis to be considered successful. With Guattari, the transference becomes vehicular, it gets away from the analyst and analysand into group relations. Transference is no longer a dual relation; it is at least triangular, but that isn't saying much. The analyst is no longer the mirror; rather, it's the group. This places the group in the position of the analyst, thus making it an *analyzer*.

Transversality is the transference become vehicular. Even so, Guattari specifies that among the power relations between the groups in a typical psychiatric hospital – i.e., between nurses and patients and doctors – the transference may be "fixed . . . obligatory, predetermined, 'territorialized' on a role, a certain stereotype"[51] For Guattari, this is "a form of the interiorization of bourgeois repression by the repetitive, archaic and artificial resurgence of the phenomena of caste, with their procession of fascinating and reactionary group phantasms".[52] Just as the transference is the cornerstone of psychoanalysis, transversality in the group – rather than the more ambiguous institutional transference, Guattari notes – is the object of institutional analysis. And institutional analysis eventually becomes, under the pressure to avoid its normalizations and professionalization as a therapy, schizoanalysis. Guattari writes: "Imagine a fenced field in which there are horses wearing adjustable blinkers, and let's say that the 'coefficient of transversality' will be precisely the adjustment of the blinkers. If the horses are completely blind, a certain kind of traumatic encounter will be produced. As soon as the blinkers are opened, one can imagine that they will move about in a more harmonious way. Let's try to represent the manner in which people comport themselves in relation to one another from the affective point of view".[53] Guattari then jumps from horses to porcupines: "According to Schopenhauer's famous parable of the freezing porcupines, nobody can stand being too close to one's fellows". Guattari slips back into the psychoanalytic bestiary, echoing Freud's use of the same idea in his "Group Psychology". The group is characterized, Freud says, by its libidinal ties. Both Guattari and Freud quote Schopenhauer:

> One cold winter's day, a company of porcupines huddled together to protect themselves against the cold by means of one another's warmth. But they were pricked by each other's quills, and it was not long before they drew apart again. The persistent cold drew them back together, but once again they felt the painful pricks. They alternately drew together and apart for some time until they

discovered an acceptable distance at which they would be free of both evils.[54]

Presumably, the degree of blindness (the coefficient of transversality) of the horses is related to the degree of blindness of the persons in the hospital; or, Freud's blinkers, like those of the horses, need to be adjusted. Official adjustments by the trainer, or by the hospital bureaucracy, come from on high, while pressure from below, from the horses and the patients, often have little effect in traditional settings. Transversality is opposed to and attempts to overcome vertical hierarchies and horizontal intra-ward relations (the hospital is one fence, the ward another) by maximizing (that is, bringing to light through analysis the latent coefficients of transversality in the group, its desires) inter-level communication, and enabling meanings to proliferate and pass between the levels, the personnel, and the patients. There is a certain harmony in the movement of the porcupines that illustrates the relations subsequent to the removal of the horses' blinkers in Guattari's mixed bestiary. But the degree of discomfort explodes the myth of group togetherness; the achievement of balance is a sign of hope that the de-rationalization of the group model, through reference to its instinctual, unconscious desires, is conducive to the actualization and analysis of the hitherto repressed or distorted desires of its members.

What should we say about these porcupines? Recall that the phrase "to find one's porcupine" was a saying that circulated in psychoanalytic circles after Freud's visit to America in 1909.[55] The idea of seeing a porcupine was for Freud "a lightning conductor" for drawing off anxiousness about his main task of lecturing at Clark University. Freud did, in fact, see a porcupine; he literally found one. Guattari finds his porcupine in Schopenhauer, which really means he was able to let Freud serve as a lighting conductor for his task of elaborating the concept of transversality. The porcupine is just another animal in the psychoanalytic bestiary which facilitates the siphoning of excess affect; after all, that is precisely the role played by animals in children's animal phobias according to Freud. Let psychoanalysis be struck by lightning, Guattari slyly suggests.

IV Schizoanalysis

" 'Do it': this could be the watchword of a micropolitical schizoanalysis", Guattari wrote in *L'Inconscient machinique*.[56] This is the sort of watchword that we need to watch out for: a yippie deterritorialization of money at the stock exchange too easily reterritorialized by the new information technologies of late capitalism. But Guattari adds: "A schizoanalytic 'watchword' will not attempt to interpret, to reorganize the significations, to compromise with them; it will postulate that beyond their system of redundancy, it is always possible to transform the semiotic assemblage which corresponds to them."[57] Despite its compromises, there's still hope for "do it". Schizoanalysis neither legitimates the significations of the dominant codes nor accepts the impositions resulting from their overcoding. The schizoanalyst won't, in other words, open a technical consultancy in pragmatics. Still, even schizoanalysts have to make a living at a social pragmatics aimed at detecting micropolitical orientations, freeing them up, and making connections between them. "Do it" means that the schizoanalyst is not sunk in a theoretical funk; pragmatics is not held in third place, as it were, behind syntactics and semantics. As Therese Grisham explains in linguistic terms: " 'Pragmatics' has historically designated all that is outside linguistic study. Using a reterritorialized term in a subversive mode is typical of Deleuze and Guattari, for they insist that pragmatics is immanent to a consideration of language. The meaning of 'pragmatic' lies in its position in a power relation, and not in representation or signification. To introduce a pragmatics into language is to analyze language politically".[58] A further example of this pragmaticization may be seen in Guattari's use of the diagram.

In *La Révolution moléculaire*, Guattari attempted to recast Peirce's inclusion of diagrams under the rubric of icons by means of his own distinction between signifying and a-signifying semiotics. For Peirce, diagrammatic reasoning is iconic: "A Diagram is mainly an Icon, and an icon of intelligible relations . . . in the constitution of its Object" (CP 4.531).[59] A diagram is, then, mainly but not exclusively an icon. It is, as Guattari admits, for Peirce a "simplified image of things", representational, and even "naturally analogous to the thing represented" (CP 4.368). Guattari first interrogates the relationship between the image and the diagram: the image is both more and less than the diagram: an image reproduces certain things a diagram does not, while a diagram captures better than an image functional articulations.[60] Guattari then situates images in the category of symbolic semiotics, that is, among substitutes for and representations of intensities and real multiplicites. Diagrammatism is, Guattari thinks, a category of a-signifying semiotics; diagrammatics is, however, another name for a-signifying semiotics, as is post-signifying semiotics. Diagrammatics produces machinic rather than significative redundancies. Guattari writes: "Peirce gives graphic representations as examples of diagrams, temperature curves, for example or, at the most complex level, algebraic equations. Signs function for and on behalf of objects to which they refer, and they do so independently of the effects of significations which may exist laterally. It is as if machines of diagrammatic signs had for an ideal the loss of all of their own inertia; it is as if they renounced all the polysemy which can exist in symbolic systems or signifying systems: the sign is refined, there are no longer thirty-six possible interpretations but a denotation and an extremely precise and strict syntax".[61]

In Guattari's terminology, a-signifying signs are more deterritorialized than those of symbolic and signifying semiotics. They blaze their own trails across dominant significations without the authority of a signifying semiology into which they can be translated and coded. While a Peircean could rightly claim that Guattari has engaged in acts of interpretive violence by playing favorites with iconic phenomena, his approach to Peirce is, I think, uncannily Peircean. To be sure, diagrams incorporate certain habits involved in the creation of graphic abstractions (in geometry and syllogistics); they also have the indexical feature of pointing "There!" (CP 3.361) without, however, describing or providing any insight into their objects. Since a diagram displays in itself the formal features of its object, it may be said to take the place of its object: "the distinction of the real and the copy disappears, and it is for the moment a pure dream" (CP 3.362). This simulation defies, Guattari specifies, the territorializing effects of representation and denotation. In Peirce's work, too, diagrams can be deterritorializing because they are iconic – icons do not lead one away from themselves to their objects, rather, they exhibit their object's characteristics in themselves. Icons can be indifferent to the demands of dominant semiotic formalizations. Guattari adopts a Peircean attitude towards Peirce by extending interpretation beyond his conventional definitions. And this is what Peirce called critical-philosophical thinking since it requires that one observe an author's line of thought, from which one then extrapolates imaginatively. In his discussion of theorematic reasoning (CP 4.233), Peirce wrote: "It is necessary that something be DONE". Guattari responds with "do it": an a-signifying abstract machine is diagrammatic. So too is theorematic reasoning. What was a necessary question for Peirce, was a question of necessity for Guattari, a question understood well by Lenin and revisited by Jerry Rubin.

Schizoanalysis will avoid the pitfalls of personological and developmental psychologies, as well as all glottocentric semiotics, by establishing, on a case to case basis, "a map of the unconscious" (including its strata, lines of deterritorialization, black holes, blockages, etc.). Ever attentive to the details of semiotic production, as well as to the "principle micropolitical lines of assemblages of enunciation and formations of power", this cartographer will not, like a psychoanalyst, close and reduce, but rather, open and produce. Such mapping opens onto experimentation.

Disparate elements make connections and achieve various consistencies of which there are different types (biological, ethical, etc); and all this without being dependent upon or beholden to a super-stratum or structure. These consistencies are neither totalizing, nor imposed from the outside. Connections are made along proliferating internal networks. Keep in mind that such connective rhizomes are formed from truly disparate elements, the partial objects of the unconscious.

A schizoanalytic pragmatics has at its disposal rhizomes that are irreducible to linguistic signifiers and systems of representation. The distinction between the rhizome and the tree is not absolute. Guattari writes of two preparations: first, "the preparation of a schizoanalytic rhizome will not have for its goal the description of a state of fact, the rebalancing of intersubjective relations, or the exploration of the mysteries of an unconscious lurking in the obscure nooks of memory".[62] This preparation doesn't capture static unconscious arrangements; it doesn't decipher what was already arranged, but remains open to experimentation in its construction of intersecting semiotics. "Maps themselves are like laboratories where tracing experiments are made to interact".[63] Tracings are "essential elements of diagrammatic semiotization", but they are, as one finds in "Introduction: Rhizome", in *A Thousand Plateaus*, part of the tree logic of reproduction, unless, of course, they are *put back on the map* (which is not, incidentally, to deny or erase them).[64] When writing with Deleuze on this matter, Guattari seems more severe in separating tracings (aligned with competence) from maps (related to performance). For Guattari, however, maps of competence, for example, remain irreducible to "competence" as such; in the same vein, there is no universal cartography of all the pragmatic maps. Guattari does note, however, that "it is only with the signifying semiologies that a hierarachical relation of double segmentarity installs itself between maps and tracings, fixing in a narrow margin possibilities of semiotic innovation".[65] This is because signifying semiologies are only relatively autonomous from the sort of formalization which makes them dependent upon a system of universal signification. Segmentation occurs in terms of a semiotic restriction of the modes of connection – too many rigid dualist segments.

The second "preparation of a tree of the generative type will not be, therefore, independent from that of a rhizome of the transformational type".[66] Before we examine in more detail these two kinds of schizoanalysis, generative and transformational, take note that rhizomes can branch out from the heart of generative trees. That is, idiolects and vernaculars are particular performances for which no dominant language or general competence may serve as a "totalizing reference". Many readers of *Anti-Oedipus*, Guattari notes, made the mistake of making Manichean principles out of the distinction between generative and

transformational pragmatics. But "a schizoanalytic pragmatics of collective assemblages of enunciation will constantly oscillate between these
two types of micro-political semiotics".[67] Still, together they call into
question dominant encodings.

Anti-Oedpius required its authors to produce much secondary
commentary and correct misunderstandings, for example, the "balance sheet" on machines published in the second French edition.[68] "Do
it" with your own example. What about the deaf-dumb-and-blind-boy
and his pinball machine? *Tommy* may be read against the grain of the
normalizing motif of the "cure". Tommy's cure is a kind of psychical
normalization for his reinsertion into the institution of the family. The
first thing to be noticed is that Tommy is the story of a boy and his
machine: a "pinball wizard". The relationship between Tommy and
the pinball machine does not need to lead us into a game of identifying correspondences between them; nor must we be led down the blind
alley of treating the machine as a kind of phantasy. What good is it to
point out, as almost every critic feels they must, that pinball is a metaphor for rock n' roll: it's the electric guitar. What makes such a displacement and substitution necessary? Gadgets only pile up: pinball, electric
guitar . . .

Anything, it seems, will do to reroute this kid's desire. This adds
nothing to the way Tommy communicates with the machine to the
amazement of the reiging "table king", whom he defeats. Tommy's
ability to connect with the machine is extraordinary because he cannot
connect with anything or anyone else, at least in a way that would
convince his parents and doctors, that his trauma is not narcissistic.
Haven't we heard enough about mirrors and psychology? His mother
neither tolerates the libidinal dynamism of his pinball playing nor his
fascination with his own reflection. Oh little blind and deaf narcissus,
listen to and look at your mommy! Over here little oedipus! When she
can't stand it anymore, she smashes the mirror, and Tommy becomes a
sensation: "Pinball Wizard in a miracle cure!" the papers read. It's the
beginning of his end.

The gesture of smashing the mirror is, however, bold, both as a
fabulous cure, and as a double anti-mirror stage. Strictly speaking,
Tommy is already too old for the child who, between six and eighteen
months, perceives and delights in his/her own mirror image, anticipating
and identifying with the bodily integrity it presents but s/he presently
lacks due to his/her physical immaturity. To the extent that the mirror
stage is fundamental to the constitution of the ego, even when it is
smashed it gives back to Tommy, perhaps even counterintuitively against
the expectations of fragmentation or cracking, a unity he apparently
lacked before then. But it wrecked his pinball game.

The "table king" thinks Tommy is part of the machine: "He stands like a statue/ Becomes part of the machine". He thinks Tommy looks like the machine – "he's got crazy flipper fingers" – and represents him as one. No wonder he has to give up the crown, he is no better than the doctor at the research laboratory who tries to "cure" Tommy with several ridiculous little noisemakers that he is supposed to cathect onto because they makes sounds when struck. Only a shrink would believe in such things! Indeed, Tommy – who is not bothered by pinball sounds – is unimpressed. There is nothing more ridiculous than the doctor's claim that "No machine can give the kind of stimulation/Needed to remove his inner block". On every occasion that Tommy plays pinball, affective intensities pass between him and the machine, to and fro. Where is the block? Let it be said that Tommy's libido withdraws into himself, except when he is playing pinball. With this auto-erotism, his ego is his sole love object, it is worth repeating, with the exception of pinball. Here we find his lines of escape. But Tommy and the pinball machine are completely independent; they are not extensions or projections of one another. They are becomings of one another. This is what allows these disparate elements to form a machinic assemblage on the basis of desire, to separate, and reform. Tommy is "unblocked" at the table, any table, even that of the local champ – who has played them all "from Soho down to Brighton" – and even if he is deaf, dumb and blind. The teenager-pinball ensemble lets desire flow. The lights, buzzers, bells, and representational iconography of the machine draw the table king into the ensemble, but do not distract Tommy since, already deterritorializing on the sensory level, "he plays by sense of smell". These "distractions" are also operational in relation to the reigning table king and his "Bally table", that is, in relation to a second structure, a tilt machine, and, of course, to followers of the game, groupies, hangers-on, capitalists, his abusive parents, cousin and uncle, shrinks, and the rest.

Schizoanalysis doesn't play the pretend mirror games dear to psychoanalysis. It "makes micro-political choices in opting, for example, for the acceleration or the slackening of an internal mutation of assemblages, for the facilitation or braking of an inter-assemblage transition . . . ."[69] It distinguishes between intra-mutations and inter-passages, and then makes decisions about them. Schizoanalysis "will explore and will experiment with an unconscious in actuality [*en acte*]".[70] Diachronic outcomes and synchronic states will both figure in its questioning of the inclusions, exclusions, confusions and refusions of assemblages. A generative schizoanalytic pragmatics will concern itself with "a pre-existing assemblage", while a transformational pragmatics will "create new [assemblages]"[71]; they are distinguished, then, on the basis of their objects, in a way Guattari considered to have been somewhat artificial but nonetheless prudent. Guattari adds: "Schizoanalysis isn't dependent upon holding up or forcing events. It never loses sight of the compromises, the regressions, the progressions, the ruptures, the revolutions exposing processes that it is not at all a question of pretending to control, or of overcoming, but only of attending to semiotically and machinically".[72]

In a generative schizoanalysis, "the role of the components of passage will be here limited to putting into play only weak interactions between the assemblages, with the goal of loosening, untangling if possible, their alienating mechanisms, their stratifications and their oppressive redundancies, their black hole-effects, indeed, even of averting or deferring the threats of catastrophe which hang over them".[73] Components of passage connect the mutant fluxes of desire. This weak approach will not lead, Guattari specifies, to a "systematic deterritorialization" of assemblages. It is not passive, however, even though it "will accommodate . . . stases of long-lasting reterritorialization", while it takes, at its own less than frantic pace, whatever opportunities present themselves for deterritorializing and re-assembling. Its motto would be, Guattari adds, "no watchword, only passwords", as it "updates new machinic senses in situations in which everything seemed played out in advance".[74]

A transformational pragmatics will involve itself in "the radical modification of intrinsic mechanisms in the nuclei of assemblages and thus the creation of new assemblages".[75] The nuclei [*noyaux*] which specify assemblages exist at the points of crossing of two types of machinic consistencies: molecular consistencies that are strongly resonant (across the semantic and poetic fields) and interactive (among the components of passage); these are "the actualized face of abstract machinisms" or the formation of unformed matter; and intrinsically abstract consistency, whose sign-particles may be manifested in different ways (as capitalist abstractions) while also remaining "undecidable" and holding a "possible potential" in reserve.[76] The machinic nucleus is where transformational schizoanalysis will work. The difference between generative and transformational lies in, then, the shift from the putting into play of "molar relations of subjection" to "molecular vectors of machinic subservience".[77] The strong interactions of the components of passage may be distinguished on the basis of their points of departure: i) "assemblages and inter-assemblage relations already constituted"; ii) "or of molecular populations, of matters of expression, in a nascent state". Still, Guattari immediately adds "it matters little, in effect, that these molecular populations and matters of expression are extracted from 'previous assemblages' or are put together for the occasion!"[78] The critical issue here is the implementation of micro-political choices which led to new assemblages; this will involve an analysis of the transformations which elevate components "to the rank of components of passage", of which Guattari distinguishes three functions: i) *discerniblization* (borrowing magnification, colorization and semiotic crossing from Proust, and acceleration, slowing down, becoming heavy, and the deformation of spatio-temporal coordinates from Kafka); ii) *proliferation* ("a component gets to work on its own account and unfastens itself from the assemblage within which it was stratified"); iii) *diagrammatization* ("a component unleashes a mutational machinism capable of crossing heterogeneous domains from the point of view of their matters of expression").[79] All of the deterritorializations are, Guattari specifies, *controlled*. In general, the two pragmatics Guattari describes involve the *extraction* of existing components (generative) and the *creation* ex nihilo of new components (transformational). And the latter, Guattari writes, "harbours no particular mystery", because a cartographic diagram of its passages would reveal that it does not stray far from matter of expression, that is, to use Brian Massumi's language, not far from a complex with neither substance nor form, but just "a bundle of potential [non-actualized] functions".[80]

Schizoanalysis is not a science, a technique, a type of cure, or a new analytic practice. It is "inseparable from a personal trajectory in specific social, political and cultural domains".[81] This means that Massumi's schizoanalysis (with its references to: baby, marriage, high school, and the rest) will differ from Eugene Holland's schizoanalysis, because in both cases their trajectories will have been determined by their specifics: experiences, contexts, and socio-political circumstances, etc.[82] Freud thought the same of psychoanalysis, even though the degree of followership he would come to require from his colleagues defied his initial recognition of methodological plurality.

Machinism is at once threatening and potentially liberatory; the former due to "the microscopic means of disciplinarization of thought and affect and the militarization of human relations", the latter to the extent that it remains open to "singularization and creative initiatives".[83] Revolutionary machines have two specific goals: to destroy the relations of capitalism and "to establish themselves at odds with every value founded on a certain micro-politics of muscle, the phallus, territorialized power, etc".[84] Perhaps a little reluctantly, but in order to avoid once more the charge that schizoanalysis is a cult of the machine, Guattari elaborated eight principles or "simple rules" in the form of aphorisms which would give direction to the analysis of the machinic unconsious[85]: 1. "Do no harm", act without prejudice, "remain just until the end"; 2. "When something's happening, this proves that something's happening". This tautology dispenses with the mystifications of the psychoanalytic understanding of the unconscious and its secrets: the shrink says: "when nothing is happening, this proves that something is happening, in reality, something unconscious"; 3. "The best position to place oneself in order to listen to the unconscious is not necessarily behind a couch". Who needs a cigar, a dog, a room full of statues, a scorecard . . .?; 4. "The unconscious compromises [*mouille*] those who come near it". Those who encounter it are carried in its wake; they are soaked by it, as it were, making the taking of a neutral position impossible; 5. "Important things never happen where one expects them". Or, "the entrance doesn't coincide with the exit". What initiates a change isn't what effects this change; 6. Transferences made by "subjective resonance, by personological identification" need to be distinguished from those made machinically – producing new assemblages by means of "a-signifying diagrammatic interactions"; 7. "Take nothing for granted". There is no fixity of identity, and no situation is guaranteed; unlike the "guaranteed symbolic consistencies" of psychoanalysis (castration), which Guattari calls "dishonest and dangerous"; 8. "Every principle must be considered suspect".

V IWC

Guattari developed a theory of post-industrial capitalism, which he referred to as integrated world capitalism (IWC), through a series of remarkable collaborations with Deleuze, Eric Alliez, and Antonio Negri. Before considering how Guattari posed in a myriad of ways the question of how to resist and defeat IWC, let's revisit the analysis of capitalism in *Anti-Oedipus* in order to better understand the relationship between desire and his theory of capitalism.

Using a tool of structuralist analysis, despite the anti-structuralism of *Anti-Oedipus*, the synchronic time of the despotic State is distinguished from the diachronic time of capitalism. Capitalism develops over time on the basis of a series of decodings and deterritorializations including the sale of accumulated property, and the circulation of money and workers. Capitalism comes into existence "in a space that takes time", then, with the conjunction of these and other contingent factors, a conjunction that "constitutes a desire" and "actually produces a desiring-machine that is at the same time social and technical".[86] It is not that these decoded flows had yet to exist. Rather, it is the conjunction of them, some of which existed for a long time in different social formations that were not so marked by decodings but, instead, consisted of codings and overcodings, upon which capitalism establishes itself. Capitalism channels, however, the flows into the guiding principle of "production for production's sake". Keep in mind that the priority of production is not peculiar to IWC. In the meantime, Deleuze and Guattari analyze in particular the encounter or conjunction of two contingent factors: deterritorialized workers and decoded money. The worker-producer was deterritorialized on the basis of the: i) privatization of the soil; ii) appropriation of the instruments of production; iii) loss of the means of consumption through the dissolution of the family and corporation; and iv) the favoring of work itself over the worker. Money was decoded on the basis of: i) monetary abstraction; ii) merchant capital's influence on the flows of production; iii) public debt and financial capital's influence on the State; and iv) industrial capital's control of the means of production.[87] Numerous contingent factors made conditions favorable for the encounter of these decoded and deterritorialized flows. Under such favorable conditions, capitalism appropriates production and becomes "the new social full body", characterized by a generalized decoding and becoming-immanent. The capitalist machine enters into relationships with itself or becomes filiative as it reproduces its immanent limits and the crises upon which it depends in ever widening extensions.

Deleuze and Guattari specify that diachronic technical machines are created by the synchronic capitalist machine and thus do not revolutionize the latter; that is, the latter revolutionizes itself through the breaks and cleavages it introduces into the former technical machines of production.[88] Technical machines are parts of social machines. The generalized theory of flows that constitutes this theory of capitalism reveals the schizophrenic process at the center of capitalist desire. The desire for strength and impotence go hand in hand with capitalism's reproduction of its immanent limits. Anti-production exists, then, at the heart of production; flows of stupidity effect the absorption of the suplus-value of analysis and information, just as the absorption of surplus-value is regulated by the introduction of lack in the face of abundance.

While there are important affinities between capitalism and schizophrenia, the two are not identical. While it may be that "our society produces schizos the same way it produces Prell shampoo or Ford cars, the only difference being that the schizos are not salable",[89] capitalist production both sets in motion and arrests the schizophrenic process. Deleuze and Guattari contrast capitalism, as the relative limit of all societies, with schizophrenia, as the absolute limit of capitalism. While capitalism's relative limits are immanent, those of schizophrenia constitute the exterior limit of capitalism that the latter wants to fill with its own immanent limits.[90] This desire to fill by means of the reproduction of capitalism's interior limits smothers the revolutionary potential of schizophrenia's decoded flows by means of apparatuses of domination and regulations enforced by the State. The relationship between the capitalist and the schizophrenic is antagonistic. The decoding of flows that is the mark of capitalism is accompanied by their immanent axiomatization. This immanent axiomatic of capitalism has three features: i) its differential relations are filled by surplus-value; ii) the absence of an exterior limit is filled by interior limits; and iii) the anti-productive aspect of production is filled by the absorption of surplus-value.[91] The social axiomatic of capitalism is never completely filled or saturated because it constantly expands its own limits and introduces new axioms. On the one hand, capitalism's energy for deterritorialization seems boundless; but, on the other hand, it constantly confronts its own limits that it allows to be overcome. Capitalism vacillates between pre-capitalist or archaic-despotic overcoding and post-capitalist or schizo decoding; between, then, reaction (paranoia) and revolution.[92] It is thoroughly mad. And it is constantly threatened by the external limit of the schizophrenic process, which it meets with the addition of new axioms. But Deleuze and Guattari are hopeful that as the decoded flows continue to overflow, the holes in the mesh of the axiomatic will be exploited, and the libidinal breaks and breaches will appear suddenly and unexpectedly here and there, at this or perhaps that precise moment, without an "order of causes", thus, escapes from the axiomatic of capital will occur, because it is exhausted from playing a catch-up game of sealing breaches, and outwitted in a game of guessing where the next renegade flow (not an individual libidinal disposition, but a multiplex desiring-machine) will emerge. While there is much more that could and perhaps needs to be said about the theory of capitalism developed in *Anti-Oedipus*, this much will suffice to get us on our way.

Let's try and place this theory within the non-general typological description of the multiple forms of capitalist modes of valorization that Guattari developed with the French philosopher Alliez.[93] Understood as a "general function of semiotization", capitalism exercises an integrative and transformative semiotic power over a diverse domain of machines (technical, economic, social, desiring). It is, moreover, as we have seen, a deterritorializing power whose processual nature relies upon its avoidance of despotism for the sake of the marginal freedoms it permits around certain key power arrangements (production, for instance). From the most diverse machinic operations (material and non-material) capitalism extracts and exploits a surplus value, having drawn them into its exchangist "framework of equivalence". The double articulation of formal economic and machinic content, that is, of a contradictory arrangement rendering equivalent diverse forces in a closed territory divided by legal and social rules, is imperfect and unequal, despite capital's happy facade of symmetry and egalitarianism. The semiotic (i.e. economic) and the machinic (i.e. libidinal) are not in opposition, but produce opportunities of renewal for one another.

Guattari and Alliez propose a minimal model consisting of three evaluative terms: processes of machinic *production*, which they do not further develop; structures of social segmentation, considered in terms of the *state*; dominant economic semiotic systems, considered in terms of the *market*. Each historic mode of capitalistic valorization is described on the basis of the priority given to one the these terms: The order of priority for IWC is: production – market – state. Colonial monopoly capitalism is also ordered by production: production – state – market. This is not exhaustive, nor is it meant to be. It reveals, however, certain tendencies and emphases which, in this case, involve rapacious imperialist powers bleeding peripheral countries by holding commercial monopolies over resources extracted for the home and world markets, with no regard for the disorganization of the colony in question, nor the disintegration and degradation of the people and the land. The state (the distant imperialist power and its feudal outposts) poses for Guattari and Alliez an interesting question in light of its collapse and reconstruction in a "highly artificial" form under certain post-colonial conditions.

What makes IWC "new" is its innovative means of semiotization and increased capacity for the "machinic integration" of molecular diversity. Here, production reterritorializes and capitalizes all of the segments of social reproduction, the latter having the axioms of racism, sexism, and conservatisms of all sorts. For this *social-machinic capital*, as Guattari and Alliez refer to it, circulation takes the form of crisis and process becomes that of permanent restructuration. Production integrates circulation, information, and resegments society, giving to capital a "maximal synergetic fluidity" (a proliferation of fluid and mobile productive networks, of temporary labour, etc.). The state becomes the trader (and even a speculator) in trans-national flows, free-trade zones, minimizing and liberalizing (or rather decentralizing and privatizing) its national responsibilities.

IWC may present itself as the "highest stage of capitalism", but for Guattari and Alliez it is only one among other modes. Given its unprecedented integrative capacity and fluidity, what are its limits? Whatever the limits actually turn out to be, Guattari and Alliez think that IWC can be brought down by "the development of new collective responses" and molecular valorizations. In short, the theory of IWC is the background against which Guattari's valorization of molecular, revolutionary practices needs to be understood in order to be fully appreciated.

Guattari's analysis of IWC is further developed in his work on generalized ecology, as well as in the project for the renewal of communism that he wrote with Negri. In "The Three Ecologies", Guattari outlines the semiotic regimes upon which IWC is founded: economic, juridical, technico-scientific, and subjectification.[94] These are not causally related since "IWC has to be regarded as all of a piece: it is simultaneously productive, economic, and subjective".[95] IWC produces certain forms of subjectivity by semiotic means and keeps them distinct by affording one legitimation while cultivating resignation in the other. Guattari specifies the two types of subjectivity produced and employed by capitalistic societies: *serial* subjectivity (wage-earners and the "insecure" or "non-guaranteed"); and *elitist* subjectivity (ruling social strata).[96] The main goal of Guattari's generalized ecology is to allow for the resingularization of individuals and collectivities through the radical questioning of the limited subjective formations of capitalism. Ecological praxis in its broadest psychical, social and environmental senses must identify "dissident vectors of subjectification" and work towards their emancipation and maximization by opening up a-signifying ruptures and creating conditions conductive to the formation of new subject-groups.[97]

One of the goals of the ecological praxis of resingularization is to shift capitalism from the era of mass media to that of post-media.[98] Guattari and Alliez have argued that with IWC information becomes a factor of production. Capital becomes cybernetic and seeks a global informatization of society which goes hand in hand with global mass-mediaization. IWC can then expand and exercise social control through its networks and information technologies. Guattari repeatedly asked with regard to this transnational computerization: "why have the immense processual potentials brought forth by the revolutions in information processing, telematics, robotics, office automation, biotechnology and so on up to now led only to a monstrous reinforcement of earlier systems of alienation, an oppressive mass-mediated culture and an infantilizing politics of consensus?"[99] Emancipatory social struggles must insist on and protect the *fundamental right to singularity*. This is precisely the goal of Guattari and Negri's communism: the continuous reaffirmation and maximization of singularization in all its processual unevenness, creativity, multiplicity and contextual variability.[100]

With Negri, however, Guattari adds a new layer to the theory of IWC. Intergrated World Capitalism remains a flexible semio-social science of exploitation, but has at its centre the nuclear state.[101] Computerization is inseparable from mechanization and militarization. Outbreaks of singularization – in the liberation movements of the 1970s, including the disastrous "terrorist interlude" – challenge the translation of life time into the "time of capital", that is, into exchangist terms. Nuclear terror "became the only way to secure the resumption to capitalistic and socialistic accumulation in the 1970s".[102] It has long been a central thesis in peace studies that the mass media, science and technology are the means for the production of militarism, especially in non-material forms. Nuclear terror is for Guattari and Negri at "the root of every kind of oppression and overdetermines the relationships of exploitation between social groups at both political and micro-political levels", including the North/South axis of domination, and the West/East (especially former socialist countries) axis of capitalistic integration.

In Negri's "Lettre archéologique" written to Guattari, the programmatic nature of their renewal of communism still leaves unanswered the question of social practice. But the answer will not be as immediately forthcoming in Negri's mind as were the practices (i.e., wildcat strikes, absenteeism, sabotage, as part of the refusal of work) that realized and justified the program in the sixties.[103] It is worth mentioning here Negri's moving refrain: "We [the struggles of the sixties] have been defeated". If such defeats were strewn across the seventies, then in the eighties they were consolidated for capitalism's sake. Negri wants us to fully appreciate the gravity of this defeat in order to avoid both reminiscence and repetition, but also to grasp the enormity of the critical task ahead. Negri sees in this defeat, however, a premature cause of the enemy's modernization. Automation, he suggests, "is freely invented by the knowledge that springs from the rejection of work but is, on the other hand, applied in order to break and mystify the generality of this proletarian and labouring need".[104] The matter of the exercise of generalized social control through information technology remains, for Negri, unresolved. The production and reproduction of cybernetic subjectivity and the dislocation and mystification of the knowledge possessed by the counter-hegemonic forces have been used by IWC to break the desire for social transformation and reinvention. Today, then, transversal and alternative struggles need to expand the little room they have to maneuver and rest desire, the material and technical transformations of modernization, and knowledge from the impositions of capitalism. There are many traps and obstacles along the way.

Guattari's commitment to a politics informed by an ecosophical perspective in its most general sense had to rise above the sectarianism that marked French Green politics in the early 1990s. Although Guattari was at times active in both Les Verts, led by Antoine Waechter, and Génération Écologie, led by the [then] Minister of the Environment, Brice Lalonde, he joined the latter group at the national level, which is perhaps not surprising given that they were the so-called "leftist" minority of the movement that threatened what Waechter saw as the sacrosanct principle of "neither left nor right" of green politics. Guattari wanted to play a moderating role and openly lamented the split, while still reserving his praise for Lalonde. Guattari's statement "Une autre vision du futur" played the savvy political card of separating the quarrel from the plurality of the ecological movement as a vehicle of reinvention in social, political and personal life.[105] Many of Guattari's political lessons delivered in Part I, "The Vicissitudes of Therapy", may be applied here in the context of the Green movement: reformism and utopianism must be resisted. The Green equivalents of these are, respectively, the competing models of so-called "shallow, short-term" ecology and mystical variants of "deep, long-term" ecology. The very notion of ecology as both subversive and scientific needs to be called into question. Whether there can be an "ecology" that is closely tied to the potentializations of subjective singularities rather than a bio-social interrelation must remain a deeply troubling question for all those concerned with a green politics inspired by Guattari's thought.

On another political front, Guattari did not live to see that his work for peace in the former Yugoslavia, initiated together with Edgar Morin and other members of the French committee of the Assemblée européenne des citoyens, as well as those enagaged in "transmediterranian dialogue" cultivated by the French through the "Citoyens de la Méditerranée" conference in Paris in early 1992, would be repeatedly frustrated by the virulent interethnic hatred and nationalist ambitions that had moved him to action on this issue in the first instance.[106]

The struggles continue.

Gary Genosko, Kingston, Ontario, April 1995

Notes

1 Guattari, "Alternative à psychiatrie", in *La Révolution moléculaire*, Fontenay-sous-Bois: Encres/Recherches, 1977, pp. 147–60.

2 Guattari, "L'étudiant, le fou et le katangais", in *psychanalyse et transversalité*, Paris: François Maspero, 1972, pp. 230–1, n. 2.

3 See Roger Gentis, *Traité de psychiatrie provisoire*, Paris: Maspero, 1977, pp. 7–27. The politics of the sector provoked the members of CERFI (Centre d'études, de recherches et de formations institutionnelles) to publish a 600-odd page issue devoted to it and related questions entitled: "histoire de la psychiatrie de secteur, ou le secteur impossible?" *Recherches* 17 (1975). *Recherches* is the journal of CERFI.

4 Guattari, *RM*, p. 147.

5 Thomas Szasz, *The Myth of Mental Illness*, New York: Harper & Row, 1961, p. 308.

6 T. Szasz, *The Myth of Psychotherapy*, Garden City: Anchor Press, 1978.

7 Guattari, "La contestation psychiatrique", *La Quinzaine littéraire* 94 (1970): 24–5.

8 Guattari, *RM*, p. 158.

9 Ibid., p. 159.

10 See Guattari, "Le 'voyage' de Mary Barnes", *Le Nouvel observateur* (28 mai 1973): 82–4, 87, 93, 96, 101, 104, 109–10. It should perhaps be noted that David Cooper, in his review of Guattari's *L'Inconscient machinique*, praised his "calling into fundamental question classical conceptions . . . of the unconscious, and communication models based on systems theory in the attempt to understand human and above all familial interactions". If, for Cooper, this was Guattari's greatest accomplishment, he also considered, for example, Laing's "paradigmatic utilization of fragments of dialogues . . . to illustrate the ways in which people, little by little, articulate (or undo) their life in relation to the life of others' as more powerfully concrete than Guattari's analysis of the characters in Proust's *La Recherche du temps perdu*", although Cooper

understood that Guattari used Proust as an example of "how to understand the assemblages and machinic territorialities in the act of untangling a certain micro-social reality". Cooper was, in the end, unhappy with this turn to Proust as a political and practical expression of Guattari's theory. Still, he looked for "zones of mutual enrichment" between Guattari and so-called "Anglo-Saxon" thinkers such as Goffman and Laing, as well as between theory and praxis (See Cooper, "Guattari, et notre implication dans les luttes quotidiennes", *La Quinzaine littéraire* 319 (fév 1980): 23.

11 Gentis, op. cit., pp. 213–14.

12 Guattari, "La contestation", p. 24.

13 Guattari, "Un entretien avec Félix Guattari" [Int. by Jean-Yves Nau], *Le Monde* (6 sept. 1989): 19.

14 Guattari, "Urgences: la folie est dans le champ", *Le Monde* (9 mars 1988): 22.

15 Ibid.

16 Guattari, *RM*, p. 152.

17 Ibid., p. 153.

18 Ibid., p. 154.

19 Guattari, "La contestation", p. 25.

20 Guattari, *RM*, p. 157.

21 J. Oury, F. Guattari, J-C. Pollack, D. Sabourin, "La Borde, un lieu psychiatrique pas comme les autres" [Interview by C. Deschamps and R. Gentis], *La Quinzaine littéraire* 250 (fév. 1977): 20.

22 Oury, "Une dialectique de l'amitié", *Le Monde* (1 sept. 1992): 11.

23 Pollack in Oury *et al* p. 21; Guattari, "La Borde, un lieu-dit", in *RM*, pp. 161–69; Sabourin and Pollack, *La Borde, or le droit à la folie*, Paris: Calmann-Lévy, 1976.

24 Guattari, "Laing divisé", *La Quinzaine littéraire* 132 (janv. 1972): pp. 22–3.

25 S. Turkle, "French Anti-psychiatry", in *Critical Psychiatry*, D. Ingleby (ed.), New York: Pantheon, 1980, p. 174; Robert Castel, *Le Psychanalysme*, Paris: Maspero, 1972, pp. 21–3.

26 Pollack in Oury, *et al* p. 21.

27 Guattari, *RM*, p. 166.

28 Ibid., p. 162.

29 In Oury, *et al* p. 21. See also Marie Depussé, *Dieu gît dans les détails*, Paris: POL, 1993, p. 102. She "quotes" Oury: "Mais, c'est une clinique, ici, on est à la campagne. C'est mauvais, tous ces intellectuels, pour les fous".

30 Depussé, p. 145.

31 Oury, in "Un rameau saint-albanais, une souche nouvelle: La Borde (1949–1954)", in *Recherches* 17 (1975): 165–66.

32 Lucien Bonnafé, "La Poète et les Proscrits", in *Eluard*, Paris: Les éditeurs français Réunis, 1972, pp. 41–68.

33 L. Bonnafé and François Tosquelles, "La Résistance: Saint-Alban", in *Recherches* 17 (1975): 80–88.

34 Ibid., p. 88.

35 Deleuze and Guattari, *What is Philosophy?* H. Tomlinson and G. Burchell (trans.), New York: Columbia University Press, 1994, p. 96.

36 Guattari, "Un nouvel axe progressiste", *Le Monde* (4 juin 1992): 2.

37 Guattari, "Un entretien avec Guattari" [J.-Y. Nau], *Le Monde* (6 sept. 1989): 19.

38 Ibid., p. 21.

39 Deleuze and Guattari, "1914: One Or Several Wolves?" in *A Thousand Plateaus*, trans. Brian Massumi, Minneapolis: University of Minnesota Press, 1987, p. 38.

40 M. Gardiner (ed.), *The Wolf-Man and Sigmund Freud*, London: Hogarth, 1972, pp. 315–16.

41 Deleuze and Guattari, "1730: Becoming-Intense, Becoming-Animal, Becoming-Imperceptible . . .", in *ATP*, p. 240.

42 Ibid., p. 275.

43 Ibid., p. 239.

44 See, for instance, the explanation given by Ernest Jones, *The Life And Work Of Sigmund Freud*, Vol. 3, New York: Basic Books, 1957, p. 141.

45 See Paul Roazen, *Freud and His Followers*, New York: New American Library, 1976, p. 499 and Mark Zborowski and Elizabeth Herzog, *Life Is With Other People: The Culture Of The Shetl*, New York: Schocken, 1952, p. 344.

46 See my "Freud's Bestiary: How Does Psychoanalysis Treat Animals?" *The Psychoanalytic Review* 80/4 (1993): 603–32; and my "Introduction" to Marie Bonaparte's *Topsy: The Story of a Golden-Haired Chow*, New Brunswick: Transaction, 1994, pp. 1–31.

47 "Wolves", *ATP*, p. 32.

48 Ibid., p. 34.

49 Christopher L Miller, "The Postidentitarian Predicament in the Footnotes of *A Thousand Plateaus*: Nomadology, Anthropology, and Authority", *diacritics* 23/3 (1993): 6–35.

50 Gardiner, p. 12.

51 Guattari, "Transversalité", in *psychanalyse et transversalité*, p. 79.

52 Ibid.

53 Ibid.

54 Ibid., p. 80; Sigmund Freud, "Group Psychology and the Analysis of the Ego" [1921], in *The Pelican Freud Library*, vol. 12, Harmondsworth: Penguin, 1985, p. 130. It needs to be said that these few remarks on the bestiary of Guattari are merely the tip of a long tale which includes his writings on ethology in *L'Inconscient machinique*, pp. 117–53, as well as, of course, his work on Little Hans, especially the animal phobia (more horses) as a child's libidinal pragmatic in face of the familialism of psychoanalysis, pp. 181–82. See also his sense of the analysis of the institutional object in extreme cases in which the imaginary of a group (miners) is suddenly destroyed (the mine is closed), and the work involved in "guiding the imaginary from one structure to another, a little like what happens in the animal world during moulting" ("Le groupe et la personne", *psychanalyse et transversalité*, p. 168). This sort of reading will not be everyone's cup of tea. It is merely one among many other ways of reading.

55 E. Jones, *The Life and Work of Sigmund Freud*, V. 2, New York: Basic Books, 1955, p. 59.

56 Guattari, *IM*, p. 182.

57 Ibid.

58 Therese Grisham, "Linguistics as an Indiscipline: Deleuze and Guattari's Pragmatics", *Sub stance* 66 (1991): 45; see my *Baudrillard and Signs*, London: Routledge, 1994, pp. 57–71. This *Reader* emphasizes Guattari's creative elaboration of concepts borrowed from Louis Hjelmslev's glossematics in the section on "Polysemiosis". Deleuze and Guattari refer to Hjelmslev as "the Danish Spinozist geologist . . . that dark prince descended from Hamlet" (*ATP*, 43). In spite of its reputation as an agent of linguistic imperialism, Guattari has made glossematics serve the pragmatic ends of schizoanalysis. Guattari makes an arid alegbra of language serve a pragmatics of the unconscious. In *Anti-Oedipus*, Deleuze and Guattari combined a critique of a linguistics of the signifier with praise for Hjelmslev: "We believe that, from all points of view and despite certain appearances, Hjelmslev's linguistics stands in profound opposition to the Saussurean and post-Saussurean undertaking" (242). Hjelmslev's theory "is the only linguistics adapted to the nature of *both* the capitalist *and* the schizophrenic flows: until now, the only modern (and not archaic) theory of language" (243). Glossematics may

be "schizo", but was Hjelmslev schizophrenic? That is, did Hjelmslev not only think like a schizo-analyst and theorize the schizo-process in order to free the flows of language, but also suffer from something called schizophrenia? Was he another Artaud, Van Gogh, Mary Barnes – a Judge Schreber whose breakthroughs enlightened us all? *Anti-Oedipus* does not answer these questions. On the floors of conferences, in obituaries, in diagnostic speculations, Hjelmslev's "depression", his "long and tragic illness", are made reference to not as breakthroughs, but as breakdowns. For all the care Deleuze and Guattari take in recognizing the dangers of turning clinical issues into metaphors, and to the extent that Guattari bases his extrapolations on decades of clinical experience, they have said nothing about Hjelmslev's "case".

59 All references to C.S. Peirce are from *The Collected Works*, eds. C. Hartshorne, P. Weiss, and A.W. Burks, Cambridge: Harvard University Press, 1935–66.
60 Guattari, *RM*, p. 310.
61 Ibid., pp. 310–11.
62 Guattari, *IM*, p. 178.
63 Ibid.
64 Deleuze and Guattari, "Introduction: Rhizome", in *ATP*, pp. 12–13.
65 Guattari, *IM*, p. 179.
66 Ibid., p. 187.
67 Ibid.
68 Deleuze and Guattari, "Bilan-Programme pour machines désirantes", in *L'Anti-Oedipe*, 2nd ed., Paris: Minuit, 1974; "Balance-Sheet: Program for Desiring-Machines", trans. Robert Hurley, *Semiotext(e)* II/3 (1977): 117–35.
69 Guattari, *IM*, p. 190.
70 Ibid.
71 Ibid., p. 191.
72 Ibid.
73 Ibid., p. 192.
74 Ibid., pp. 192–3.
75 Ibid., p. 193.
76 Ibid., pp. 47–8.
77 Ibid., p. 193.
78 Ibid.
79 Ibid., p. 194.
80 Massumi, *A User's Guide to Capitalism and Schizophrenia: Deviations from Deleuze and Guattari*, Cambridge: Swerve, 1992, p. 152, n. 36.
81 Guattari, *IM*, pp. 196–7.
82 Holland, "Schizoanalysis: The Postmodern Contextualization of Psychoanalysis", in *Marxism and the Interpretation of Culture*, eds. C. Nelson and L. Grossberg, Urbana: University of Illinois Press, 1988, pp. 405–16. Guattari would have recoiled in horror at Holland's notion of a "postmodern schizoanalysis", but may have been relieved at what it actually entailed.
83 Guattari, *IM*, p. 200.
84 Ibid., p. 201.
85 Ibid., pp. 201–3.
86 Deleuze and Guattari, *Anti-Oedipus*, p. 224.
87 Ibid., p. 225.
88 Ibid., p. 233.
89 Ibid., p. 245.
90 Ibid., p. 246.
91 Ibid., p. 250.

92 Ibid., pp. 259–60.
93 See Guattari and Alliez, "Capitalistic Systems, Structures and Processes", trans. Brian Darling, in *The Molecular Revolution*, Harmondsworth: Penguin, 1984.
94 Guattari, "The Three Ecologies", trans. Chris Turner, *New formations* 8 (1989): 137.
95 Ibid., p. 138.
96 Ibid., pp. 143–44.
97 At issue here is Guattari's long-standing, non-absolute distinction between subjugated groups and subject-groups. The former follow a path of reference received passively from the outside; their cause is heard but by whom? The latter follow a path of self-reference (they have the ability to assume an internal law), that is, of interpreting their own position, with regard to their elaboration of projects and tools, and vocation in general. At first glance, this distinction, while non-absolute, may not be as dialectical as the Sartrean concepts to which it is indebted. The subjugated group is very similar to serial being, with its exterior focus on an object in which a prior praxis is embodied and its passive internal structure of mutual Otherness. The subject-group is a kind of group in fusion, a genuine group, that has achieved fusion, having liquidated its seriality and accomplished an active restructuration. But this would take us beyond Sartre, because for him the group in fusion is still, even if it is united in "the flash of a common *praxis*", united, that is, in mutual determination by reciprocity, through a common object (a danger, an enemy) like serial being. See Sartre, *The Critique of Dialectical Reason*, Vol. I, trans. Alan Sheridan-Smith, London: NLB, 1976, p. 253 ff.
98 On Guattari's hopes for the transition from the consensual mass-media era to the dissensual post-media era see, "Pour une éthique des médias", *Le Monde* (6 nov. 1991): 2. Guattari envisages this transition on the basis of four factors: i) forseeable technological developments; ii) the necessary redefinition of the relations between producers and consumers; iii) the institution of new social practices and their inter-ference with the development of media; iv) the development of information techno-logies. But for many communication theorists, "post-mass media" culture merely provides yet another opportunity to demonstrate that the transition has not been decisive, and to drag out and dust off old models. These theorists should be, as Umberto Eco once put it, "pensioned off".
99 Guattari, "Regimes, Pathways, Subjects", trans. B. Massumi, in *Incorporations*, eds. J. Crary and S. Kwinter, New York: Urzone, 1992, p. 29.
100 Guattari and Negri, *Communists Like Us*, trans. M. Ryan, New York: Semiotext(e), 1990, pp. 39–40. The questions of subjectivation and singularization run through *The Guattari Reader*. I have emphasized the thematic of queer subjectivation in Part V on "Queer/Subjectivities".
101 Ibid., p. 54.
102 Ibid., pp. 53–4.
103 Negri, "Letter to Félix Guattari on Social Practice", in *The Politics of Subversion: A Manifesto for the Twenty-First Century*, trans. J. Newell, Oxford: Polity, 1989, p. 156.
104 Ibid., p. 157.
105 Guattari, "Une autre vision du futur", *Le Monde* (15 fév. 1992): 8.
106 Guattari, "Un appel d'Edgar Morin, Edgard Pisani et Félix Guattari", *Le Monde* (10 juin 1992): 2.

PART I

The Vicissitudes of Therapy

1

The Divided Laing

The clear-cut alternatives between good and evil, normal and pathological, sane and mad, are perhaps about to undergo a radical modification,
falling short of the full understanding which could potentially be gained
from such a process. We notice only that a number of judgments, which
yesterday seemed self-evident, are now wavering, and that a number of
roles no longer function according to the norm of common sense. Deviance has taken charge. There is now a revolutionary front for homosexuals [FHAR, *Front homosexuel d'action révolutionnaire*], a legal support
group for prisoners (*Groupe d'information sur les prisonniers de droit com-
mun*), and the "Cahiers de la folie", etc.

According to this new context, the importance of Ronald Laing, one of
the originators of English anti-psychiatry, lies in this "countercultural
movement which combines politics with the problematic of the university",[1] as Daniéle Sabourin has said. Laing is firstly a deviant psychiatrist.
For us, he was in the first place this frenzied and somewhat euphoric
character, whose flare up with David Cooper had the effect of a bomb in
the days of the study group Enfance Aliénée, organized in Paris in 1957
by Maud Mannoni and the journal *Recherches*.

All of psychiatry speaks of the anti-psychiatry of Laing. But does Laing
himself still speak of psychiatrists? He is far, already very far from their
world and their preoccupations. He has undertaken this "trip", which he
recommends to schizophrenics, on his own account, and he has abandoned his activities in London in order to meditate, so some say, in a
monastery in Ceylon. On the other hand, his books are surely there too.
It's impossible to avoid them. They irritate and disrupt specialized
gatherings. Public opinion gets mixed up with them. The French translations have succeeded one another: after *The Politics of Experience* [*La
politique de l'expérience*], and *The Divided Self* [*Le Moi divisé*]; a theoretical
work appeared: *Self and Others* [*Soi et les autres*]; this was followed by
Sanity, Madness and the Family [*L'équilibre mental, la folie et la famille*]; a
collection of eleven clinical monographs written in collaboration with A.
Esterson, and a disconcerting, unclassifiable book entitled *Knots*
[*Noeuds*], sort of a collection of logico-psychological poems.[2] How can we
understand the public's infatuation with Laing? Since May 1968, it

seems that a public has emerged which is particularly sensitive to everything that touches upon the problems of madness. It is more than twenty
years after the death of Antonin Artaud, and to pick up one of Laing's
terms, the mad are about to become the *hierophants* of our society. The
order of things, the institutions have received such a blow that one can
no longer refrain from pondering the future, and scrutinizing with apprehension every form of contestation, every protestation which considers itself exemplary – the emotion aroused by the Caro affair was, only
five years ago, altogether unimaginable!

Seen in this light, one might expect that the oeuvre of Laing will find
in the future an even larger readership. Is it not significant in this regard
that an anti-establishment movement of urbanists, known as CRAAAK,[3]
has used a poem on childhood from *Knots* as an epigraph of its manifesto?
Laing, Cooper, Basaglia, Gentis and several others have, in several
months, done more to change opinions about madness than decades of
patient and serious research carried out, for example, by the French
stream of Institutional Psychotherapy which is committed to never de-
parting from the concrete terrain of institutions of mental hygiene.

Nevertheless, it will always be necessary, in order to get to the heart of
the problem, to return to the overwhelming reality of the alienation of
psychiatric "populations", and to the inextricable predicaments in which
mental health workers find themselves every day.

In the last instance, it is on this terrain that the value of anti-psychiatric
theories must be appreciated. Anti-psychiatry will either be renewed by a
widespread, profound modification of the attitudes and the relations of
force in everyday practice, or it will remain what it is by circumstance: a
literary phenomenon and, as such, already largely "recuperated" by the
most reformist, indeed the most reactionary, currents which never shrink
from making verbal concessions.

It is necessary to admit that, up to the present, no anti-psychiatric
experiment has been long-lasting. All have been only gallant last stands
which have been liquidated by orthodox institutions. So far no mass
movement has suggested imposing a genuine anti-psychiatry (Cooper's
experiment at Pavillon 21 in London has had no repercussions; there has
not been another household like Kingsley Hall; and Basaglia had to leave
Gorizia, etc.).

Anti-psychiatry lays itself open all the more to reformist "recuper-
ations" because on the doctrinal level it has not freed itself from a
personalist and humanist ideology. This is true of Laing less than others,
but he is, at least a little, the leftist support for a current of thought that
one has to recognize as, altogether, in frank retreat from the contributions of Marx and Freud to the understanding of social alienation and
mental alienation.

Laing is in himself divided: revolutionary when he breaks with psychiatric practice, his written work gets away from him and, whether he likes it or not, is used for purposes alien to its inspiration. This is perhaps how his current Asian retreat must be interpreted.

When Laing writes that the most important new fact for about twenty years is "the more and more marked discontent which greets every theory or study of the individual that isolates him from his own context" (*Soi et les autres*, p. 98), this credits the most traditional forms of family psychotherapy and psychiatry of the sector. When he holds society responsible for the genesis of psychosis, one especially recalls that, for him, the remedy will have to come from an "honest confirmation between the parents" (*Ibid.*, p. 123). We are, then, soothed by such a return to the finer feelings, and prepared to be liberated from this object-cause of desire revealed by Lacan following Freud; an object radically heterogeneous to the person, whose identity and localization escape into intersubjective coordinates and the world of significations.

In a note Laing worries about giving the reader the impression that he would underestimate "the action of the person on himself" or that he would minimize "what relates to sexuality awakened by members of the family, that is, to incest" (*L'équilibre mental*, p. 32). No sooner has he evoked the spectre of sexual machinism, than he reduces it to familialism and incest. His search for a 'schizogenius' will never escape from the personological "nexus". His project of an existential phenomenology of madness amounts, in fact, to following "the twists and turns of the person in relation to the diverse manners in which one is more or less involved in what one does" (*Soi et les autres*, p. 160). It will be a matter of nothing other than "recognizing a person as an agent" (*Ibid.*, p. 124). It is "false situations" (*Ibid.*, 157) that are pathogenic. What must be recovered is the "true self" and "real confidence in the future" based on the "true encounter", as Martin Buber puts it (*Ibid.*, pp. 134 and 164).

We are not always convinced that Laing completely grasps the implications of his writings. At certain points he only commits himself with reservations to the themes which constitute the common ground of anti-psychiatry. For example, he is much more prudent than Cooper,[4] or even Hochmann,[5] when it comes to promoting this famous family psychotherapy which is essentially only a disguised return to techniques of readaptation, indeed, of suggestion at the scale of the small group.

It is also with some reservation that he adheres to the neo-behaviorist theory of Bateson called the "double bind" which consists of the reduction of the etiology of schizophrenia to a system of logical impasses and to an essentially deceptive personological alienation in the order of communication. Laing in particular shrinks from Bateson's affirmation that "there will be a collapse, in any individual, of the ability to establish a distinction between logical types[6] each time a situation of the double bind occurs" (*Soi et les autres*, pp. 183 and 186).

Is it not obvious that a series of interpersonal breakdowns might not suffice to produce a psychosis, even a neurosis nor, conversely, the resolution of these breakdowns might not sufficiently modify them! One sometimes connects too quickly Laing's phenomenological exercises with those in the work of Sartre. In actual fact Sartre never tied himself up in the mirror games which seem to fascinate Laing:

She wants him to want her
He wants her to want him
To get her to want him
He pretends he wants her . . .
(*Noeuds*, p. 48)

Sartre is a man of history and real engagement. He would certainly challenge the contemplative ideal which leads Laing to declare that we can do no more than "reflect the decomposition that surrounds and is in us".[7]

Is it possible today, when it is a question of madness, to ignore the contributions of Freud and Lacan? Is it possible to take refuge in a personalist and mystical wisdom without becoming the unconscious prisoner of ideologies whose mission is to suppress desire in every way?

Let's hope that Laing, who has sought to dissociate himself in an exemplary fashion from the traditional role of the psychiatrist, returns to the concrete struggle against the repression of the mentally ill and that he will be able to define more rigorously the conditions of a revolutionary psychiatric practice, that is, of a non-utopian psychiatry that is susceptible to being taken up en masse by the avant garde of mental health workers and by the mentally ill themselves.

Notes

This is a review of three books by R.D. Laing in French translation: *Soi et les autres*, trad. par Gilberte Lambrichs (Paris: Gallimard, 1971); a book written with A. Esterson, *L'équilibre mental, la folie et la famille*, trad. par Micheline Laguilhommie (Paris: Maspero, 1971); and *Noeuds*, trad. par Claude Elsen (Paris: Stock, 1971). It first appeared in *La Quinzaine littéraire* 132 (janv. 1972): 22–3. References to the French texts have been retained.

1 'L'avenir d'une utopie', *La Nef* 42 (1971): 222.
2 The translation of the book by Mary Barnes, one of principle figures of Kingsley Hall, is forthcoming. [Mary Barnes and Joseph Berke, *Two accounts of a journey through madness* (London: MacGibbon and Kee, 1971)]
3 Cirque Rurbain d'Animation, d'Action, d'Agitation Koultourelle.

4 Cooper, *Psychiatrie et antipsychiatrie* (Paris: Editions du Seuil, 1970).

5 Hochmann, *Pour une psychiatrie communautaire* (Paris: Editions du Seuil, 1971).

6 At issue are the logical types of Bertrand Russell.

7 Laing, *Politique de l'expérience* (Paris: Stock, 1970).

Translated by Gary Genosko

2

Franco Basaglia: Guerrilla
Psychiatrist

A war of liberation, waged for ten years to overthrow the traditional institution is presented to us in terms of militant struggle, in a literary fortnightly containing recorded accounts, book reviews, discussions, journal extracts, personal opinions and articles. And it is done without the least bit of pedantry. There is straightaway a violent refusal of all scientific pseudo-neutrality in this domain which is, for the authors, eminently political.

It all started in 1961. Under the impetus of Dr. Basaglia, the new direction of the hospital brought about "a sudden rupture of working solidarity" among the personnel and the breaking away of an "avant garde" which refused to any longer fulfill the "mandate of the cure and of surveillance" entrusted to them by a repressive society. Step by step all services were to be opened: general meetings would be open to the institutionalized, communications, the organization of leisure, and socio-therapy would be intensified. . . .

At first "nobody would open their mouth"; but then there was a thaw, and intense interest spread to all the departments. The hospital held over fifty meetings a week, spectacular improvements were made, and patients were sent home after 10, 15 or 20 years in the hospital.

Basaglia and Minguzzi then decided to undertake a detailed investigation into similar experiments in institutional psychotherapy in France and therapeutic communities in England (i.e. at Dingleton, under the direction of Maxwell Jones). They gradually developed their own conceptions, distancing themselves from other attempts that they considered to be too reformist, and questioning their own initial approaches.

Until then it had been the advance group – the "avant garde" – who "granted privileges" to patients. The dice were loaded. In 1965, Basaglia and his group decided to develop more thoroughly the "community culture" which, little by little, gained ground and modified the real relations of force between the personnel and the patients. Maxwell Jones's ideas were subjected to criticism. They decided that the techniques involved in *reaching a consensus* were, after all, only a new method of integrating the mentally ill into a society answering to the "ideal of the panorganization of neo-capitalist society" (Lucio Schiter, p. 149). The famous "third psychiatric revolution" would be merely, as they put it, "a belated adaptation of modalities of social control of pathological behavior to the methods of production perfected over the last forty years by sociologists and technicians of mass communication" (p. 149).

Thus, they rejected every politics of improvement and the consolidation of hospitals, a politics which in France had lead the most innovative trends in psychiatry to collaborate directly with the Minister of Health, and to elaborate, with the top-ranking civil servants, ministerial circulars for the reform of psychiatric hospitals, etc. In the long run, this experience was deceptive and bitter, and it drove certain of the best of French psychiatrists to despair. In addition, the recent psychiatric reform of teaching, finalized by Edgar Faure[1] for the departments, must have contributed to the spread of confusion among the ranks of the psychiatric opposition after May 1968. The society of institutional psychotherapy itself took cover during the May movement, certain psychiatrists estimating "that nothing happened in May", nothing in any case that could possibly concern institutional psychotherapy. Violently contradictory positions confronted one another during an international congress in Vienna in 1968, which Basaglia concluded by leaving and slamming the door behind him.

In Italy, where the state of the hospitals and the legislation is undoubtedly one of the most archaic in Europe, such illusions can hardly be dismissed – given the infamous stamp on the police record of psychiatric inmates; inmates denied their civil rights; and torture by strangulation: "a sheet, usually wet, is twisted tightly around the neck to prevent breathing: the loss of consciousness is immediate" (Basagila, p. 164). Basaglia harbors no illusions about the experiment of Gorizia: its future was doomed; at best, events would unfold as they did in Maxwell Jones's therapeutic communities at Dingleton, that is to say, in a "didactic and therapeutic engagement pursued on the staff level, but which retreats into the particular domain of institutional interests" (p. 100).

Unlike what generally happened elsewhere, the "psychiatric revolution" of Basaglia and his group was not "for laughs." From year to year, we witness an absolute escalation which has, moreover, lead to serious difficulties for its instigators. The *open door* [policy], ergotherapy, sociotherapy, sectorization – all these were implemented but did not cohere in a satisfying way. Was it the context of the Italian "creeping May" that entailed this permanent refusal of all self-satisfaction? Or was it the indifference of the Italian state and its inability to promote reform which discouraged every attempt at renewal? In any case, the "avant garde" of

Gorizia was no longer there: the "common goal" became "institutional change", the "negation of the institution", the Italian equivalent of the anti-psychiatry of Laing and Cooper in England.[2]

The very honesty of this book leads us to question the desperate nature of this endeavor. Is it not secretly preoccupied by a desire to bring things to the verge of collapse? Isn't the dialectical process on the way to transforming itself in forward flight and, in a sense, betraying itself? For *anti-psychiatry*, political intervention constitutes the prerequisite of all therapeutics. But doesn't the agreement around the "negation of the institution", which has meaning only if it is taken up by a real avant garde and securely achored in social reality, risk serving as a springboard for a new form of social repression, this time at the level of global society and aiming at the very status of madness?

Basaglia states that with the medications that he administers "the doctor calms his own anxiety in the face of a patient with whom he does not know how to enter into contact nor find a common language" (p. 117). An ambiguous and perhaps demagogic expression: psychopharmacology is not, in itself, a reactionary science! It is the context of its use that must be called into question.

Nosography, too, is perhaps a little rashly thrown overboard. The ways of repression are sometimes subtle! Those who uphold normality at any price can become more effective than the police! With the best moral and political intentions in the world, one may come to refuse the mad the right to be mad; the claim that "society is to blame" can disguise a way of suppressing all deviance. Institutional negation would then become a denegation – *Verneinung* in the Freudian sense – of the singular fact of derangement. Before taking out an option on nosography, Freud devoted himself to *really* giving a voice to neurotics, freeing them from all the effects of suggestion. Giving up the idea of medical suggestion in order to fall into collective suggestion would only create an illusory benefit.

I think that Basaglia and his comrades might be led incisively beyond some of their current formulations and "bend" their ears to mental alienation without systematically reducing it to social alienation. Matters are relatively straightforward and rightfully violent when it is a matter of repudiating repressive institutions. Things are much more difficult when they concern our understanding of madness. Then a few formulas from Sartrean or Maoist sources will not in this case suffice.

Political causality does not completely govern the causality of madness. It is perhaps, conversely, in an unconscious signifying assemblage that madness dwells, and which predetermines the structural field in which political options, drives, and revolutionary inhibitions are deployed, beside and beyond social and economic determinisms.

Fortunately, Basaglia's project has not fallen into a theoretical dogmatism. This book is invaluable in that it poses a thousand questions that the learned of contemporary psychiatry meticulously avoid.

Notes

This is a review of Franco Basaglia's *L'institution en négation*, trad. de l'italien par Louis Bonalumi (Paris: Editions du Seuil, 1970). The original title of the article was 'La contestation psychiatrique'. It appeared in *La Quinzaine littéraire* 94 (1970): 24–5 and was reprinted as 'Guerrilla en psychiatrie' in Guattari's *psychanalyse et transversalité* (Paris: François Maspero, 1972), pp. 261–64.

In the Maspero edition Guattari added an explanatory footnote: "The final lines of this article, arbitrarily cut by *La Quinzaine*, affirmed that above all the divergences a militant solidarity is imperative. I believe this point must be reaffirmed at the moment when the problems Basaglia has with Italian repression have presented an opportunity for the medical chronicler of *Le Monde*, Madame Escoffier-Lambiotte, for an underhand attack which, through this affair, looks at various attempts at renovation and innovation in psychiatry" (p. 264).

1 Edgar Faure was named Minister of [National] Education immediately following the events of May 1968.

2 Cf. Laing, *Politique de l'expérience* (Paris: Stock, 1970), and *Recherches*, "Spécial enfance aliénée", II (Déc. 1968); D. Cooper, *Psychiatrie et antipsychiatrie* (Paris: Editions du Seuil, 1970).

Translated by Gary Genosko

3

Mary Barnes's "Trip"

In 1965, a community of about 20 people formed around Ronald Laing. They settled in an old building, Kingsley Hall,[1] in a suburb of London which had been for a long time a Labour stronghold. Over the course of five years the leaders of the anti-psychiatry movement and the patients who, as they say, "made a career of schizoprenia", collectively explored the world of madness. Not the madness of the mental hospital, but the madness that dwells in each of us, a madness they proposed to liberate in order to release inhibitions and symptoms of every kind. At Kingsley Hall they disregarded – or tried to disregard – the division of roles among patients, psychiatrists, nurses, etc. No one had the right to give or receive orders, or to issue prescriptions. Kingsley Hall became a liberated parcel of land, a base for the counter-cultural movement.

The anti-psychiatrists want to move beyond the experiments of community psychiatry: according to them, such experiments were only reformist ventures which did not truly question the repressive institution and the traditional framework of psychiatry. Maxwell Jones and David Cooper,[2] two of the principal instigators of such experiments, actively participated in the life of Kingsley Hall. Thus, anti-psychiatry had at its disposal its own surface of inscription, a kind of body without organs in which every corner of the house – cellar, roof, kitchen, staircase, chapel – and each episode in the life of the collectivity, functioned like the gears of a big collective machine, drawing each person out of their immediate self and their own little problems, either to put themselves at the service of others, or to descend into themselves in a sometimes vertiginous process of regression.

This liberated parcel of land, Kingsley Hall, came under attack from all sides: the old world oozed through the cracks; the neighbours complained about its nighttime activities; local kids threw stones at the windows; on the slightest pretext the cops were ready to cart off any of the agitated residents to the *real* psychiatric hospital.[3]

But the real threat to Kingsley Hall came from within: the residents were free from identifiable constraints but secretly continued to interiorize repression and, furthermore, they remained under the yoke of simplistic reductions to the tired triangle – father, mother, child – which presses any situation considered to be outside the bounds of normality into the mold of Oedipal psychoanalysis.

Was it necessary to maintain a minimum of discipline at Kingsley Hall, or not? The atmosphere was poisoned by internal power struggles. Aaron Esterson, *leader* of the "hardline" faction – he walked around with a book by Stalin under his arm, while Laing carried Lenin – was eventually ousted and, despite this fact, it was always difficult for the community to establish its system of self-regulation. Moreover, the press, television, and "hangers-on" filtered in and out; Kingsley Hall became the object of obtrusive publicity. One of the residents, Mary Barnes, became a star of madness, which made her the focus of implacable jealousies.

Mary Barnes and her psychiatrist, Joseph Berke, wrote a book based on her experience at Kingsley Hall. It is a confession of disconcerting naïvety. It is both an exemplary exercise in the liberation of "mad desire" and neo-behaviorist dogmatism,[4] as well as being full of brilliant discoveries and an unrepentant familialism akin to the most traditional puritanism. The "mad" Mary Barnes explains in several confessional chapters what no "anti-psychiatrist" has ever revealed: the hidden side of Anglo-Saxon anti-psychiatry.

Mary Barnes is a former nurse who was labelled schizophrenic. She might also have been classified among the hysterics. She understands literally Laing's advice on the "trip". Her "regression into childhood" is undertaken in the manner of a *kamikaze*. Her "down" periods on several occasions lead her to the verge of death by starvation. Everyone would get in a panic: should she be taken to the hospital, or not? This precipitated a "monumental crisis" in the community. But it should be said that during her "up" periods, the problems of the group did not improve: she agreed to deal only with those whom she had heavily endowed with her familialism and mysticism, which is to say above all Ronnie (Laing), whom she idolizes like a god, and Joe (Berke), who becomes simultaneously her father, mother, and spiritual lover.

In this way she establishes for herself a little oedipal territory that echoes all of the paranoaic tendencies of the institution. Her pleasure is concentrated in the painful awareness, which pitilessly torments her, of the *evil* she unleashes around her. She is opposed to Laing's project; yet, it is her dearest possession. The more guilt she feels, the more she punishes herself, the worse her condition gets, unleashing reactions of panic all around her. She restores the infernal circle of familialism but, by putting more than twenty people into it, only makes matters worse!

She behaves like a baby and needs to be bottle-fed. She walks around naked, covered in shit, pissing in all the beds, breaking everything, or lets herself starve to death. She tyrannizes Joe Berke, prevents him from leaving, and harasses his wife to the extent that, one day, unable to bear it, he hits her. Inexorably, one is tempted to resort to the well known methods of the psychiatric hospital! Joe Berke asks himself how it happens that "a group of people devoted to demystifying the social relations of disturbed families come to behave like one of them"?

Fortunately, Mary Barnes is an exceptional case. Not everyone at Kingsley Hall behaves like her! But doesn't she present the real problems? Is it certain that understanding, love, and all the other Christian virtues, combined with a technique of mystical regression, suffice to exorcize the demons of oedipal madness?

Laing is without doubt among those who are the most deeply engaged in the attempt to demolish psychiatry. He has scaled the walls of the asylum, but gives the impression that he remains a prisoner of other walls he carries inside himself; he has not yet managed to free himself from the worst constraint, the most dangerous of *double binds*,[5] that of "psychoanalysm" – to recall Robert Castel's felicitous expression – with its delirious signifying interpretation, representations with hidden levels, and derisive abysses.

Laing thought that one could outwit neurotic alienation by centering the analysis on the family, on its internal "knots". For him, everything starts with the family. He would like, however, to break away from it. He would like to merge with the cosmos, to burst the everydayness of existence. But his mode of explanation cannot release the subject from the grip of the familialism that he wanted only as a point of departure and which reappears at every turn. He tries to resolve the problem by taking refuge in an Oriental style of meditation which could not definitively guard against the intrusion of a capitalist subjectivity with the most subtle means at its disposal. One doesn't bargain with Oedipus: as long as this essential structure of capitalist repression is not attacked head-on, one will not be able to make any decisive changes in the economy of desire and thus, in the status of madness.

This book is filled with flows of shit, piss, milk and paint. But it is significant to note that it is practically never a question of the flow of money. It is not certain how matters stand from this perspective. Who handles the money, who decides what to buy, and who gets paid? The community seems to live on air: Mary's brother Peter, who is without doubt much more engaged than she in a schizo process, cannot bear the bohemian style of Kingsley Hall. There is too much noise, too much chaos, and besides, what he wants is to hold onto his job.

But his sister harasses him and he has to settle in Kingsley Hall. Implacable proselytism of regression: you will discover, you will take your trip, you will be able to paint, you will see your madness through to its end . . . . But Peter's madness is far more disturbing. He is not very eager to embark on this sort of venture! Here, perhaps, one can under-

stand the difference between a real schizo trip and a petit-bourgeois style
of familialist regression. The schizo is not all that interested in "human
warmth". His dealings are elsewhere, on the side of the most deterritorialized fluxes: the flux of the "miraculating" cosmic signs, but also the
flux of monetary signs. The schizo is not unaware of the reality of money
– even if it is put to extraordinary uses – any more than he is unaware of
any other reality. The schizo does not behave like a child. For him money
is a reference point like any other and he needs to have at his disposal a
maximum number of systems of reference, precisely to enable him to
keep his distance. Exchange is, for him, a way of avoiding confusions. In
short, Peter does not want to put up with these interfering stories of
community which threaten his singular relation to desire.

Mary's familial neurosis is quite another thing; she is continually
establishing little familial territories; it is a kind of vampirism of "human
warmth". Mary clings to the image of the other; for example, she asked
Anna Freud to analyze her – but, in her mind, this meant that Anna
would move into her place, with her brother, and that they would
become her children. It's this process that she tried to begin again with
Ronnie and Joe.

Familialism consists in magically denying social reality, and avoiding
all connections with real fluxes. There remain only the possibilities of the
dream and the infernal locked-door of the conjugal-familial system or,
still, in great moments of crisis, a little ratty territory into which one can
withdraw, alone. It is on this level that Mary Barnes functioned at
Kingsley Hall: as a missionary of Laing's therapy, as a militant of madness, and as a professional.

This confession teaches us more than a dozen theoretical works on
anti-psychiatry. We can finally catch a glimpse of the implications of
'psychoanalysm' in the methods of Laing and his friends.

From Freud's *Studies on Hysteria* to the structuralist analysts currently
in fashion, all psychoanalytic method consists in sifting any situation
through three screens [*cribles*]: i) *Interpretation*: a thing must always
signify something other than itself. The truth is never to be found in the
actuality of intensities and relations of force, but only through a game of
signifying clues; ii) *Familialism*: these signifying clues are essentially
reducible to familial representations. To reach them one proceeds by
means of regression; one will induce the subject to "rediscover" his
childhood. In point of fact, this means a "powerless" representation of
childhood, a childhood of memory, myth, refuge, the negative of current
intensities which have no possible relation to its positive aspects; iii)
Transference: in the continuation of the interpretive sifting and familialist
regression, desire is reinstalled in a cramped space, a miserable little
identificatory world (the couch of the analyst, his look, his supposed

attention). The rule of the game is that everything which presents itself must be reduced by means of interpretation and images of papa–mama. All that remains is to proceed to the ultimate reduction of the signifying battery itself, which must function with only a single term: the silence of the analyst, against which all questions come up against. Psychoanalytic transference, a kind of churn used to cream off the reality of desire, leaves the subject hanging in a vertigo of abolition, a narcissistic passion, which, though less dangerous than russian roulette, still leads – if it goes well – to an irreversible fixation on valueless subtleties which will end by taking him away from all other social investment.

We have known for a long time that these three screens operate poorly with the mad: their interpretations, their images are too distant from dominant social coordinates. Instead of giving up this method, at Kingsley Hall they tried to improve the screens in order to reinforce their effects. Thus, the silent interpretation of dual analysis was replaced by a collective – and boisterous – interpretation, a kind of communal delirious interpretation. The method did find a new efficacy: it is no longer satisfied with a mirror game between the words of the analysand and the silence of the analyst; there are also objects, gestures, and the interaction of forces. Joe Berke gets into the big game of Mary Barnes' regression in a way that is still rare among typical psychoanalysts: he grunts, acts like a crocodile, bites and pinches her, rolls her in her bed.

We're almost there! We are on the verge of breaking into another practice, another semiotic. We will break the shackles with the sacred principles of signifiance and interpretation. Not quite, though, since each time the psychoanalyst recovers and reinstates his familialist coordinates. He is caught in his own game: when Joe Berke wants to leave Kingsley Hall, Mary does everything to keep him there. Not only has the analysis become interminable, but the session has as well! It is only by losing his temper that Berke manages to free himself from his "patient" for a few hours in order to attend a meeting on the Vietnam war.

The interpretive contamination has become limitless. Paradoxically, it is Mary who first broke the cycle through her painting. Over the course of a few months she became a famous painter.[6] Yet even here interpretation has not relinquished its claims: if Mary feels guilty when she takes a drawing class, it is because her mother's hobby was painting and she would be upset if she knew that her daughter was a better painter. On the paternal side, things are scarcely better: "Now, with all these paintings, you possess the penis, the power, and your father feels threatened".

With touching industriousness, Mary tries hard to absorb all of the psychoanalytic hodgepodge. Thus, in the communal atmosphere of Kingsley Hall, Mary stands out like a sore thumb because she does not want to work with just anyone. She turns away some people because she wants to be assured that they are completely immersed in Ronnie's thought: "When I got the idea of a breast, a safe breast, Joe's breast, a breast I could suck without being stolen from myself, nothing could hold me back . . . When Joe put his finger in my mouth he was saying to me. 'Look, I can come into you without controlling you, possessing, stealing you'."

Even the psychoanalyst ends up being overwhelmed by the interpretive machine he helped to set into motion. He admitted that: "Mary interpreted everything that was done for her (or for anyone else for that matter) as therapy. If the coal was not delivered on time, that was therapy. And so on, to the most absurd conclusions". This didn't prevent Joe from continuing to struggle with his own interpretations, which had no other goal than to make his relationship with Mary fit into the oedipal triangle: "By 1966, however, I had a pretty good idea of what and who I was for her when we were together. 'Mama' took the lead when she was Mary the baby. 'Papa' and 'brother Peter' vied for second place. In order to protect my own sense of reality, and to help Mary break through her web of illusion, I always took the trouble to point out when I thought Mary was using me as someone else". But it would be impossible for him to break free of this spider web. Mary had caught the whole household up in it.

Let's now turn to the technique of regression into childhood and the transference: their "derealizing" effects were accentuated by being developed in a communal milieu. In the traditional analytic encounter, the dual relation, the artificial and limited nature of the session establishes a barricade of sorts against imaginary outbursts. At Kingsley Hall, it was a real death that confronted Mary Barnes at the end of each of her trips, and the entire institution was overcome with a sadness and distress equally as real. At this point Aaron Esterson resorted to the old methods of authority and suggestion: Mary was on the verge of death by starvation, and he forcefully ended her fast.

A few years earlier a Catholic psychoanalyst had forbidden her, with the same measure of brutality, to masturbate, explaining to her, as she recalled, that it was an even graver sin than sleeping with a man out of wedlock. It worked then as well. In fact, isn't this return to authority and suggestion the inevitable correlate of this technique of regression on all fronts? Suddenly returning from the brink of death, a papa-cop comes out into the open. The imaginary, especially that of the psychoanalyst, does not constitute a defense against social repression; on the contrary, it secretly invites it.

One of the most valuable lessons of this book perhaps is that it shows us the extent to which it is illusory to hope to recover raw desire, pure and simple, by embarking on a search for the knots hidden in the unconscious and the secret keys of interpretation. Nothing can unravel, by the sole magic of the transference, the real micropolitical conflicts in which the subject is imprisoned; no mystery, no hidden universe. There is nothing to discover in the unconscious. The unconscious is something to be built. If the Oedipus of the transference does not resolve the familial Oedipus, it is because it is deeply attached to the familialized individual.

Alone on the couch or in a group, in an institutional regression, the "normal-neurotic" (you and I) or the psychiatrist's neurotic (the "mad") continues to ask again and again for Oedipus. Psychoanalysts, whose entire training and practice has saturated them with the reductionist drug of interpretation, can only reinforce this policy of crushing desire: transference is a technique of diverting the investments of desire. Far from slowing the race towards death, it seems on the contrary to accelerate it, accumulating, as in a cyclotron, "individuated" oedipal energies, in what Joe Berke calls "the vicious spiral of punishment-anger-guilt-punishment". It can only lead to castration, self-denial, and sublimation: a shoddy sort of asceticism. The objects of collective guilt succeed one another, accentuating the punitive, self-destructive impulses by doubling them with a real repression composed of anger, jealousy and fear.

Guilt becomes a specific form of the libido – capitalist Eros – when it enters into conjunction with the deterritorialized fluxes of capitalism. It then finds a new way, a novel solution, outside the confines of family, asylum, or psychoanalysis. I shouldn't have, what I did was bad and, the more I feel it's bad, the more I want to do it, because then I can live in this zone of intensity of guilt. However, this zone, instead of being "embodied", of being attached to the body of the subject, to the ego, to the family, takes possession of the institution – Mary Barnes was the real boss of Kingsley Hall. She knew it intimately. Everything revolved around her. She just played with Oedipus, while the others were well and truly caught in a collective oedipalism.

One day Joe Berke finds her covered in shit and shivering from the cold, and his nerves crack. He then becomes aware of "her extraordinary ability to conjure up everyone's favorite nightmare and embody it for them". Thus, at Kingsley Hall, the transference is no longer "contained" by the analyst, but goes in all directions and threatens even the psychoanalyst. Everyone becomes a psychoanalyst! And yet, it very nearly happened that nobody was the analyst, and that the desiring intensities, the "partial objects", followed their own lines of force without being haunted by systems of interpretation, and duly codified by the social grids of the "dominant reality".

Why did Berke desperately attempt to reglue the scattered multiplicity through which Mary "experiments" with the dissolution of her ego and gives free rein to her neurosis? Why this return to familial poles, to the unity of the person which prevents Mary from becoming aware of the world outside with its potential rewards? "The initial process of her coming together was akin to my trying to put together a jigsaw puzzle without having all the pieces. Of those pieces at hand, many had had their tabs cut off and their slots plugged. So it was practically impossible to tell what went where. This puzzle, of course, was Mary's emotional life. The pieces were her thoughts, her actions, her associations, her dreams, etc."

What proof do we have that the solution for Mary Barnes lies with infantile regression? What proof do we have that the origin of her problems stem from disturbances, from blockages in the intrafamilial system of communication of her childhood? Why not consider instead what was happening around the family? In fact, we note that all the doors to the outside were firmly shut on her when she tried to open them; that's how she came up against a familialism that was, without doubt, even more repressive than what she had known during her childhood. What if poor father and mother Barnes were only the pitiful, unknowing relays of the repressive tempest raging outside? Mary was not *fixated* in childhood; she simply never found the exit! Her desire for a real exit was too violent and too demanding to adapt itself to the compromises of the outside world.

The first episode occurred at school. "School was dangerous". She sat in her chair, paralysed, terrorized, and she fought with the teacher. "Most things at school worried me . . ." She pretended to read, sing, draw . . . She wanted, however, to be a writer, a journalist, a painter, a doctor! One day it was explained to her that all that meant she wanted to become a man. "I was ashamed of wanting to be a doctor. I know this shame was bound up – and here the interpretation kicks in again – with the enormous guilt I had in connection with my desire to be a boy. Everything masculine in myself must remain hidden, secret, unexperienced."

Priests and cops of every type tried to make her feel guilty, about everything and nothing and, in particular, about masturbation. When she resigned herself to being a nurse and enlisted in the army, she hit another dead end. Once she wanted to go to Russia because she had heard that there "women with babies and no husbands were quite acceptable". When she decided to enter a convent, her religious faith was doubted: "What brought you into the Church?"

And the priests were undoubtedly right; her desire for saintliness seemed fishy. Finally, all this led to the asylum. Even there, she was prepared to do something, to dedicate herself to others. One day she brought a bouquet of flowers for a nurse and was told: "Get out! You should not be in here!" There is no end to recounting the social traumas and subjugations she suffered. Having become a nurse, her right to higher education was challenged. Mary Barnes was not, at the outset, interested in the family, but in society! But everything brought her back to the family. And, this is hard to say, even her stay at Kingsley Hall! Since the familialist interpretation was the game of choice of the place, and since she adored everyone there, she also played along. But did she ever play!

She was the real analyst of Kingsley Hall; she fully explored all the neurotic forces and subjacent paranoia of her father and mother of Kingsley Hall. Has Mary-the-missionary at least helped the anti-psychiatrists to clarify the reactionary implications of their psychoanalytic postulates?

Notes

"Le 'voyage' de Mary Barnes" appeared in *Le nouvel observateur* (28 mai, 1973): 82–4, 87, 93, 96, 101, 104, 109–10. It was first translated into English by Rosemary Sheed as "Mary Barnes, or Oedipus in Anti-Psychiatry", in *Molecular Revolution* (Harmondsworth, Middlesex: Penguin, 1984), pp. 51–59. Sheed's title was the one used by Guattari in the 10–18 reedition of *La révolution moléculaire* (1980). A second translation by Ruth Ohayon, "Mary Barnes' 'Trip'", appeared in *semiotext(e) Anti-Oedipus* II/2 (1977): 63–71. I have consulted both translations.

1 Kingsley Hall, in Bow (East London), was leased for a five year period from 1965–1970. It was one of seven experimental therapeutic community households in London administered by the Philadelphia Association, whose chairman was R. D. Laing.
2 David Cooper, *Psychiatry and Antipsychiatry* (London: Tavistock, 1967).
3 Nothing is comparable, however, with the Italian repression which has destroyed less 'provocative' attempts and, above all, with the truly barbaric German repression, currently inflicted upon the SPK (Sozialistiches Patientenkollectiv) in Heidelberg.
4 Behaviorism: a turn of the century theory which reduced psychology to the study of behavior, defined as the interaction between external stimuli and the responses of the subject. The neo-behaviorism of today tends to reduce all human problems to questions of communication and information, ignoring the socio-political problems of power at all levels.
5 A contradictory double constraint situated on the level of the communication between a subject and his family, and which is completely disturbing.
6 Her exhibitions, in Great Britain and abroad, brought her a certain notoriety. Much could be said about this sort of recuperation, "art brut" style, which consists in promoting a mad artist . . . like the star of a variety show, for the benefit of the producers of this kind of spectacle. The essence of mad art is to be above and beyond notions of oeuvre and authorial functions.

Translated by Gary Genosko

4

The Four Truths of Psychiatry

The slump that psychiatry and its shaky therapeutic grounds have found themselves mired in over the last few decades cannot be accounted for independently of contemporary economic and social upheavals. Some of the anti-establishment and counter-cultural movements of the sixties may have appeared, to many who had intensely lived through those times, as the premises for profound transformations which later on became woven into the social fabric. None of these transformations, however, actually took place! History, of course, may have a few surprises in store for us! But, while we wait, we may conclude that the recurring crises of these last few years justified these movements. One can even ask whether this was not one of their prime *objectives*. Whatever the hopes, utopias, and innovative experiments of this epoch amounted to, all that remains of them today is a dim memory – cherished by some, full of spite and revenge in others or, deemed to be quite indifferent by the majority. This doesn't mean that alternative efforts and movements have been definitively swept away, having lost all legitimacy. Other generations have taken up the challenge where they left off, perhaps with less dreaming, more realism, and less mythical and theoretical baggage. As for me, I remain convinced that far from having gone *beyond* the issues of that period, the same problems continue to haunt the future of our societies, in that the choice at the time was either to gear efforts towards human ends by bringing about, through every possible means, the task of reappropriating individual and collective existential territories, or fast-forwarding towards collective murderous and suicidal madness – our present situation providing an abundance of symptoms and indices to this effect.

I believe it is in the context of this more or less roughly sketched state of affairs that the notions of transformation within the field of psychiatry over the last few years should be re-examined. To give a brief sketch of the most notable events: the movement of institutional therapy in its early period under the impact of people like Daumezon, Le Guillant, Bonnafé, etc., who were committed to the humanization of old psychiatric hospitals; the initial implementation of a psychiatry of the sector, with its day hospitals, supervised workshops, home visits, etc.; institutional psychiatry in its later phase, rearticulated by François Tosquelles, Jean Oury and GTPSI [Groupe de travail de psychothérapie institutionelle] in terms of psychoanalytic concepts and practices; the different movements aimed at offering an alternative to psychiatry . . . . All of these carried within them a fraction of the truth without ever having had to face or consider the effects of upheavals in society at large. In addition to their particular contributions – which I would certainly be the last to underestimate – the question of a truly radical reconfiguration, a paradigmatic change of psychiatry, always seemed to loom in the background as a possibility.

Without putting myself in a situation of having to provide an exhaustive mapping of this problem, I would like to delineate a few characteristics of the necessary conditions for a complete progressive *revival* of this languishing field – after all, this is the place to spill the beans! It seems to me that we have to connect this exclusively to at least four levels of intervention, to four kinds of truths:

1 the transformation of existing cumbersome apparatuses;

2 the maintenance of alternative experiments;

3 the sensitization and mobilization of these themes with the most diverse social partners;

4 the development of revamped methods for the analysis of unconscious subjectivity, both at the individual as well as the collective level.

The task, in other words, is to free ourselves, in a most radical way, from the dogmatic shortsightedness and corporate quarrels that, for such a long period, have fed parasitically on our reflections and practices. In this domain, much like any other, one truth does not hound the other. Since there is no universal remedy that one could prescribe and apply univocally to all situations, the first criterion of concrete *feasibility* would be to take on a project in which committed social functionaries would accept responsibility for the consequences of all plans.

In the following few examples let us try to illustrate, for the moment, how recent efforts directed at the transformation of psychiatry already implied at least a minimum consideration of one of our *four truths* and how they have also come up against their own limits by not having concurrently weighed all of them – which, in turn, would have necessitated a sufficiently consistent presupposition of the existence of collective assemblages required for their commencement.

What has been termed as the *first psychiatric revolution* of the post-war years, which had taken the tangible material and moral amelioration of a number of French psychiatric hospitals as its aim, could only succeed because of its appeal to the following coordinates:

1 a strong progressive psychiatric standard;

2 a powerful majority of militant psychiatric nurses all in favor of transforming the conditions of the asylum (leading, for example, to the formative stages of the *Centre d'entraînement aux méthodes actives*: CEMEA);

3 a nucleus of Ministry of Health officials pursuing similar aims.

It was by way of these exceptionally well linked conditions that an effective intervention was made possible at the first level. On the other hand, neither of the other three levels – alternatives, social mobilization, and analysis of subjectivity – were taken up in spite of the fact that there had been many questions revolving around these issues at the very heart of the psychiatry of the sector.

The English communitarian experiments, developed in the wake of Maxwell Jones, and then by R. D. Laing, David Cooper and the Philadelphia Association, have proved that they were endowed with a certain social intelligence and an indisputable analytic sensibility. Yet they received no support whatsoever from the state or from what we might conveniently call the forces of the left. This denial of patronage had so profoundly affected their personal efforts that the movement lacked the potential for rapid development within the field.

If we now turn to an experiment like that of La Borde – a clinic of a hundred beds where Jean Oury has been the main inspirational force over the last thirty years and to whom I remain personally indebted – we will find ourselves in the presence of an extraordinary institutional clockwork constituting a *collective analyzer* which, to my mind, is of the utmost importance. There is no shortage of flaws attributed to its work by external supporters, although according to different modalities than the examples listed above. Let us only invoke the fact that in spite of Social Security, this clinic has always been systematically marginalized from an economic point of view while its lot, paradoxically, has not improved under a socialist regime. On the contrary, it has deteriorated. While some believe it ought to be treated as an historical relic, the clinic has remained more alive than ever and has even found itself "carried" on a wave of sympathy that has never failed it, and is attested to by the enrolment of over a hundred French and foreign trainees. Meanwhile, it can very well be regarded as having been condemned to isolation. An experiment like this cannot acquire its full meaning unless it is placed within the context of a proliferating network of alternative initiatives. The issue to be pinpointed here is the reevaluation of the role of hospitalization. It is quite evident that one must urgently do away with all the incarcerative methods of accommodation. This by no means implies the unnuanced renunciation of structures of hospitality and collective life. For many dissidents of the psyché, the question can no longer be posed in terms of a reintegration into the so-called normal structures of the socius. In this respect, all too often we have mythified the more or less forced and guilt-ridden maintenance of, or a return to, the heart of the family. Other modes of individuality and collectivity need to be found and it is here that an immense site for research and experimentation is suddenly opened up.

I could list other figures to put into relief the discord of the four levels of intervention that would illustrate a less ambivalent attitude on the part of French public powers vis-à-vis alternative communities in the South-West region of France where, for example, my friend Claude Sigala has been caught up in a strange coming-and-going between the halls of the ministry, those of the Department of Justice, and a cell in the prison of Health! But I will content myself with a final example by referring to Psichiatria Democratica and to the work of Franco Basaglia, whose memory I honor here. This was the first movement to explore, with similar intensity, the potential for work in the field that would align itself with the forces of the left in order to seek ways of creating public awareness and systemic action with respect to public powers. Unfortunately – and this had been the object of a friendly debate between Basaglia and myself – it was the analytic dimension that had blurred the situation and which had often been vehemently rejected.

Why, you may ask, are you insisting, as a leitmotif, on your fourth, analytic dimension? Should it really be considered as one of the principle jurisdictions of our problem? Without getting bogged down in further elaborations, it seems to me that there is a possible cure for the leprosy of our psychiatric institutions and, beyond the entirety of welfare arrangements, I would like to speak to this desperate serialization of misguided individuals, not only with reference to them as "users", but also to their therapeutic, technical, and administrative roles. To conduct an institutional analysis on a grand scale, one would need to make a permanent effort to study the subjectivity produced in all relations of social assistance, education, etc. A certain type of subjectivity which I will qualify as capitalist, is poised to sweep the planet: a subjectivity of equivalence, of standard fantasy, of massive consumption and infantilizing reassurance. This is the source of all passivity, all the forms of the degeneration of democratic values, the collective abandonment to racism . . . . It is today secreted in massive doses by the mass media, by collective apparatuses, by the allegedly cultural industries. It does not merely concern conscious ideological formations, but equally encompasses the sphere of unconscious collective affects. Psychiatry and the entire range of therapies have a particular responsibility: either they caution us regarding their present forms, or they strive to branch out in non-alienating directions. It is relative to this problematic that alternative approaches to psychiatry and psychoanalysis acquire their significance. They will have no real impact unless they align themselves with other movements aimed at transforming subjectivity and can present themselves in multiple ways through ecological, nationalist, and feminist interest groups that are sympathetic towards the fight against racism and, in general, through conscientious and well thought out alternative practices that are able to properly gauge the perspectives of an ever increasing crowd of *marginalized* and non-guaranteed people.

But this implies correlatively that parties, groupuscules, communities, collectives and individuals desiring to work in his direction must be capable of self-transformation and break the pattern of modelling their functions and unconscious representations on dominant repressive models. In order to accomplish this, they must operate towards themselves and the exterior, not only as a social and political instrument, but also as a collective analytic assemblage of these unconscious processes. And here, I repeat, everything has yet to be invented. Everything is ahead of us. It is the ensemble of social practices that need to be questioned and which demand to be rethought and retried.

This is basically what we have attempted to accomplish with the "Réseau alternative à la psychiatrie" since its inception in 1975, and which periodically organizes an international debate between the most diverse, the most heterogeneous components of the therapeutic profession and its alternative movements. There are, of course, other initiatives along these lines. I am thinking, in particular, about the gatherings in Italy on mental ecology to be held at the end of this year, thanks to the initiatives of the Topia group in Bologna, under the direction of Franco Berardi.

The aim is to reaffirm, stronger than ever, the right to singularity, to the freedom of individual and collective creation, and the removal of technocratic conformisms; the goal is to do away with the arrogance of all forms of postmodernism and to conjure up and call attention to the dangers inherent in the levelling out of all subjectivity that is being promoted in the wake of new technologies.

Here are a few elements I would like to bring to your debate. Allow me again, by way of concluding, to add three remarks pertaining to your Bill 180:

1 It was by all considerations of crucial importance to redress the previous legislation and the complete return to the reinstitution of the old structures of asylums and confront them as wholly reaction-

ary and absurd. In France, the debate continues to go round in circles with respect to the modification of the old law of 1838 (a law that is segregative and contrary to human rights).[1] I fully agree with Henri Ey in this matter: that the only solution is its suppression pure and simple, and that all the questions that have been shelved should only be taken up in the spirit of the Code of Health.

2　If one is to recreate the specific facilities of the reception hospital – and I believe this is absolutely necessary – these need to be conceived of as evolutive places of research and experimentation, which is to restate just how much I am against having them reestablished within general hospitals.

3　Only renewed forms of social mobilization will allow for the growth and development of mentalities and for the possibility of overcoming the always menacing 'anti-mad' racism. The initiative and decisions in this domain ultimately do not lie with traditional political formations, hampered as they generally are by their bureaucratic shackles, but with the reinvention of a new type of social and alternative movement.

Notes

"Les quatres vérités de la psychiatrie" was presented in Rome (28/6/1985) at a conference organized by the Italian Socialist Party on the theme of "Psychiatry and Institutions". It was collected in *Les Années D'Hiver* 1980–1985 (Paris: Bernard Barrault, 1986), pp 223–232.

1　References to the law of 30 juin 1838 are commonplace in progressive French psychiatric circles. The result of cooperation between proto-psychiatrists and the government of the period, the law had several far-reaching effects: i) it provided a legal justification for the theory of isolation as a therapeutic method; ii) it gave legal status to the sequestering of so-called "lunatics"; iii) it legitimated psychiatry as a profession; and iv) led to the establishment of a nation-wide, public departmental network of asylums.

Translated by Charles Dudas

5

The Transference

J. Schotte[1] was right in highlighting the nature of signifying operations that allow us to identify transferential phenomena with those of speech and language. This ought to help us clarify the question of the transference outside of the strict field of psychoanalytic experience, that is to say, of the transference as it manifests itself in the group or institution. To the extent that we can regard the group as also "structured like a language" – to transpose one of Lacan's expressions regarding the unconscious – the question can also be posed, perhaps, as to how it speaks, and, above all, if it is even legitimate to consider that it gives us access to speech. Can a group be the subject of its own enunciation? If so, would this be by virtue of consciousness or the unconscious? To whom does the group speak? Is the subjugated group, alienated from the discourse of other groups, condemned to remain prisoner of the non-meaning of its own discourse? Is there a possible, even if only partial, way out for such a group that would allow for it to step back a little from its own utterances and, in spite of its subjugation, become both subject and object?

Under what sort of conditions could we hope to see a full speech emerge from a field of empty speech – to borrow other expressions from Lacan? Can we, for example, envisage in good faith and without betrayal that there may be "for all that something to do" in situations as alienating as those to be found in psychiatric hospitals, schools, and so forth? Or must we give up in sheer despair, and live a politics where we resign ourselves to the worst possible outcome, and make social revolution the absolute precondition for any intervention in the local running of institutions by its "users"?

Or does the group and its non-meaning maintain a kind of secret dialogue – harbouring a potential alterity? In this way, could not the group be, even on the basis of its impotence, the carrier of an unconscious call that might render this alterity possible? Even if only to speak this impotence together as a group: "What does the unconscious [ça] think of all this around us?" "What good is it?" "What the hell are we doing there . . . ?" So, the subjugated group and the subject-group should not be regarded as being mutually exclusive. A formerly

revolutionary contingent, that is now more or less subject to the dominant order, can still occupy, in the eyes of the masses, the empty place
left by the subject of history, and may even, in certain circumstances
become, despite itself, the subject of the enunciation of a revolutionary
struggle, that is, the spokesperson of a discourse that is not its own,
though it may mean betraying this discourse when the development of
the relation of forces give it the hope of a "return to normalcy". Thus,
however subject it may be to socio-economic restraints, such a group will
– as a transformation of context would reveal – unintentionally retain the
possibility of a subjective cut. It is, therefore, not a question for us of
conceiving the alienating and disalienating phenomena of the group as
things-in-themselves, but rather as the varying sides – that would be
differently expressed and developed depending on the context – of a
similar institutional object.

On the side of the subjection of the group, we will need to decode those
phenomena that encourage the group to withdraw into itself: leaderships,
identifications, effects of suggestion, disavowals, scape-goating, and so
forth. We will also need to decode anything that tends to promote local
laws and idiosyncratic formations involving interdictions, rites, and anything else that tends to protect the group by buttressing it against
signifying storms in which – as the result of a specific operation of
misrecognition – the threat is experienced as issuing from the outside.
This has the effect of producing those deceitful outlooks peculiar to
group delusions. This kind of group is thus involved in a perpetual
struggle against any possible inscription of non-meaning: various roles
are reified by a phallic appropriation along the model of the leader or of
exclusion. One is part of such a group so as to collectively refuse to face
up to the nothingness, that is, to the ultimate meaning of the projects in
which we are engaged. This group is a kind of a syndicate or lobby of
mutual defense against solitude, and of anything that might be classified
as having a transcendental nature.

As concerns the other side, the subject-group does not employ the
same means to secure itself. One is here threatened with being sub-
merged in a flood of problems, tensions, internal battles, and risk of
secession. This is so for the very reason of the opening of this group onto
other groups. Dialogue – the intervention into other groups is an accepted aim of the subject-group – compels this group to have a certain
clarity in relation to its finitude, that is, it brings into profile its distinct
death, or its rupture. The calling of the subject-group to speak tends to
compromise the status and security of the group's members. There thus
develops a kind of vertigo, or madness peculiar to this group. A kind of
paranoid contraction is substituted for this calling to be subject: the
group would like to be subject at any cost, including being in the place of

the other, and in this way, it will fall into the worst alienation, the kind that is at the origin of all the compulsive and mortiferous mechanisms employed by religious, literary, and revolutionary coteries.

What might be the balancing factors of a group placed between these diverse sides of alienation; that is, between the external one of the subjugated-group, and that of the internal or borderline madness that is the project of the subject-group?

Our experience in hospitals might shed some light on this question. We know quite well that the "socialization" or reintegration of someone who is ill into a group does not simply depend on the good will of the therapists. In their attempts to reintegrate into a group or society, some of the ill in institutions encounter zones of tolerance, but also thresholds of absolute impossibility. We are here in the presence of a similar mechanism that is to be found in the rites of passage of primitive societies when initiating or welcoming into the culture a sub-group that has come of age. What happens if a person does not accept being marked by the group? If we force things to their limit, we arrive at one of two possibilities: either the group, or the recalcitrant individual, is shattered. Now, it is precisely in those groups that do not cultivate their symptoms by rituals – the subject-groups – that the risk of a face to face encounter with non-meaning is much greater, but, consequently, so is the possibility of a lifting of individual symptomatic impasses.

So long as the group remains an object for other groups and receives its non-meaning, that is, death, from the outside, one can always count on finding refuge in the group's structures of misrecognition. But from the moment the group becomes a subject of its own destiny and assumes its own finitude and death, it is then that the data received by the superego is modified, and, consequently, the threshold of the castration complex, specific to a given social order, can be locally modified. Thus one belongs to such a group not so as to hide from desire and death, engaging in a collective process of neurotic obsession, but owing to a particular problem which is ultimately not eternal in nature, but transitory. This is what I have called the structure of "transversality".

Schotte emphasizes the fact that in the transference there is virtually never any actual dual relation. This is very important to note. The mother–child relationship, for example, is not a dual relation, at whatever level it is considered. At the moment that we envisage this relation in a real situation we recognize that it is, at the very least, triangular in character. In other words, there is always in a real situation a mediating object that acts as an ambiguous support or medium. For there to be displacement, transference, or language, there must also by necessity exist something there that can be cut or detached. Lacan strongly emphasized this feature of the object as decisive for making one's way through those questions concerning the transference and counter-transference. One is displaced in the order of the transference only insofar as *something* can be displaced. Something that is neither the subject nor the object. There is no intersubjective relation, dual or otherwise, that would suffice to establish a system of expression, that is to say, a position of alterity. The face to face encounter with the other does not account for the opening onto the other, nor does it establish access to the other's understanding. The founder of metaphor is this something outside or adjacent to the subject that Lacan described under the heading of the *objet "a"*.

But what about this *"a"*? One must not make of it a universal key of linguistic essence, an experiment of some new genre, or a new kind of tourism that would permit one to visit ancient Greece, for example, by effortless linguistic means. I am thinking here in particular of this perverse etymological practice brought into fashion by Heidegger. These kinds of imaginary retrospectives have basically nothing to do with Freud's genuine work on the signifier. I do not think that these etymological retrospectives are the carriers of some special message from the unconscious. In my opinion, whatever Freud borrowed, rightly or wrongly, from the realm of mythologies in order to translate his conceptual arrangements, should not be interpreted "imagingly" [*pied de l'image*]. It is the "literality" [*pied de la lettre*], in all its *artificiality*, indeed the combination which is the key to interpretation for Freud. This is clear in a book like *Jokes and their Relation to the Unconscious* wherein we see that the unconscious signifying chains in the term "joke" [*mot d'esprit*], for example, do not maintain any special relation with etymological laws. For the link can just as easily be made with a phoneme, an accentuation, syntactic play or semantic displacement. Unfortunately – and it is not by chance – what was reified by Freud, and practically deified by his successors, were the mythical references that initially came to him somewhat arbitrarily in his attempt to chart out and locate the dramatization and impasses of the conjugal family. But let us not make a myth of myth! As references, the ancient myths dealing with the topic of Oedipus, for example, have nothing to do with the imaginary forces and symbolic articulations of the present conjugal family, nor with our system of social coordinates!

It is an illusion to think that there is something to read in the order of being, or of a lost world – or to think that recovering a mythical being, on this side of all historical origins, could be institutionalized as a psychoanalytic propaedeutic or maieutic. Considering the actual processes involved in the therapeutic cure or in setting up a therapeutic organization, reference to these kinds of mythico-linguistic reductions lead one nowhere except directly into the pitfalls of speculative frameworks. The important thing here is to get to the remarkable message, as well as to the object-carrier and founder of this message. But such an object would only derive its meaning on the basis of a similar retrospective illusion. We cannot hope to recover the specificity of the Freudian message unless we are able to disconnect it or sever it from its desire to return to the origins – a modern myth that established its diet for a full outpouring of sentiments beginning with Romanticism: the infinite quest for an impossible truth that supposedly lies beyond the manifest, in the heart of nature and the dark night of existence.

The remedy for this desire consists in orienting oneself in the direction of history, and the direction of the diachronic cut-out of the real and its provisional and partial attempts towards totalization – what I would call the *bricolage* of history and social constructions. It is impossible to carry out such a reconfiguration if we do not as a precondition ask the question: where is the law? Is it behind us? Behind history? Does it fall short of our actual situation, in which case it would lie outside our grasp? Or is it, perhaps, before us, within our reach, and potentially retrievable? As Bachelard says: nature must be pushed at least as far as our minds.[2] Who will ask this question? Certainly not the groupings and societies who establish their reason for being on ahistorical systems of religious and political legitimacy. The only groups to ask this question are the ones that accept from the start the precarious and transient nature of their existence: lucidly accept the situational and historical contingencies that confront them; accept an encounter with nothingness; and, finally, refuse to mystically reestablish and justify the existing order.

Today, a psychoanalyst would be content if his analysand overcame his anachronistic fixations; if he were able, for example, to get married, have children, reconcile himself to his biological contingencies, and integrate himself into the status quo. Regardless of the particular psychoanalytic curriculum, a reference to a predetermined model of normality remains implicit within its framework. The analyst, of course, does not in principle expect that this normalization is the product of a pure and simple identification of the analysand with the analyst, but it works no less, and even despite him (if only from the point of view of the continuity of the treatment, that is to say, often from the capacity of the analysand to continue to pay), as a process of identification of the analysand with a human profile that is compatible with the existing social order, and the acceptance [*assumation*] of his branding by the cogs of production and institutions. The analyst does not find this model ready-made in present society. His work is to create just that: to forge a new model in the place where his patient is lacking one. Moreover, and generally, this has to be his work, given that the modern bourgeois, capitalist society no longer

has any satisfactory model at its disposal. It is in order to respond to this
deficiency that psychoanalysis borrows its myths from earlier societies. It
is thus that psychoanalysis proposes a model of drives and an ideal type
of subjectivity and of familial relations that is at once new and composite;
a kind of syncretism that encompasses elements of an archaic nature, and
some that are quite modern. As far as the dominant social order is
concerned, what is important is that the model be in a position to
function in the present society. Such is the meaning of this requisite
acceptance [*assumation*] of the castration complex – a kind of initiation
substitution for modern societies – as the possible outcome of Oedipal
impasses. This also accounts for the success and profitability of psychoanalysis.

For us the question is of a completely different kind. Our problem is to
find out whether this recourse to alienating models can be limited,
whether it is possible to establish the laws of subjectivity in places other
than social constraint and the mystifying means of these mythical composite references. My question, therefore, is: can man become the
founder of his own law?

Let us attempt afresh to resituate certain key concepts. If a totalizing
god of values exists, every system of metaphoric expression will remain
connected to the subjugated group by a kind of fantasmatic umbilical
cord connecting it to this system of divine totalization. So as to not
stretch this formulation, and in order to avoid, at whatever cost, falling
into an idealist option, let us begin with the idea that we no longer need
consider that such a totalizing system is to be sought at the level of *human
ramification*, as if transmitted from sperm to sperm. While a *medium* of
transmission certainly exists, this does not translate into it being an
actual message. Spermatozoids, after all, do not speak! Also, from the
point of view of meaning, this transmission eludes all the orders which
are said to be "structured like a language". Taken as a system of reference, the order of human values is but an inch away from the systems of
divine positionality. What is transmitted from the pregnant woman to her
child? Quite a bit: nourishment and antibodies, for example. But not just
these obvious things. For what is transmitted above all are the fundamental models of our industrial society. While there is still no speech here
there is already a message. The message concerns industrial society; it is
a specific message and differs according to the place one occupies within
this order. We are here already in the signifier, though not yet in speech
or in language. While the transmitted message has hardly anything to do
with the structural laws of linguistics or etymology, it has a great deal to
do with all those heterogeneous things that converge in the aforemen-
tioned idea of human ramification. Everything that concerns man in his
relation to the most primitive demand is clearly marked by the signifier,

but not necessarily by a signifier that partakes of a more or less universal linguistic essence.

All that attempts to speak in this way–though is not yet at the level of speech, but rather has to do with transference, transmission, or exchange –can be characterized as what can be cut, and as something that allows for the signifiers' play of articulation. If the objects of transmission, gestures, and glances result in rendering possible the nourishment of a child this is because, at all levels, these things have already been marked and have a direct effect on this system of signifying chains. What is the law of exchange at this level? It is impossible to avoid this question! It is played out and exposes itself anew at every turn. We are faced with a fundamental precariousness in the structure of exchange, as this signifier that is not "crystallized" like a language is clearly at the foundation of society and, in the final analysis, at the foundation of all the signifying systems, including linguistics.

If speech does not exist in the animal realm, this is because the system of transmission and of totalization of this order has until now been able to do without speech, which is not the case for the degenerate branch of humanity; this is so because the relations of speech, image, and the transference in man are tied to a fundamental deficiency – what Lacan calls a "dehiscence at the heart of the organism"[3] – which, furthermore, constrains man to have recourse to various forms of social division of labor in order to survive. In the future, this survival will depend on the capacity of cybernetic machines to resolve humanity's problems. It will, therefore, be impossible to respond to the attack of a new virus without the intervention of continuously advancing computers.

If I evoke this myth of the machine, it is to highlight the absurdity of the situation. Is the computer in question God? Or perhaps it is God himself who predetermined these successive versions so that they would respond to all sorts of more or less contingent problems such as, for example, the novel strategic calculations that would be required in a new cold war. After all, this myth illustrates better the impasses of present society than the staid references to the habitual imagery of familialism, regionalism, nationalism, which, moreover, suffer the disadvantage of serving to reinforce forms of social neurosis to the same extent that they are unable to respond to the goals they have set out for themselves. In fact, this traditional imagery would probably be incapable of sustaining its subjugating function were it not for the incessant work of misrecognition and the neurosis of civilization, forever condemning the subject to compulsively resort to degenerate forms of need – needs that are at once blind and without object, and addressed to a god that has become idiotic and evil.

Notes

This short presentation to the GTPSI (Groupe de travail de psychothérapie institutionnelle, which is also referred to as the Groupe de travail de psychologie et sociologie institution-nelle) appeared in *Psychanalyse et transversalité* (Paris: Maspero, 1972), pp. 52–58. It dates from 1964. GTPSI was founded in 1960. Upon expansion in 1965 it became known as the SPI (Société de psychothérapie institutionnelle).

1 See J. Schotte, "Le Transfert dit fondamental de Freud pour poser le problème: psychanalyse et institution", *Revue de psychothérapie institutionnelle* 1 (1965). All issues of this *Revue* are to my knowledge out of print.

2 Gaston Bachelard, *Philosophie du non* (Paris: PUF), p. 36.

3 Jacques Lacan, *Écrits* (Paris: Éditions du Seuil, 1966), p. 96. [*Écrits: A Selection*, trans. Alan Sheridan (New York: W.W. Norton, 1977), p. 4.]

Translated by John Caruana

6

Psychoanalysis Should Get a Grip on Life

Anti-Oedipus managed to stir things up a bit with its severe criticism of the "familialism" of psychoanalysis. After about ten years, however, this has now become a banal issue. Nearly everyone realized that that criticism had the ring of truth. I duly respect Freud, for what he represents; he was incredibly creative. His strokes of both genius and folly were rejected as he remained marginalized, kept at the peripheries of the scientific and medical arenas, over a rather long period of his life, and it was during this period of marginalization that he managed to draw attention to subjective facts which had been, until then, totally mistaken. His successors, however, in particular those of the Lacanian structuralist strain, have transformed psychoanalysis into a cult, turning psychoanalytic theory into a kind of theology celebrated by affected and pretentious sects which are still proliferating. At the time of my studies at the École freudienne, I was struck by the schism that inserted itself between the sophistication of the theoretical propositions taught there and the attitude people had developed vis-à-vis the clinical domain. Those with discourses that were not particularly brilliant and short on razzle-dazzle, still managed to hold down a fairly reasonable practice while, inversely, those known for distinguished and elegant discourses employed in their monkey-see-monkey-do mimicking of the *Master,* often behaved outright irresponsibly in therapy. To take charge of someone's life and direct its outcome, all the while running the risk of perhaps having all efforts lead one down a blind alley, is a matter of no little significance! There are people who come to you in total disarray, who are very vulnerable and very responsive to your suggestions, so much so that if the transference gets off on a bad footing the peril of alienating the person becomes a real threat. This phenomenon is not peculiar to the domain of psychoanalysis. Most of us are certainly aware of other examples of grand theories that have been employed for religious and perverted purposes and have had dreadful consequences (I can think of the Pol Pot regime in Cambodia or of certain Marxist-Leninist groups in South America . . .).

In short, this method of furthering the cause of psychoanalysis no longer holds much water; others continue to do it with great talent – for example, Robert Castel.[1] On the other hand, one must admit that it is also important not to tip the scale and sink into reductionist, neo-behaviourist or systemist perspectives so typical of the Anglo-Saxon tradition which are currently conveyed by trends in family therapy.

Should one wish to go beyond this critical point to envision possibilities for the reconstruction of analysis on a different basis, I feel it is important to restate the question in terms of its status as a *myth of reference*. In order to live one's life – one's madness as well as one's neurosis, desire, melancholy, or even one's quotidian "normality" – each individual is bound to refer to a certain number of public or private myths. In ancient societies these myths had social consistency sufficient to allow for a system of reference with respect to morals, religion, sex, etc., in a manner that was much less dogmatic compared to what we have today; hence, in the case of a sacrificial exploration, the collectivity sought out ways to locate the kind of spirit dwelling within the sick person and to uncover the cultural, social, mythical and affective nature of the transgression. If a practical ritual no longer worked, one oriented oneself in another direction without pretending that one had come up against a resistance. These people probed subjectivity with an indisputable pragmatism and with an appeal to codes of conduct shared by the whole social body that provided the *testing grounds* for the effects of these codes. This is far from being the case with our psychological and psychoanalytic methods!

In societies where human faculties are highly integrated, the mythical systems of reference, at the very beginning, were taken over by great monotheistic religions which strived to respond to the cultural demand of castes, national groups and social classes. In time, all this collapsed with the deterritorialization of the ancient forms of filiation, of the clan, the community, the chiefs, etc. Consequently, the great monotheistic religions in their turn declined and lost a major portion of the direct sway they once held over collective subjective realities. (Aside from certain paradoxical situations today like those of Poland or Iran where religious ideologies have recovered their structural function for a whole nation. I draw on these two examples for their symmetric and, at the same time, antinomic nature: the latter leaning towards fascism, the former towards social liberation.) Generally speaking, however, reference to sin, confession, and prayer no longer carry the same weight as they once did; nor can they intervene any longer in the same manner in the problems of individuals held in the grip of psychotic intensity, neurosis or whatever form of mental distress. To make up for this loss, we can often see spectacular and daring ventures to bring back onto the modern scene animistic religions and traditional approaches to medicine in countries like Brazil with the *candomblé*, Macumba and Voodoo, etc.

To compensate for the relapse of these religions, great devices of subjectivation have emerged as conduits of modern myths: from the bourgeois novel of Jean-Jacques Rousseau to James Joyce, from the star-system of cinema to hit songs and sports and, generally speaking, the whole array of what we recognize today as mass-mediated culture. Only here we are talking of ruptured family myths. Psychoanalysis and family therapy constitute in their own right a kind of background reference, providing a body and a serious demeanor for this profane subjectivation. To restate my point, it seems to me that nobody can possibly organize their life independently of these subjective formations of reference. When one is through with one of them – whether it has lost its motivating force, or whether it is reduced to the level of banality – one sees that in spite of its degeneration and impoverishment, it continues to survive. This is perhaps the case with Freudianism and Marxism. Unless they are replaced in their role as collective myths, they will never wither away! They have, in fact, become a kind of chronic collective delirium. Take the end of the Hitlerian paradigm, for example: the matter was already lost in 1941 and 1942; but it was seen through to the end, to total disaster, and it has managed to linger well after its end. As Kuhn pointed out so well with reference to scientific paradigms, a body of explication that loses its consistency is never simply replaced by a more credible alternative. It retains its place and hangs on like an ailing patient.

Under these conditions it is useless even to attempt to demonstrate in a rational way the absurdity of most psychoanalytic hypotheses. One has to drain one's own cup to the last drop! And this probably applies just as well to the systematization of family therapy. Psychologists and social workers today display a certain avidity for rediscovering frames of reference. The university is poised as a resource to supply them with scientific bases. In most of the cases, however, all we are dealing with are reductionist theories that position themselves side-by-side with real problems – a metonymic scientificity, in a manner of speaking. In fact, when the *users* go to see a shrink, they know very well that they are not dealing with real scientists, but with people who present themselves as *servers* in a particular problematic order. In the past, when people went to see a priest, the servant of God, they were to some extent familiar with his methods of proceeding, his intimate ties with his maid, with the neighbours, and had some idea of his way of thinking. Psychoanalysts are, no doubt, people held in high esteem! However, they are far more isolated and, in my opinion, will not continue to carry on with their business much longer by referring to deflated myths.

Once the necessity, or dare I say even the legitimacy, of mythic references is understood, the question is no longer aimed at their scientific validity but is redirected towards their *social functionality*. This is the true site of theoretical research in this domain. One can theorize a production of subjectivity in a given context, within a particular group or with respect to a neurosis or psychosis, without having to resort to the authority of science in the matter and refer instead to something that would imply a formalization of a sense of the universal in order to affirm itself as a universal truth. I feel a strong urge to underline that we are not talking about ways to create a general theory for the human sciences – not even for the social and juridical sciences – since theorization, in all the matters it may encompass, cannot amount to more than what I call a descriptive or functional *cartography*. In my estimation, this would involve an invitation to all parties and groups concerned, in accordance with the appropriate modalities, to participate in the activity of creating models that touch on their lives. Furthermore, it is precisely the study of these modalities that I perceive as being the essence of analytic theorizing. I read in the papers quite recently that twenty million Brazilians are on the brink of dying of hunger in the north-east part of the country, which may lead to the engendering of a race of *autistic dwarfs*. In order to understand and help this population, references to symbolic castration, the signifier or the Name of the Father would hardly amount to more than a paltry form of support!

On the other hand, people who need to confront these types of challenges would make unmistakable gains were they able to create a certain number of social instruments and functional concepts to deal with the situation. The political dimension of the production of subjectivity is clearly evident in such a case. Yet it goes beyond that under the auspices of other modalities and into different contexts. I repeat, therefore, the less the shrinks see themselves as scientists, the more they will take heed of their responsibilities; we are not talking about an air of guilt ridden responsibility displayed by those who pretend to be speaking in the name of truth or history. I belong to a generation who witnessed the attacks on J.-P. Sartre, where some people imagined, in the age of *La Nausée*, that they knew for certain the reasons behind suicide and delinquency among the youth of that period, and held him responsible for all of it. Intellectuals who labor on the building of theories sometimes caution us against states of affairs they disapprove of and will even take some responsibility for the consequences that follow from the theory. This, however, only seldom amounts to a direct assuming of responsibility. On the other hand, they often frequently exert an inhibiting function by treading, unwarranted, on a terrain where they constrain the emergence of certain problems that could be looked at from more constructive angles. I always find myself politically involved in various ways and degrees. I have been participating in social movements since my childhood and, moreover, I became a psychoanalyst. This has led me to reject any tight compartmentalization between the individual and society. In my view, the singular and collective dimensions always tend to merge. If one refuses to situate a problem in its political and micropolitical context, one ends up sterilizing its impact of truth. To intervene with one's intelligence and one's means, as feeble as they may be, or as simple as they may appear, nevertheless, remains quite essential. And this is an integral part of any propaedeutic, of any conceivable didactic process.

After 1968, psychologists, psychiatrists, caretakers on mental wards, were all seen as cops. This we have to admit! But where does this begin, where does this end? What is important is to determine whether the position one occupies will, or will not, contribute to the overcoming of the realities of segregation, social and psychological mutilation, and whether one will, at least, be able to minimize the damage.

Notes

This article "La psychanalyse doit être en prise directe avec la vie" [propos recueillis par Michèle Costa-Magna et Jean Suyeux], appeared first in *Psychologies* 5 (nov. 1983), and was collected in *Les Années d'hiver* 1980–1985 (Paris: Bernard Barrault, 1986), pp. 193–200.

1 Robert Castel, *Le Psychanalysme* (Paris: Maspero, 1972).

Translated by Charles Dudas

PART II

From Schizo Bypasses to Postmodern Impasses

7

The First Positive Task of Schizoanalysis

With Gilles Deleuze

The negative or destructive task of schizoanalysis is in no way separable from its positive tasks – all these tasks are necessarily undertaken at the same time. The first positive task consists of discovering in a subject the nature, the formation, of the functioning of *his* desiring-machines, independently of any interpretations. What are your desiring-machines, what do you put into these machines, what is the output, how does it work, what are your nonhuman sexes? The schizoanalyst is a mechanic, and schizoanalysis is solely functional. In this respect it cannot remain at the level of a still interpretative examination – interpretative from the point of view of the unconscious – of the social machines in which the subject is caught as a cog or as a user; nor of the technical machines that are his prized possession, or that he perfects or even produces through handiwork; nor of the subject's use of his machines in his dreams and his fantasies. These machines are still too representative, and represent units that are too large – even the perverted machines of the sadist or the masochist, even the influencing machines of the paranoiac. We have seen in general that the pseudo-analyses of the "object" were really the lowest level of analytic activity, even and especially when they claim to double the real object with an imaginary object; and better a how-to-interpret-your-dreams book than a psychoanalysis of the market place.

The consideration of all these machines, however, whether they be real, symbolic, or imaginary, must indeed intervene in a specific way – but as functional indices to point us in the direction of the desiring-machines, to which these indices are more or less close and affinal. The desiring-machines in fact are only reached starting from a certain threshold of dispersion that no longer permits either their imaginary identity or their structural unity to subsist. (These instances still belong to the order of interpretation, that is to say the order of the signified *or* the signifier.) Partial objects are what make up the parts of the desiring-machines; partial objects define the working machine or the working parts, but in a state of dispersion such that one part is continually referring to a part from an entirely different machine, like the red clover and the bumble bee, the wasp and the orchid, the bicycle horn and the dead rat's ass. Let's not rush to introduce a term that would be like a phallus structuring the whole and personifying the parts, unifying and totalizing everything. Everywhere there is libido as machine energy, and neither the horn nor the bumble bee have the privilege of being a phallus: the phallus intervenes only in the structural organization and the personal relations deriving from it, where everyone, like the worker called to war, abandons his machines and sets to fighting for a war trophy that is nothing but a great absence, with one and the same penalty, one and the same ridiculous wound for all – castration. This entire struggle for the phallus, this poorly understood will to power, this anthropomorphic representation of sex, this whole conception of sexuality that horrifies Lawrence precisely because it is no more than a conception, because it is an idea that "reason" imposes on the unconscious and introduces into the passional sphere, and is not by any means a formation of this sphere – here is where desire finds itself trapped, specifically limited to human sex, unified and identified in the molar constellation. But the desiring-machines live on the contrary under the order of dispersion of the molecular elements. And one fails to understand the nature and function of partial objects if one does not see therein such elements, rather than parts of even a fragmented whole. As Lawrence said, analysis does not have to do with anything that resembles a concept or a person, "the so-called human relations are not involved".[1] Analysis should deal solely (except in its negative task) with the machinic arrangements grasped in the context of their molecular dispersion.

Let us therefore return to the rule so clearly stated by Serge Leclaire, even if he sees this only as a fiction instead of the real-desire [*réel-désir*]: the elements or parts of the desiring-machines are recognized by their mutual independence, such that nothing in the one depends or should depend on something in the other. They must not be opposed determinations of a same entity, nor the differentiations of a single being, such as the masculine and the feminine in the human sex, but different or really-distinct things [*des réellement-distincts*], distinct "beings," as found in the dispersion of the nonhuman sex (the clover and the bee). As long as schizoanalysis has not arrived at these *disparate* elements, it has not yet discovered the partial objects as the ultimate elements of the unconscious. It is in this sense that Leclaire used the term "erogenous body" not to designate a fragmented organism, but an emission of preindividual and prepersonal singularities, a pure dispersed and anarchic multiplicity, without unity or totality, and whose elements are welded, pasted together by the real distinction or the very absence of a link. Such is the case in the schizoid sequences of Beckett: stones,

pockets, mouth; a shoe, a pipe bowl, a small limp bundle that is undefined, a cover for a bicycle bell, half a crutch (if one indefinitely runs
up against the same set of pure singularities, one can feel confident that
he has drawn near the singularity of the subject's desire).[2] To be sure,
one can always establish or re-establish some sort of link between these
elements: organic links between organs or fragments or organs that
eventually form part of the multiplicity; psychological and axiological
links – the good, the bad – that finally refer to the persons or to the scenes
from which these elements are borrowed; structural links between the
ideas or the concepts apt to correspond to them. But it is not in this
respect that the partial objects are elements of the unconscious, and we
cannot even go along with the image of the partial objects that their
inventor, Melanie Klein, proposes. This is because, whether organs or
fragments of organs, the partial objects do not refer in the least to an
organism that would function phantasmatically as a lost unity or a totality
to come. Their dispersion has nothing to do with a lack, and constitutes
their mode or presence in the multiplicity they form without unification
or totalization. With every structure dislodged, every memory abolished,
every organism set aside, every link undone, they function as raw partial
objects, dispersed working parts of a machine that is itself dispersed. In
short, *partial objects* are the *molecular functions* of the *unconscious*. That is
why, when we insisted earlier on the difference between desiring-machines and all the figures of molar machines, we were fully aware that
they were both contained in, and did not exist without, one another, but
we had to stress the difference in regime and in scale between these two
machinic species.

It is true that one might instead wonder how these conditions of
dispersion, of real distinction, and of the absence of a link permit any
machinic regime to exist – how the partial objects thus defined are able
to form machines and arrangements of machines. The answer lies in the
passive nature of the syntheses, or – what amounts to the same thing – in
the indirect nature of the interactions under consideration. If it is true
that every partial object emits a flow, it is also the case that this flow is
associated with another partial object and defines the other's potential
field of presence, which is itself multiple (a multiplicity of anuses for the
flows of shit). The synthesis of connection of the partial objects is
indirect, since one of the partial objects, in each point of its presence
within the field, always breaks the flow that another object emits or
produces relatively, itself ready to emit a flow that other partial objects will break. The flows are two-headed, so to speak, and it is by means
of these flows that every productive connection is made, such as we
have tried to account for with the notion of flow-schizz or break-
flow. So that the true activities of the unconscious, causing to flow and

breaking flows, consist of the passive synthesis itself insofar as it ensures the relative coexistence and displacement of the two different functions.

Now let us assume that the respective flows associated with two partial
objects at least partially overlap: their production remains distinct in
relation to the objects x and y that emit them, but not the fields of
presence in relation to the objects a and b that inhabit and interrupt
them, such that the partial a and the partial b become in this regard
indiscernible (thus the mouth and the anus, the mouth-anus of the
anorexic). And they are not indiscernible solely in the mixed region,
since one can always assume that, having exchanged their function within
this region, they cannot be further distinguished by exclusion there where
the two flows no longer overlap: one then finds oneself before a new
passive synthesis where a and b are in a paradoxical relationship of
included disjunction. Finally there remains the possibility, not of an
overlapping of the flows, but of a permutation of the objects that emit
them: one discovers fringes of interference on the edge of each field of
presence, fringes that testify to the remainder of a flow in the other, and
form residual conjunctive syntheses guiding the passage or the heartfelt
becoming from the one to the other. A permutation involving 2, 3, n
organs; deformable abstract polygons that make game of the figurative
Oedipal triangle, and never cease to undo it. Through binarity, overlapping, or permutation, all these indirect passive syntheses are one and the
same engineering of desire. But who will be able to describe the desiring-
machines of each subject, what analysis will be exacting enough for this?
Mozart's desiring-machine? "Raise your ass to your mouth, . . . ah, my
ass burns like fire, but *what can be the meaning of that?* Perhaps a turd
wants to come out . . . Yes, yes, turd, I know you, I see you, I feel you.
What is this – is such a thing possible?"[3]

These syntheses necessarily imply the position of a body without
organs. This is due to the fact that the body without organs is in no way
the contrary of the organs-partial objects. It is itself produced in the first
passive synthesis of connection, as that which is going to neutralize – or
on the contrary put into motion – the two activities, the two heads of
desire. For as we have seen, it can be produced as the amorphous fluid of
antiproduction, just as it can be produced as the support that appropriates for itself the flow production. It can as well *repel* the organs-objects
as *attract* them, and appropriate them for itself. But in repulsion as in
attraction, the body without organs is not in opposition to these organ-
objects; it merely ensures its own opposition, and their opposition, with
regard to an organism. The body without organs and the organs-partial
objects are opposed conjointly to the organism. The body without organs
is in fact produced as a whole, but a whole alongside the parts – a whole

that does not unify or totalize them, but that is added to them like a new, really distinct part.

When it repels the organs, as in the mounting of the paranoiac machine, the body without organs marks the external limit of the pure multiplicity formed by these organs themselves insofar as they constitute a nonorganic and nonorganized multiplicity. And when it attracts them and fits itself over them, in the process of a miraculating fetishistic machine, it still does not totalize them, unify them in the manner of an organism: the organs-partial objects cling to the body without organs, and enter into the new syntheses of included disjunction and nomadic conjunction, of overlapping and permutation, on this body – syntheses that continue to repudiate the organism and its organization. Desire indeed passes through the body, and through the organs, but not through the organism. That is why the partial objects are not the expression of a fragmented, shattered organism, which would presuppose a destroyed totality or the freed parts of a whole; nor is the body without organs the expression of a "de-differentiated" [*dé-différencié*] organism stuck back together that would surmount its parts. The organs-partial objects and the body without organs are at bottom one and the same thing, one and the same multiplicity that must be conceived as such by schizoanalysis. *Partial objects are the direct powers of the body without organs, and the body without organs, the raw material of the partial objects.*[4] The body without organs is the matter that always fills space to given degrees of intensity, and the partial objects are these degrees, these intensive parts that produce the real in space starting from matter as intensity = 0. The body without organs is the immanent substance, in the most Spinozist sense of the word; and the partial objects are like its ultimate attributes, which belong to it precisely insofar as they are really distinct and cannot on this account exclude or oppose one another. The partial objects and the body without organs are the two material elements of the schizophrenic desiring-machines: the one as the immobile motor, the others as the working parts; the one as the giant molecule, the others as the micromolecules – the two together in a relationship of continuity from one end to the other of the molecular chain of desire.

The chain is like the apparatus of transmission or of reproduction in the desiring-machine. Insofar as it brings together – without unifying or uniting them – the body without organs and the partial objects, the desiring-machine is inseparable both from the distribution of the partial objects on the body without organs, and from the leveling effect exerted on the partial objects by the body without organs, which results in appropriation. The chain also implies another type of synthesis than the flows: it is no longer the lines of connection that traverse the productive parts of the machine, but an entire network of disjunction on the recording surface of the body without organs. And we have doubtless been able to present things in a logical order where the disjunctive synthesis of recording seemed to follow after the connective synthesis of production, with a part of the energy of production (Libido) being converted into a recording energy (Numen). But in fact, from the stand-point of the machine itself, there is no succession that ensures the strict coexistence of the chains and the flows, as well as of the body without organs and the partial objects. The conversion of a portion of the energy does not occur at a given moment, but is a preliminary and constant condition of the system. The chain is the network of included disjunc-tions on the body without organs, inasmuch as these disjunctions resect the productive connections; the chain causes them to pass over to the body without organs itself, thereby channeling or "codifying" the flows. However, the whole question is in knowing whether one can speak of a code at the level of this molecular chain of desire. We have seen that a code implied two things – one or the other, or the two together: on the one hand, the specific determination of the full body as a territoriality of support; on the other hand, the erection of a despotic signifier on which the entire chain depends. In this regard, in vain is the axiomatic in profound opposition to codes; since it works on the decoded flows, it cannot itself proceed except by effecting reterritorializations and by reviving the signifying unity. The very notions of code and axiomatic therefore seem to be valid only for the molar aggregates, where the signifying chain forms a given determinate configuration on a support that is itself specifically determined, and in terms of a detached signifier. These conditions are not fulfilled without exclusions forming and ap-pearing in the disjunctive network – at the same time as the connective lines take on a global and specific meaning.

But it is another case altogether with the properly molecular chain: insofar as the body without organs is a nonspecific and nonspecified support that marks the molecular limit of the molar aggregates, the chain no longer has any other function than that of deterritorializing the flows and causing them to pass through the signifying wall, thereby undoing the codes. The function of the chain is no longer that of coding the flows on a full body of the earth, the despot, or capital, but on the contrary that of decoding them on the full body without organs. It is a chain of escape, and no longer a code. The signifying chain has become a chain of decoding and deterritorialization, which must be apprehended – and can only be apprehended – as the reverse of the codes and the territorialities. This molecular chain is still signifying because it is composed of signs of desire; but these signs are no longer signifying, given the fact that they are under the order of the included disjunctions where *everything is possible*. These signs are points whose nature is a matter of indifference, abstract machinic figures that play freely on the body without organs and as yet form no structured configuration – or rather, they form one no longer. As Jacques Monod says, we must conceive of a machine that is such by its functional properties but not by its structure, "where nothing but the play of blind combinations can be discerned".[5] It is precisely the ambiguity of what the biologists call a genetic code that enables us to understand this kind of situation: for if the corresponding chain effectively forms codes, inasmuch as it folds into exclusive molar configurations, it undoes the code by unfolding along a molecular fibre that includes all the possible figures. Similarly in Lacan, the symbolic organization of the structure, with its exclusions that come from the function of the signifier, has as its reverse side the real inorganization of desire.

It would seem that the genetic code points to a genic decoding: one need only grasp the decoding and deterritorialization functions in their own positivity, inasmuch as they imply a particular chain state that is metastable and distinct both from any axiomatic and from any code. The molecular chain is the form in which the genic unconscious, always remaining subject, reproduces itself. And as we have seen, that is the primary inspiration of psychoanalysis: it does not add a code to all those that are already known. The signifying chain of the unconscious, Numen, is not used to discover or decipher codes of desire, but to cause absolutely decoded flows of desire, Libido, to circulate, and to discover in desire that which scrambles all the codes and undoes all the territorialities. It is true that Oedipus will restore psychoanalysis to the status of a simple code, with the familial territoriality and the signifier of castration. Worse yet, it will happen that psychoanalysis itself wants to act as an axiomatic, which is the famous turning point where it no longer even relates to the familial scene, but solely to the psychoanalytic scene that supposedly answers for its own truth, and to the psychoanalytic operation that supposedly answers for its own success – the couch as an axiomatized earth, the axiomatic of the "cure" as a *successful* castration! But by recoding or axiomatizing the flows of desire in this way, psychoanalysis makes a molar use of the signifying chain that results in a misappreciation of all the syntheses of the unconscious.

The body without organs is the model of death. As the authors of horror stories have understood so well, it is not death that serves as the model for catatonia, it is catatonic schizophrenia that gives its model to death. Zero intensity. The death model appears when the body without organs repels the organs and lays them aside: no mouth, no tongue, no teeth – to the point of self-mutilation, to the point of suicide. Yet there is no real opposition between the body without organs and the organs as partial objects; the only real opposition is to the molar organism that is their common enemy. In the desiring-machine, one sees the same catatonic inspired by the immobile motor that forces him to put aside his organs, to immobilize them, to silence them, but also, impelled by the working parts that work in an autonomous or stereotyped fashion, to reactivate the organs, to reanimate them with local movements. It is a question of different parts of the machine, different and coexisting, different in their very coexistence. Hence it is absurd to speak of a death desire that would presumably be in qualitative opposition to the life desires. Death is not desired, there is only death that desires, by virtue of the body without organs or the immobile motor, and there is also life that desires, by virtue of the working organs. There we do not have two desires but two parts, two kinds of desiring-machine parts, in the dispersion of the machine itself. And yet the problem persists: how can all that function together? For it is not yet a functioning, but solely the (non-structural) condition of a molecular functioning. The functioning appears when the motor, under the preceding conditions – i.e. without ceasing to be immobile and without forming an organism – attracts the organs to the body without organs, and appropriates them for itself in the apparent objective movement. Repulsion is the condition of the machine's functioning, but attraction is the functioning itself. That the functioning depends on repulsion is clear to us, inasmuch as it all works only by breaking down. One is then able to say what this running or this functioning consists of: in the cycle of the desiring-machine it is a matter of constantly translating, constantly converting the death model into something else altogether, which is the experience of death. Converting the death that rises from within (in the body without organs) into the death that comes from without (on the body without organs).

But it seems that things are becoming very obscure, for what is this distinction between the experience of death and the model of death? Here again, is it a death desire? A being-for-death? Or rather an investment of death, even if speculative? None of the above. The experience of death is the most common of occurrences in the unconscious, precisely because it occurs in life and for life, in every passage or becoming, in every intensity as passage or becoming. It is in the very nature of every intensity to invest within itself the zero intensity starting from which it is produced, in one moment, as that which grows or diminishes according to an infinity of degrees (as Pierre Klossowski noted, "an afflux is necessary merely to signify the absence of intensity"). We have attempted to show in this respect how the relations of attraction and repulsion produced such states, sensations, and emotions, which imply a new energetic conversion and form the third kind of synthesis, the synthesis of conjunction. One might say that the unconscious as a real subject has scattered an apparent residual and nomadic subject around the entire compass of its cycle, a subject that passes by way of all the becomings corresponding to the included disjunctions: the last part of the desiring-machine, the adjacent part. These intense becomings and feelings, these intensive emotions, feed deliriums and hallucinations. But in themselves, these intensive emotions are closest to the matter whose zero degree they invest in itself. They control the unconscious experience of death, insofar as death is what is felt in every feeling, *what never ceases and never finishes happening in every becoming* – in the becoming-another-sex, the becoming-god, the becoming-a-face, etc., forming zones of intensity on the body without organs. Every intensity controls within its own life the experience of death, and envelops it. And it is doubtless the case that every intensity is extinguished at the end, that every becoming itself becomes a becoming-death! Death, then, does actually happen. Maurice Blanchot distinguishes this twofold nature clearly, these two irreducible aspects of death; the one, according to which the apparent subject never ceases to live and travel as a *One* – "one never stops and never has done with dying"; and the other, according to which this same subject, fixed as *I*, actually dies – which is to say it finally ceases to die since it ends up dying, in the reality of a last instant that fixes it in this way as an *I*, all the while undoing the intensity, carrying it back to the zero that envelops it.[6]

From one aspect to the other, there is not at all a personal deepening, but something quite different: there is a return from the experience of death to the model of death, in the cycle of the desiring-machines. The cycle is closed. For a new departure, since this *I* is another? The experience of death must have given us exactly enough broadened experience, in order to live and know that the desiring-machines do not die. And that the subject as an adjacent part is always a "one" who conducts the experience, not an *I* who receives the model. For the model itself is not the *I* either, but the body without organs. And *I* does not rejoin the model without the model starting out again in the direction of another experience. Always going from the model to the experience, and starting out again, returning from the model to the experience, is what *schizophrenizing death* amounts to, the exercise of the desiring-machines (which is their very secret, well understood by the terrifying authors). The machines tell us this, and make us live it, feel it, deeper than delirium and further than hallucination; yes, the return to repulsion will condition other attractions, other functionings, the setting in motion of other working parts on the body without organs, the putting to work of other adjacent parts on the periphery that have as much a right to say *One* as we ourselves do. "Let him die in his leaping through unheard-of and unnamable things: other horrible workers will come; they will begin on the horizons where the other collapsed"![7] The Eternal Return as experience, and as the deterritorialized circuit of all the cycles of desire.

How odd the psychoanalytic venture is. Psychoanalysis ought to be a song of life, or else be worth nothing at all. It ought, *practically*, to teach us to sing life. And see how the most defeated, sad song of death emanates from it: *eiapopeia*. From the start, and because of his stubborn dualism of the drives, Freud never stopped trying to limit the discovery of a subjective or vital essence of desire as libido. But when the dualism passed into a death instinct against Eros, this was no longer a simple limitation, it was a liquidation of the libido. Reich did not go wrong here, and was perhaps the only one to maintain that the product of analysis should be a free and joyous person, a carrier of the life flows, capable of carrying them all the way into the desert and decoding them – even if this idea necessarily took on the appearance of a crazy idea, given what had become of analysis. He demonstrated that Freud, no less than Jung and Adler, had repudiated the sexual position: the fixing of the death instinct in fact deprives sexuality of its generative role on at least one essential point, which is the genesis of anxiety, since this genesis becomes the autonomous cause of sexual repression instead of its result; it follows that sexuality as desire no longer animates a social critique of civilization, but that civilization on the contrary finds itself sanctified as the sole agency capable of opposing the death desire. And how does it do this? By in principle turning death against death, by making this turned-back death [*la mort retournée*] into a force of desire, by putting it in the service of a pseudo-life through an entire culture of guilt feeling.

There is no need to tell all over how psychoanalysis culminates in a theory of culture that takes up again the age-old task of the ascetic ideal, Nirvana, the cultural extract, judging life, belittling life, measuring life against death, and only retaining from life what the death of death wants very much to leave us with – a sublime resignation. As Reich says, when psychoanalysis began to speak of Eros, the whole world breathed a sigh of relief: one knew what this meant, and that everything was going to unfold within a mortified life, since Thanatos was now the partner of Eros, for worse but also *for better*.[8] Psychoanalysis becomes the training ground of a new kind of priest, the director of bad conscience: bad conscience has made us sick, but that is what will cure us! Freud did not hide what was really at issue with the introduction of the death instinct: it is not a question of any fact whatever, but merely of a principle, a question of principle. The death instinct is pure silence, pure transcendence, not givable and not given in experience. This very point is remarkable: it is because death, according to Freud, has neither a model nor an experience, that he makes of it a transcendent principle.[9] So that the psychoanalysts who refused the death instinct did so for the same reasons as those who accepted it: some said that there was no death instinct *since* there was no model or experience in the unconscious; others, that there was a death instinct precisely *because* there was no model or experience. We say, to the contrary, that there is no death instinct because there is both the model and the experience of death in the unconscious. Death then is a part of the desiring-machine, a part that must itself be judged, evaluated in the functioning of the machine and the system of its energetic conversions, and not as an abstract principle.

If Freud needs death as a principle, this is by virtue of the requirements of the dualism that maintains a qualitative opposition between the drives (you will not escape the conflict): once the dualism of the sexual drives and the ego drives has only a topological scope, the qualitative or dynamic dualism passes between Eros and Thanatos. But the same enterprise is continued and reinforced – eliminating the machinic element of desire, the desiring-machines. It is a matter of eliminating the libido, insofar as it implies the possibility of energetic conversions in the machine (Libido-Numen-Voluptas). It is a matter of imposing the idea of an energetic duality rendering the machinic transformations impossible, with everything obliged to pass by way of an indifferent neutral energy, that energy emanating from Oedipus and capable of being added to either of the two irreducible forms – neutralizing, mortifying life.[10] The purpose of the topological and dynamic dualities is to thrust aside the point of view of *functional multiplicity* that alone is economic. (Szondi situates the problem clearly: why two kinds of drives qualified as molar, functioning mysteriously, which is to say oedipally, rather than *n* genes of drives – eight molecular genes, for example – functioning machinically?)

If one looks in this direction for the ultimate reason why Freud erects a transcendent death instinct as a principle, the reason will be found in Freud's practice itself. For if the principle has nothing to do with the facts, it has a lot to do with the psychoanalyst's conception of psychoanalytic practice, a conception the psychoanalyst wishes to impose. Freud made the most profound discovery of the abstract subjective essence of desire – Libido. But since he realienated this essence, reinvesting it in a subjective system of representation of the ego, and since he recoded this essence on the residual territoriality of Oedipus and under the despotic signifier of castration, he could no longer conceive the essence of life except in a form turned back against itself, in the form of death itself. And this neutralization, this turning against life, is also the last way in which a depressive and exhausted libido can go on surviving, and dream that it is surviving: "The ascetic ideal is an artifice for the *preservation* of life . . . even when he *wounds* himself, this master of destruction, of self-destructing – the very wound itself compels him to live . . ."[11] It is Oedipus, the marshy earth, that gives off a powerful odor of decay and death; and it is castration, the pious ascetic wound, the signifier, that makes of this death a conservatory for the Oedipal life. Desire is in itself not a desire to love, but a force to love, a virtue that gives and produces, that engineers. (For how could what is in life still desire life? Who would want to call that a desire?) But desire must turn back against itself in the name of a horrible Ananke, the Ananke of the weak and the depressed, the contagious neurotic Ananke; desire must produce its shadow or its monkey, and find a strange artificial force for vegetating in the void, at the heart of its own lack. For better days to come? It must – but who talks in this way? what abjectness – become a desire to be loved, and worse, a sniveling desire to have been loved, a desire that is reborn of its own frustration: no, daddy–mommy didn't love me enough. Sick desire stretches out on the couch, an artificial swamp, a little earth, a little mother. "Look at you, stumbling and staggering with no use in your legs. . . . And it's nothing but your wanting to be loved which does it. A maudlin crying to be loved, which makes your knees go all ricky".[12] Just as there are two stomachs for the ruminant, there must also exist two abortions, two castrations for sick desire: once in the family, in the familial scene, with the knitting mother; another time in an asepticized clinic, in the psychoanalytic scene, with specialist artists who know how to handle the death instinct and "bring off" castration, "bring off" frustration.

Is this really the right way to bring on better days? And aren't all the destructions performed by schizoanalysis worth more than this psycho-analytic conservatory, aren't they more a part of an affirmative task? "Lie down, then, on the soft couch which the analyst provides and try to think up something different . . . if you realize that he is not a god but a human being like yourself, with worries, defects, ambitions, frailties, that he is not the repository of an all-encompassing wisdom [= code] but a wanderer, along the [deterritorialized] path, perhaps you will cease pouring it out like a sewer, however melodious it may sound to your ears, and rise up on your own two legs and sing with your own God-given voice [Numen]. To confess, to whine, to complain, to commiserate, always demands a toll. To sing it doesn't cost you a penny. Not only does it cost nothing – you actually enrich others (instead of infecting them). . . . The phantasmal world is the world which has not been fully conquered over. It is the world of the past, never of the future. To move forward clinging to the past is like dragging a ball and chain. . . . We are all guilty of crime, the great crime of not living life to the full".[13] You weren't born Oedipus, you caused it to grow in yourself; and you aim to get out of it through fantasy, through castration, but this in turn you have caused to grow in Oedipus – namely, in yourself: the horrible circle. Shit on your whole mortifying, imaginary, and symbolic theatre. What does schizoanalysis ask? Nothing more than a bit of a *relation to the outside*, a little real reality. And we claim the right to a radical laxity, a radical incompetence – the right to enter the analyst's office and say it smells bad there. It reeks of the great death and the little ego.

Freud himself indeed spoke of the link between his "discovery" of the death instinct and World War I, which remains the model of capitalist war. More generally, the death instinct celebrates the wedding of psychoanalysis and capitalism; their engagement had been full of hesitation. What we have tried to show a propos of capitalism is how it inherited much from a transcendent death-carrying agency, the despotic signifier, but also how it brought about this agency's effusion in the full immanence of its own system: the full body, having become that of capital-money, suppresses the distinction between production and anti-production; everywhere it mixes antiproduction with the productive forces in the immanent reproduction of its own always widened limits (the axiomatic). The death enterprise is one of the principal and specific forms of the absorption of surplus value in capitalism. It is this itinerary that psychoanalysis rediscovers and retraces with the death instinct: the death instinct is now only pure silence in its transcendent distinction from life, but it effuses all the more, throughout all the immanent combinations it forms with this same life. Absorbed, diffuse, immanent death is the condition formed by the signifier in capitalism, the empty locus that is everywhere displaced in order to block the schizophrenic escapes and place restraints on the flights.

The only modern myth is the myth of zombies – mortified schizos, good for work, brought back to reason. In this sense the primitive and the barbarian, with their ways of coding death, are children in comparison to modern man and his axiomatic (so many unemployed are needed, so many deaths, the Algerian War doesn't kill more people than weekend automobile accidents, planned death in Bengal, etc.). Modern man "raves to a far greater extent. His delirium is a switchboard with thirteen telephones. He gives his orders to the world. He doesn't care for the ladies. He is brave, too. He is decorated like crazy. In man's game of chance the death instinct, the silent instinct is decidedly well placed, perhaps next to egotism. It takes the place of zero in roulette. The house always wins. So too does death. The law of large numbers works for death".[14] It is now or never that we must take up a problem we had left hanging. Once it is said that capitalism works on the basis of decoded flows as such, how is it that it is infinitely further removed from desiring-production than were the primitive or even the barbarian systems, which nonetheless code and overcode the flows? Once it is said that desiring-production is itself a decoded and deterritorialized production, how do we explain that capitalism, with its axiomatic, its statistics, performs an infinitely vaster repression of this production than do the preceding regimes, which nonetheless did not lack the necessary repressive means?

We have seen that the molar statistical aggregates of social production were in a variable relationship of affinity with the molecular formations of desiring-production. What must be explained is that the capitalist aggregate is the least affinal, at the very moment it decodes and deterritorializes with all its might.

The answer is the death instinct, if we call instinct in general the conditions of life that are historically and socially determined by the relations of production and antiproduction in a system. We know that molar social production and molecular desiring-production must be evaluated both from the viewpoint of their identity in nature and from the viewpoint of their difference in regime. But it could be that these two aspects, nature and regime, are in a sense potential and are actualized only in inverse proportion. Which means that where the regimes are the closest, the identity in nature is on the contrary at its minimum; and where the identity in nature appears to be at its maximum, the regimes differ to the highest degree. If we examine the primitive or the barbarian constellations, we see that the subjective essence of desire as production is referred to large objectivities, to the territorial or the despotic body, which act as natural or divine preconditions that thus ensure the coding or the overcoding of the flows of desire by introducing them into systems of representation that are themselves objective. Hence it can be said that the identity in nature between the two productions is completely hidden there: as much by the difference between the objective socius and the subjective full body of desiring-production, as by the difference between the qualified codes and overcodings of social production and the chains of decoding or of deterritorialization belonging to desiring- production, and by the entire repressive apparatus represented in the savage prohibitions, the barbarian law, and the rights of antiproduction. And yet the difference in regime, far from being accentuated and deepened, is on the contrary reduced to a minimum, because desiring-production as an absolute limit remains an exterior limit, or else stays unoccupied as an internalized and displaced limit, with the result that the machines of desire operate on this side of their limit within the framework of the socius and its codes. That is why the primitive codes and even the despotic overcodings testify to a polyvocity that functionally draws them nearer to a chain of decoding of desire: the parts of the desiring-machine function in the very workings of the social machine; the flows of desire enter and exit through the codes that continue, however, to inform the model and experience of death that are elaborated in the unity of the sociodesiring-apparatus. And it is even less a question of the death instinct to the extent that the model and the experience are better coded in a circuit that never stops grafting the desiring-machines onto the social machine and implanting the social machine in the desiring-machines.

Death comes all the more from without as it is coded from within. This is especially true of the system of cruelty, where death is inscribed in the primitive mechanism of surplus value as well as in the movement of the finite blocks of debt. But even in the system of despotic terror, where debt becomes infinite and where death experiences an elevation that tends to make of it a *latent* instinct, there nonetheless subsists a model in the overcoding law, and an experience for the overcoded subjects, at the same time as antiproduction remains separate as the share owing to the overlord.

Things are very different in capitalism. Precisely because the flows of capital are decoded and deterritorialized flows; precisely because the subjective essence of production is revealed in capitalism; precisely because the limit becomes internal to capitalism, which continually reproduces it, and also continually occupies it as an internalized and displaced limit; precisely for these reasons, the identity in nature must appear for itself between social production and desiring-production. But in its turn, this identity in nature, far from favoring an affinity in regime between the two modes of production, increases the difference in regime in a catastrophic fashion, and assembles an apparatus of repression the mere idea of which neither savagery nor barbarism could provide us. This is because, on the basis of a general collapse of the large objectivities, the decoded and deterritorialized flows of capitalism are not recaptured or co-opted, but directly apprehended in a codeless axiomatic that consigns them to the universe of subjective representation. Now this universe has as its function the splitting of the subjective essence (the identity in nature) into two functions, that of abstract labor alienated in private property that reproduces the ever wider interior limits, and that of abstract desire alienated in the privatized family that displaces the ever narrower internalized limits. The double alienation – labor-desire – is constantly increasing and deepening the difference in regime at the heart of the identity in nature. At the same time that death is decoded, it loses its relationship with a model and an experience, and becomes an instinct; that is, it effuses in the immanent system where each act of production is inextricably linked to the process of antiproduction as capital. There where the codes are undone, the death instinct lays hold of the repressive apparatus and begins to direct the circulation of the libido. A mortuary axiomatic. One might then believe in liberated desires, but ones that, like cadavers, feed on images. Death is not desired, but what is desired is dead, already dead: images. Everything labors in death, everything wishes for death. In truth, capitalism has nothing to co-opt; or rather, its powers of co-option coexist more often than not with what is to be co-opted, and even anticipate it. (How many revolutionary groups as such are already in place for a co-option that will be carried out only in the future, and form an apparatus for the absorption of a surplus value not even produced yet – which gives them precisely an apparent revolutionary position.) In a world such as this, there is no living desire that could not of itself cause the system to explode, or that would not make the system dissolve at one end where everything would end up following behind and being swallowed up – a question of regime.

Here are the desiring-machines, with their three parts: the working parts, the immobile motor, the adjacent parts; their three forms of energy: Libido, Numen, and Voluptas; and their three syntheses: the connective syntheses of partial objects and flows, the disjunctive syntheses of singularities and chains, and the conjunctive syntheses of intensities and becomings. The schizoanalyst is not an interpreter, even less a theatre director; he is a mechanic, a micromechanic. There are no excavations to be undertaken, no archaeology, no statues in the unconscious: there are only stones to be sucked, à la Beckett, and other machinic elements belonging to deterritorialized constellations. The task of schizoanalysis is that of learning what a subject's desiring-machines are, how they work, with what syntheses, what bursts of energy in the machines, what constituent misfires, with what flows, what chains, and what becomings in each case. Moreover, this positive task cannot be separated from indispensable destructions, the destruction of the molar aggregates, the structures and representations that prevent the machine from functioning. It is not easy to rediscover the molecules – even the giant molecule – their paths, their zones of presence, and their own syntheses, amid the large accumulations that fill the preconscious, and that delegate their representatives in the unconscious itself, thereby immobilizing the machines, silencing them, trapping them, sabotaging them, cornering them, holding them fast. *In the unconscious it is not the lines of pressure that matter, but on the contrary the lines of escape.* The unconscious does not apply pressure to consciousness; rather, consciousness applies pressure and straitjackets the unconscious, to prevent its escape. As to the unconscious, it is like the Platonic opposite whose opposite draws near: it flees or it perishes. What we have tried to show from the outset is how the unconscious productions and formations were not merely repelled by an agency of psychic repression that would enter into compromises with them, but actually covered over by antiformations that disfigure the unconscious in itself, and impose on it causations, comprehensions, and expressions that no longer have anything to do with its real functioning: thus all the *statues*, the Oedipal images, the phantasmal *mise en scène*, the Symbolic of castration, the effusion of the death instinct, the perverse reterritorializations. So that one can never, as in an interpretation, read the repressed through and in repression, since the latter is constantly inducing a false image of the thing it represses: illegitimate and transcendent uses of the syntheses according to which the unconscious can no longer operate in accordance with its own constituent machines, but merely "represent" what a repressive apparatus gives it to represent. It is the very form of interpretation that shows itself to be incapable of attaining the unconscious, since it gives rise to the inevitable illusions (including the structure and the signifier) by means of which the conscious makes of the unconscious an image consonant with its wishes: we are still pious, psychoanalysis remains in the precritical stage.

Doubtless these illusions would not take hold if they did not benefit from a coincidence and a support in the unconscious itself that ensures the "hold". We have seen what this support was: primal repression, as exerted by the body without organs at the moment of repulsion, at the heart of molecular desiring-production. Without this primal repression, a psychic regression in the proper sense of the word could not be delegated in the unconscious by the molar forces and thus crush desiring-production. Regression properly speaking profits from an occasion without which it could not interfere in the machinery of desire.[15] In contrast to psychoanalysis, which itself falls into the trap while causing the unconscious to fall into its trap, schizoanalysis follows the lines of escape and the machinic indices all the way to the desiring-machines. If the essential aspect of the destructive task is to undo the Oedipal trap of regression properly speaking, and all its dependencies, each time in a way adapted to the "case" in question, the essential aspect of the first positive task is to ensure the machinic conversion of primal repression, there too in an adapted variable manner. Which is to say: undoing the blockage or the coincidence on which the repression properly speaking relies; transforming the apparent opposition of repulsion (the body without organs/the machines-partial objects) into a condition of real functioning; ensuring this functioning in the forms of attraction and production of intensities; thereafter integrating the failures in the attractive functioning, as well as enveloping the zero degree in the intensities produced; and thereby causing the desiring-machines to start up again. Such is the delicate and focal point that fills the function of transference in schizoanalysis – dispersing, schizophrenizing the perverse transference of psychoanalysis.

Notes

This selection is taken from the English translation of Deleuze and Guattari's *Anti-Oedipus: Capitalism and Schizophrenia* (New York: The Viking Press, 1977), pp. 322–39.

1 D.H. Lawrence, "Psychoanalysis and the Unconscious", in *Psychoanalysis and the Unconscious and Fantasia of the Unconscious* (New York: Viking Press, 1969), p. 30.

2 Serge Leclaire, "La réalité du désir", in *Sexualité humaine* (Paris: Aubier, 1970), p. 245. And *Séminaire Vincennes*, 1969, pp. 31–4 (the opposition between the "erogenous body" and the organism).

3 From a letter by Mozart, cited by Marcel Moré, *Le Dieu Mozart et le monde des oiseaux* (Paris: Gallimard, 1971), p. 124: "Having come of age, he found the means of concealing his divine essence, by indulging in scatological amusements". Moré shows convincingly how the scatological machine works underneath and against the Oedipal "cage".

4 In his study on "Objet magique, sorcellerie et fétichisme" in *Nouvelle revue de psychanalyse* 2 (1970), Pierre Bonnafé clearly demonstrates in this respect the inadequacy of a notion like that of a fragmented body: "There is indeed a fragmenting of the body, but not at all with a feeling of loss or degradation. Quite to the contrary, as much for the holder as for the others, the body is fragmented by multiplication: the others no longer have to do with a simple person, but with a man to the $x + y + z$ *power* whose life has been immeasurably increased, dispersed while being united with other natural forces . . . , since its existence no longer rests at the center of its person, but has hidden itself in several far-off and impregnable locations" (pp. 166–67). Bonnafé recognizes in the magic object the existence of the three desiring syntheses: the connective synthesis, which combines the fragments of the person with those of animals or plants; the included disjunctive synthesis, which records the man-animal composite; the conjunctive synthesis, which implies a veritable migration of the remainder or residue.

5 Jacques Monod, *Chance and Necessity*, trans. A. Wainhouse (New York: Knopf, 1971), p. 98.

6 On the "double death", see Maurice Blanchot, *L'Espace littéraire* (Paris: Gallimard, 1955), pp. 104, 160.

7 Arthur Rimbaud, letter to Paul Demeny, 15 May, 1871.

8 W. Reich, *The Function of the Orgasm*. A correct interpretation – marked throughout by idealism – of Freud's theory of culture and its catastrophic evolution concerning guilt feeling, can be found in Paul Ricoeur: on death, and "the death of death", see *De l'interpretation* (Paris: Editions du Seuil, 1965), pp. 299–303.

9 Freud, *The Problem of Anxiety*, trans. Henry Alden Bunker (New York: Psychoanalytic Quarterly Press, and Norton, 1936); or *Inhibitions, Symptoms, and Anxiety*, trans. Alix Strachey (London: Hogarth Press, 1936).

10 On the impossibility of immediate qualitative conversions, and the necessity for going by way of neutral energy, see Freud, *The Ego and the Id*, trans. Joan Riviere (New York: Norton, 1961). This impossibility, this necessity is no longer understandable, it seems to us, if one agrees with Jean Laplanche that "the death drive has no energy of its own" (*Vie et mort en psychanalyse* [Paris: Flammarion, 1970], p. 211). Therefore the death drive could not enter into a veritable dualism, or would have to be confused with the neutral energy itself, which Freud denies.

11 Nietzsche, *On the Genealogy of Morals*, II. 13.

12 D.H. Lawrence, *Aaron's Rod* (New York: Penguin, 1976), p. 101.

13 Henry Miller, *Sexus* (New York: Grove Press, 1965), pp. 429–30 (words in brackets added). One would do well to consult the exercises of comic psychoanalysis in *Sexus*.

14 L.-F. Céline, in *L'Herne* no. 3, p. 171.

15 Ibid.

Translated by Robert Hurley and Mark Seem

8

Regimes, Pathways, Subjects

Classical thought distanced the soul from matter and separated the essence of the subject from the cogs of the body. Marxists later set up an opposition between subjective superstructures and infrastructural relations of production. How then ought we talk about the production of subjectivity today? Clearly, the contents of subjectivity have become increasingly dependent on a multitude of machinic systems. No area of opinion, thought, images, affects or spectacle has eluded the invasive grip of "computer-assisted" operations, such as databanks and telematics. This leads one to wonder whether the very essence of the subject – that infamous essence, so sought after over the centuries by Western philosophy – is not threatened by contemporary subjectivity's new "machine addiction". Its current result, a curious mix of enrichment and impoverishment, is plainly evident: an apparent democratization of access to data and modes of knowledge, coupled with a segregative exclusion from their means of development; a multiplication of anthropological approaches, a planetary intermixing of cultures, paradoxically accompanied by a rising tide of particularisms, racisms and nationalisms; and a vast expansion in the fields of technoscientific and aesthetic investigation, taking place in a general atmosphere of gloom and disenchantment. Rather than joining the fashionable crusades against the misdeeds of modernism, or preaching a rehabilitation of worn-out transcendent values, or indulging in the disillusioned indulgences of postmodernism, we might instead try to find a way out of the dilemma of having to choose between unyielding refusal or cynical acceptance of this situation.

The fact that machines are capable of articulating statements and registering states of fact in as little as a nanosecond, and soon in a picosecond,[1] does not in itself make them diabolical powers that threaten to dominate human beings. People have little reason to turn away from machines; which are nothing other than hyperdeveloped and hyperconcentrated forms of certain aspects of human subjectivity, and emphatically not those aspects that polarize people in relations of domination and power. It will be possible to build a two-way bridge between human beings and machines and, once we have established that, to herald new and confident alliances between them.

In what follows, I shall address the following problem: that today's information and communication machines do not merely convey representational contents, but also contribute to the fabrication of new *assemblages* of enunciation, individual and collective.

Before going any further, we must ask whether subjectivity's "entry into the machine" – as in the past, when one "entered" a religious order – is really all that new. Weren't precapitalist or archaic subjectivities already engendered by a variety of initiatory, social and rhetorical machines embedded in clan, religious, military and feudal institutions, among others? For present purposes, I shall group these machines under the general rubric of *collective apparatuses* [*équipements*] *of subjectification*. Monastic machines, which passed down memories from antiquity to the present day, thereby enriching our modernity, are a case in point. Were they not the computer programs, the "macroprocessors", of the Middle Ages? The neoplatonists, in their own way, were the first programmers of a processuality capable of spanning time and surviving periods of stasis. And what was the Court of Versailles, with its minutely detailed administration of flows of power, money, prestige and competence, and its high-precision etiquette, if not a machine deliberately designed to churn out a new and improved aristocratic subjectivity – one far more securely under the yoke of the royal State than the seignorial aristocracy of the feudal tradition, and entertaining different relations of subjection to the values of the rising bourgeoisie?

It is beyond the scope of this article to sketch even a thumbnail history of these collective apparatuses of subjectification. As I see it, neither history nor sociology is equal to the task of providing the analytical or political keys to the processes in play. I shall therefore limit myself to highlighting several fundamental paths/voices [*voie/voix*] that these apparatuses have produced, and whose crisscrossing remains the basis for modes and processes of subjectification in contemporary Western societies. I distinguish three series:

1   Paths/voices of *power* circumscribing and circumventing human groupings from the outside, either through direct coercion of, and panoptic grip on, bodies, or through imaginary capture of minds.

2   Paths/voices of *knowledge* articulating themselves with technoscientific and economic pragmatics from within subjectivity.

3   Paths/voices of *self-reference* developing a processual subjectivity that defines its own coordinates and is self-consistent (what I have discussed elsewhere under the category of the 'subject-group'), but can nevertheless establish transversal relations to mental and social stratifications.

(1) Power over exterior territorialities, (2) deterritorialized modes of knowledge about human activities and machines, and (3) the creativity proper to subjective mutations: these three paths/voices, though inscribed in historical time and rigidly incarnated in sociological divisions and segregations, are forever entwining in unexpected and strange dances, alternating between fights to the death and the promotion of new figures.

I should note in passing that the schizoanalytic perspective on the processes of subjectification I am proposing will make only very limited use of dialectical or structuralist approaches, systems theory or even genealogical approaches as understood by Michel Foucault. In my view, all systems for defining models are in a sense equal, all are tenable, but only to the extent that their principles of intelligibility renounce any universalist pretensions, and that their sole mission be to help map real existing territories (sensory, cognitive, affective and aesthetic universes) – and even then only in relation to carefully delimited areas and periods. This relativism is not in the least embarrassing, epistemologically speaking: it holds that the regularities, the quasi-stable configurations, for which our immediate experiences first emerge are precisely those systems of self-modeling invoked earlier as self-reference, the third path/voice. In this kind of system, discursive links, whether of expression or of content, obey ordinary logics of larger and institutional discursive ensembles only remotely, against the grain, or in a disfiguring way. To put it another way: at this level, absolutely anything goes – any ideology, or even religion will do, even the most archaic: all that matters is that it be used as the raw material of existence.[2]

The problem is to situate appropriately this third path/voice, of creative, transforming self-reference, in relation to the first two, modes of power and modes of knowledge. I have said both that self-reference is the most singular, the most contingent path/voice, the one that anchors human realities in finitude, and that it is the most universal one, the one that effects the most dazzling crossings between heterogeneous domains. I might have used other terms: it is not so much that this path/voice is "universal" in the strict sense, but that it is the richest in what may be called universes of virtuality, the best endowed with lines of processuality. (I ask the reader here not to begrudge me my plethora of qualifiers, or the meaning-overload of certain expressions, or even the vagueness of their cognitive scope: there is no other way to proceed!)

The paths/voices of power and knowledge are inscribed in external referential coordinates guaranteeing that they are used extensively and that their meaning is precisely circumscribed. The Earth was once the primary referent for modes of power over bodies and populations, just as capital was the referent for economic modes of knowledge and mastery of the means of production. With the figureless and foundationless Body without Organs of self-reference we see spreading before us an entirely different horizon, that of a new machinic processuality considered as the continual point of emergence of all forms of creativity.

I must emphasize that the triad territorialized power-deterritorialized knowledge-processual self-reference has no other aim than to clarify certain problems – for example, the current rise of neoconservative ideologies and other, even more pernicious archaisms. It goes without saying that so perfunctory a model cannot even claim to begin to map concrete processes of subjectification. Suffice it to say that these terms are instruments for a speculative cartography that makes no pretense of providing a universal structural foundation or increasing on-the-ground efficiency. This is another way of saying, by way of a reminder, that these paths/voices have not always existed and undoubtedly will not always exist (at least, not in the same form). Thus, there may be some relevance in trying to locate their historical emergence, and the thresholds of consistency they have crossed in order to enter and remain in the orbit of our modernity.

It is safe to assume that their various consistencies are supported by collective systems for "memorizing" data and modes of knowledge, as well as by material apparatuses of a technical, scientific and aesthetic nature. We can, then, attempt to date these fundamental subjective mutations in relation, on the one hand, to the historical birth of large-scale religious and cultural collective arrangements, and on the other, to the invention of new materials and energies, new machines for crystallizing time and, finally, to new biological technologies. It is not a question of material infrastructures that directly condition collective subjectivity, but of components essential for a given setup to take consistency in space and time as a function of technical, scientific and artistic transformations.

These considerations have led me to distinguish three zones of historical fracture on the basis of which, over the last thousand years, the three fundamental capitalist components have come into being: *the age of European Christianity*, marked by a new conception of the relations between the Earth and power; *the age of capitalist abstraction or deterritorialization of knowledge and technique*, founded on principles of general equivalence; and the age of *planetary computerization*, creating the possibility for creative and singularizing processuality to become the new fundamental point of reference.

With respect to the last point, one is forced to admit that there are very few objective indications of a shift away from oppressive mass-mediatic modernity toward some kind of more liberating postmedia era in which subjective assemblages of self-reference might come into their own.

Nevertheless, it is my guess that it is only through "remappings" of the production of computerized subjectivity that the path/voice of self-reference will be able to reach its full amplitude. Obviously, nothing is a foregone conclusion – and nothing that could be done in this domain could ever substitute for innovative social practices. The only point I am making is that, unlike other revolutions of subjective emancipation – Spartacus and other slave rebellions, peasant revolts during the Reformation, the French Revolution, the Paris Commune and so on – individual and social practices for the self-valorization and self-organization of subjectivity are now within our reach and, perhaps for the first time in history, have the potential to lead to something more enduring than mad and ephemeral spontaneous outpourings – in other words, to lead to a fundamental repositioning of human beings in relation to both their machinic and natural environments (which, at any rate, now tend to coincide).

The Age of European Christianity

In Western Europe, a new figure of subjectivity arose from the ruins of the late Roman and Carolingian empires. It can be characterized by a double articulation combining two aspects: first, the relatively autonomous base territorial entities of ethnic, national or religious character, which originally constituted the texture of feudal segmentarity, but have survived in other forms up to the present day; and second, the deterritorialized subjective power entity transmitted by the Catholic Church and structured as a collective setup on a European scale.

Unlike earlier formulas for imperial power, Christianity's central figure of power did not assert a direct, totalitarian-totalizing hold over the base territories of society and of subjectivity. Long before Islam, Christianity had to renounce its desire to form an organic unity. However, far from weakening processes for the integration of subjectivity, the disappearance of a flesh-and-blood Caesar and the promotion of a deterritorialized Christ (who cannot be said to be a substitute for the former) only reinforced them. It seems to me that the conjunction between the partial autonomy of the political and economic spheres proper to feudal segmentarity and the hyperfusional character of Christian subjectivity (as seen in the Crusades and the adoption of aristocratic codes such as the Peace of God, as described by Georges Duby) has resulted in a kind of fault line, a metastable equilibrium favoring the proliferation of other equally partial processes of autonomy. This can be seen in the schismatic vitality of religious sensibility and reflection that characterized the medieval period; and of course in the explosion of aesthetic creativity, which has continued unabated since then; the first great "takeoff" of techno-logies and commercial exchange, which is known to historians as the "industrial revolution of the eleventh century", and was a correlate of the appearance of new figures of urban organization. What could have given this tortured, unstable, ambiguous formula the surfeit of consistency that was to see it persist and flourish through the terrible historical trials awaiting it: barbarian invasions, epidemics, never-ending wars? Sche-matically, one can identify six series of factors:

First: The promotion of a monotheism that would prove in practice to be quite flexible and evolutionary, able to adapt itself more or less successfully to particular subjective positions – for example, even those of "barbarians" or slaves. The fact that flexibility in a system of ideologi-cal reference can be a fundamental asset for its survival is a basic given, which can be observed at every important turning point in the history of capitalist subjectivity (think, for example, of the surprising adaptive abilities enabling contemporary capitalism literally to swallow the so-called socialist economies whole). Western Christianity's consoli-dation of new ethical and religious patterns led to two parallel markets of subjectification: one involves the perpetual reconstitution of the base territorialities (despite many setbacks), and a redefini-tion of filiation suzerainty and national networks; the other involves a predisposition to the free circulation of knowledge, monetary signs, aesthetic figures, technology, goods, people, and so forth. This kind of market prepared the ground for the deterritorialized capitalist path/voice.

Second: The cultural establishment of a disciplinary grid onto Christian populations through a new type of religious machine, the original base for which was the parish school system created by Charlemagne, but which far outlived his empire.

Third: The establishment of enduring trade organizations, guilds, mon-asteries, religious orders and so forth, functioning as so many "data-banks" for the era's modes of knowledge and technique.

Fourth: The widespread use of iron, and wind and water mills; the development of artisan and urban mentalities. It must be emphasized, however, that this first flowering of machinism only implanted itself in a somewhat parasitic, "encysted" manner within the great human assemb-lages on which the large-scale systems of production continued essen-tially to be based. In other words, a break had not yet been made with the fundamental and primordial relation of human being to tool.

Fifth: The appearance of machines operating by much more advanced subjective integration: clocks striking the same canonical hours throughout all of Christendom; and the step-by-step invention of various forms of religious music subordinated to scripture.

Sixth: The selective breeding of animal and plant species, making possible a rapid quantitative expansion of demographic and economic parameters, and therefore leading to a rescaling of the assemblages in question.

In spite or because of the colossal pressures – including territorial restrictions but also enriching acculturations – associated with the Byzantine Empire, then Arab imperialism, as well as with nomadic and "barbarian" powers (which introduced, most notably, metallurgical innovations), the cultural hotbed of protocapitalist Christianity attained a relative (but long-term) stability with respect to the three fundamental poles governing its relations of power and knowledge: peasant, religious and aristocratic subjectification. In short, the "machinic advances" linked to urban development and the flowering of civil and military technologies were simultaneously encouraged and contained. All this constitutes a kind of "state of nature" of the relation between human being and tool, which continues to haunt paradigms of the "Work, Family, Fatherland" type even today.

The Age of Capitalist Deterritorialization of Modes of Knowledge and Technique

The second component of capitalist subjectivity begins effectively in the eighteenth century. It is marked above all by a growing disequilibrium in the relation of human being to tool. Human beings also witnessed the disappearance and eradication of social territorialities that, until then, were thought to be permanent and inalienable. Their landmarks of social and physical corporeality were profoundly shaken. The universe of reference for the new system of generalized exchange was no longer territorial segmentarity, but rather capital as a mode of semiotic reterritorialization of human activities and structures uprooted by machinic processes. Once, a real Despot or imaginary God served as the operational keystone for the local recomposition of actual territories. Now, though, that role would be played by symbolic capitalization of abstract values of power bearing on economic and technological modes of knowledge indexed to newly deterritorialized social classes, and creating a general equivalence between all valorizations of goods and human activities. A system of this sort cannot preserve its historical consistency without resorting to a kind of endless headlong race, with a constant renegotiation of the stakes. The new "capitalist passion" would sweep up everything in its path, in particular the cultures and territorialities that had succeeded to one degree or another in escaping the Christian steamroller. The principal consistency factors of this component are the following:

First: The general spread of the printed text into all aspects of social and cultural life, correlated with a certain weakening of the performative force of direct oral communication; by the same token, capabilities of accumulating and processing knowledge are greatly expanded.

Second: The primacy of steam-powered machines and steel, which multiplied the power of machinic vectors to propagate themselves on land, sea and air, and across every technological, economic and urban space.

Third: The manipulation of time, which is emptied of its natural rhythms by: chronometric machines leading to a Taylorist rationalization of labor power; techniques of economic semiotization, for example, involving credit money, which imply a general virtualization of capacities for human initiative and a predictive calculus bearing on domains of innovation – checks written on the future – all of which makes possible an unlimited expansion of the imperium of market economies.

Fourth: The biological revolutions, beginning with Pasteur's discoveries, that have linked the future of living species ever more closely to the development of biochemical industries.

Human beings find themselves relegated to a position of quasi-parasitic adjacency to the machinic phyla. Each of their organs and social relations are quite simply repatterned in order to be reallocated, overcoded, in accordance with the global requirements of the system. (The most gripping and prophetic representations of these bodily rearrangements are found in the work of Leonardo da Vinci, Breughel, and especially Arcimboldi.)

The paradox of this functionalization of human organs and faculties and its attendant regime of general equivalence between systems of value is that, even as it stubbornly continues to invoke universalizing perspectives, all it ever manages to do historically is fold back on itself, yielding reterritorializations of nationalist, classist, corporatist, racist and nationalist kinds. Because of this, it inexorably returns to the most conservative, at times caricatured, paths/voices. The "spirit of enlightenment", which marked the advent of this second figure of capitalist subjectivity, is necessarily accompanied by an utterly hopeless fetishization of profit – a specifically bourgeois libidinal power formula. That formula distanced itself from the old emblematic systems of control over territories, people and goods by employing more deterritorialized mediations – only to secrete the most obtuse, asocial and infantilizing of subjective groundworks. Despite the appearance of freedom of thought that the new capitalist monotheism is so fond of affecting, it has always presupposed an archaistic, irrational grip on unconscious subjectivity, most notably through hyperindividuated apparatuses of responsibility – and guilt-production, which, carried to a fever pitch, lead to compulsive self-punishment and morbid cults of blame – perfectly repertoried in Kafka's universe.

The Age of Planetary Computerization

Here, in the third historical zone, the preceding pseudo-stabilities are upset in an entirely different way. The machine is placed under the control of subjectivity – not a reterritorialized human subjectivity, but a new kind of machinic subjectivity. Here are several characteristics of the taking-consistency of this new epoch:

First: Media and telecommunications tend to "double" older oral and scriptural relations. It is worth noting that in the resulting polyphony, not only human but also machinic paths/voices link into databanks, artificial intelligence and the like. Public opinion and group tastes are developed by statistical and modelizing apparatuses, such as those of the advertising and film industries.

Second: Natural raw materials are replaced by a multitude of new custom-made, chemically produced materials (plastics, new alloys, semi-conductors and so on). The rise of nuclear fission, and perhaps soon nuclear fusion, would seem to augur a considerable increase in energy resources – providing, of course, that irreparable pollution disasters do not occur! As always, everything will depend on the new social assemblages' capacity for collective reappropriation.

Third: The temporal dimensions to which microprocessors provide access allow enormous quantities of data and huge numbers of problems to be processed in infinitesimal amounts of time, enabling the new machinic subjectivities to stay abreast of the challenges and issues confronting them.

Fourth: Biological engineering is making possible unlimited remodeling of life forms; this may lead to a radical change in the conditions of life on the planet and, consequently, to an equally radical reformulation of all of its ethological and imaginary references.

The burning question, then, becomes this: Why have the immense processual potentials brought forth by the revolutions in information processing, telematics, robotics, office automation, biotechnology and so on up to now led only to a monstrous reinforcement of earlier systems of alienation, an oppressive mass-media culture and an infantilizing politics of consensus? What would make it possible for them finally to usher in a postmedia era, to disconnect themselves from segregative capitalist values and to give free rein to the first stirrings, visible today, of a revolution in intelligence, sensitivity and creativity? Any number of dogmatisms claim to have found the answer to these questions in a violent affirmation of one of the three capitalist paths/voices at the expense of the others. There are those who dream of returning to the legitimated powers of bygone days, to the clear circumscription of people, races, religions, castes and sexes. Paradoxically, the neo-Stalinists and social democrats, both of whom are incapable of conceiving of the socius in any terms other than its rigid insertion into State structures and functions, must be placed in the same category. There are those whose faith in capitalism leads them to justify all of the terrible ravages of modernity – on people, culture, the environment – on the grounds that in the end they will bring the benefits of progress. Finally, there are those whose fantasies of a radical liberation of human creativity condemn them to chronic marginality, to a world of false pretense, or who turn back to take refuge behind a facade of socialism or communism.

Our project, on the contrary, is to attempt to rethink these three necessarily interwoven paths/voices. No engagement with the creative phyla of the third path/voice is tenable unless new existential territories are concurrently established. Without hearkening back to the post-Carolingian pathos, they must nevertheless include protective mechanisms for the person and the imaginary and create a supportive environment. Surely the mega-enterprises of the second path/voice – the great collective scientific and industrial adventures, the administration of knowledge markets – still have legitimacy: but only on the condition that they redefine their goals, which remain today singularly deaf and blind to human truths. Is it still enough to claim profit as the only goal? In any case, the aim of the division of labor, and of emancipatory social practices, must be redirected toward a *fundamental right to singularity*, toward an ethic of finitude that is all the more demanding of individuals and social entities, because its imperatives are *not* founded on transcendent principles. It has become apparent in this regard that ethicopolitical universes of reference now tend to institute themselves as extensions of aesthetic universes, which in no way authorize the use of such terms as "perversion" or "sublimation". It will be noted that not only the existential operators pertaining to these ethicopolitical matters but the aesthetic operators as well inevitably reach the point at which meaning breaks down, entailing irreversible processual engagements whose agents are, more often than not, incapable of accounting for anything (least of all themselves) – and are therefore exposed to a panoply of risks, including madness. Only if the third path/voice takes consistency in the direction of self-reference – carrying us from the consensual media era to the dissensual postmedia era – will each be able to assume his or her processual potential and, perhaps, transform this planet – a living hell for over three quarters of its population – into a universe of creative enchantments.

I imagine that this language will ring false to many a jaded ear, and that even the least malicious will accuse me of utopianism. Utopia, it is true, gets bad press these days, even when it acquires a charge of realism and efficiency, as it has with the Greens in Germany. But let there be no mistake: these questions of subjectivity production do not only concern a handful of illuminati. Look at Japan, the prototypical model of new capitalist subjectivities. Not enough emphasis has been placed on the fact that one of the essential ingredients of the miracle mix showcased for visitors to Japan is that the collective subjectivity produced there on a massive scale combines the highest of "high-tech" components with feudalisms and archaisms inherited from the mists of time. Once again, we find the reterritorializing function of an ambiguous monotheism – Shinto-Buddhism, a mix of animism and universal powers – contributing to the establishment of a flexible formula for subjectification going far beyond the triadic framework of capitalist Christian paths/voices. We have a lot to learn!

For now, though, consider another extreme, the case of Brazil. There, phenomena involving the reconversion of archaic subjectivities have taken an entirely different turn. It is common knowledge that a considerable proportion of the population is mired in such extreme poverty that it lives outside the money economy, but that does not prevent Brazil's industry being ranked sixth among Western powers. In this society, a dual society if there ever was one, there is a double sweep of subjectivity: on the one hand, there is a fairly racist Yankee wave (like it or not) beamed in on one of the most powerful television transmitting networks in the world, and on the other, an animist wave involving religions like *candomblé*, passed on more or less directly from the African cultural heritage, which are now escaping their original ghettoization and spreading throughout society, including the most well-connected circles of Rio and Sao Paulo. It is interesting that, in this case, mass- media penetration is preceding capitalist acculturation. What did President Sarney do when he wanted to stage a decisive coup against inflation, which was running as high as 400 percent per year? He went on television. Brandishing a piece of paper in front of the cameras, he declared that from the moment he signed the order he held in his hand everyone watching would become his personal representative and would have the right to arrest any merchant who did not respect the official pricing system. It seems to have been surprisingly effective – but at the price of considerable regression in the legal system.

Capitalism in permanent crisis (Integrated Worldwide Capitalism) is at a total subjective impasse. It knows that paths/voices of self-reference are indispensable for its expansion, and thus for its survival, yet it is under tremendous pressure to efface them. A kind of superego – that booming

Carolingian voice – dreams only of crushing them and reterritorializing them onto archaic images. Let us attempt to find a way out of this vicious circle by resituating our three capitalist paths/voices in relation to the geopolitical coordinates – First, Second and Third Worlds – commonly used to establish a hierarchy of the major subjective formations. For Western Christian subjectivity, everything was (and, unconsciously, remains) quite simple: it has no restrictions in latitude and longitude. It is the transcendent center around which everything is deemed to revolve. The paths/voices of capital, for their part, have continued their onward rush – first westward, toward elusive "new frontiers", more recently toward the East, in conquest of what remains of the ancient Asiatic empires (Russia included). However, this mad race has reached the end of the road, from one direction in California, from the other in Japan. The second path/voice of capital has closed the circle; the world has buckled, the system is saturated. Henceforth, the North–South axis will perhaps function as the third path/voice of self-reference. This is what I call "the barbarian compromise". The old walls marking the limits of "barbarism" have been torn down, deterritorialized once and for all. The last shepherds of monotheism have lost their flocks, for it is not in the nature of the new subjectivity to be herded. Moreover, capitalism itself is now beginning to shatter into animist and machinic polyvocity. What a fabulous reversal, if the old African, pre-Columbian and aboriginal subjectivities became the final recourse for subjective reappropriation of machinic self-reference! The very same blacks, Indians, even South Sea Islanders whose ancestors chose death over submission to Christian and capitalist ideals of power: first slavery, then the exchange economy.

I hope that my last examples are not faulted for being overly exotic. Even in Old World countries such as Italy there has been a proliferation of small family enterprises in symbiosis with cutting-edge sectors of the electronics industry and telematics; this has happened over the last few years in the northeast-center triangle of Italy. If an Italian Silicon Valley develops there, it will be founded on a reconversion of subjective archaisms originating in the country's antiquated patriarchal structures. Some futurologists, who are in no way crackpots, predict that certain Mediterranean countries – Italy and Spain, in particular – will overtake the great economic centers of northern Europe in a few decades' time. So when it comes to dreaming and utopia, the future is wide open! My wish is that all those who remain attached to the idea of social progress – all those for whom the social has not become an illusion or a "simulacrum" – look seriously into these questions of subjectivity production. The subjectivity of power does not fall from the sky. It is not written into our chromosomes that divisions of knowledge and labor must necessarily lead to the hideous segregations humanity now suffers. Unconscious figures of power and knowledge are not universals. They are tied to reference myths profoundly anchored in the psyche, but they can still swing around toward liberatory paths/voices. Subjectivity today remains under the massive control of apparatuses of power and knowledge, thus consigning technical, scientific and artistic innovations to the service of the most reactionary and retrograde figures of sociality. In spite of that, other modalities of subjective production – processual and singularizing ones – are conceivable. These alternate forms of existential reappropriation and self-valorization may in the future become the *reason for living* for human collectivities and individuals who refuse to give in to the deathlike entropy characterizing the period we are passing through.

Notes

This essay was published in *Incorporations*, eds. Jonathan Crary and Sanford Kwinter (New York: Urzone, 1992). It corresponds to the "Liminaire" of Guattari's *Cartographies schizoanalytiques* (Paris: Gallilée, 1989).

1 A nanosecond is 10^{-9} seconds; a pico-second is 10^{-12}. On the futurological themes touched on here, see the special issue of *Science et technique* entitled "Rapport sur l'état de la technique", ed. Thierry Gaudin.

2 The immediate aim of their expressive chains is no longer to denote states of fact or to embed states of sense in significational axes but – I repeat – to activate existential crystallizations operating, in a certain way, outside the fundamental principles of classical reason: identity, the excluded middle, causality, sufficient reason, continuity . . . . The most difficult thing to convey is that these materials, which can set processes of subjective self-reference in motion, are themselves extracted from radically heterogeneous, not to mention heteroclite, elements: rhythms of lived time, obsessive refrains, identificational emblems, transitional objects, fetishes of all kinds . . . . What is affirmed in this crossing of regions of being and modes of semiotization are traits of singularization that date – something like existential postmarks – as well as "event", "contingent" states of fact, their referential correlates and their corresponding assemblages of enunciation. Rational modes of discursive knowledge cannot fully grasp this double capacity of intensive traits to singularize and transversalize existence, enabling it, on the one hand, to persist locally, and on the other hand, to consist transversally (giving it transconsistency). It is accessible to apprehension only on the order of affect, a global transferential grasp whereby that which is most universal is conjoined with the most highly contingent facticity: the loosest of meaning's ordinary moorings becomes anchored in the finitude of being-there. Various traditions of what could be termed "narrow rationalism" persist in a quasi-militant, systemic incomprehension of anything in these metamodelizations pertaining to virtual and incorporeal universes, fuzzy worlds of uncertainty, the aleatory and the probable. Long ago, narrow rationalism banished from anthropology those modes of categorization it considered "prelogical", when they were in reality metalogical or paralogical, their objective essentially being to give consistency to individual and/or collective assemblages of subjectivity. What we need to conceptualize is a continuum running from children's games and the makeshift ritualizations accompanying attempts at psychopathological recompositions of "schizoid" worlds, through the complex cartographies of myth and art, all the way to the sumptuous speculative edifices of theology and philosophy, which have sought to

apprehend these same dimensions of existential creativity (examples are Plotinus's "forgetful souls" and the "unmoving motor" which, according to Leibniz, preexists any dissipation of potential.)

Translated by Brian Massumi

9

The Postmodern Impasse

A certain conception of progress and modernity has become bankrupt and, in the process, compromised collective confidence in the notion of an emancipatory social practice. At the same time, a sort of glaciation has got the upper hand in social relations: hierarchies and segregations have hardened, misery and unemployment tend today to be accepted as necessary evils, while the unions hang onto the last institutional branches conceded to them. The unions, as well, are glued to corporatist practices that lead them to adopt conservative attitudes, which at times resemble those of reactionary circles. The communist left is sinking into ossification and dogmatism, while the socialist parties, concerned with presenting themselves as reliable technocratic partners, have given up any progressive questioning of existing structures. It should come as no surprise, then, that the ideologies that once claimed to serve as guides for reconstructing society on a more just and egalitarian basis have lost their credibility.

Does it follow, then, that we are condemned to remain helpless before the rise of this new order of cruelty and cynicism that is about to overwhelm the planet, an order that seems determined, it would seem, to persist? It is to this regrettable conclusion that a number of intellectuals and artists, especially those influenced by postmodernist thought, have arrived.

I will have to leave aside, for the purposes of this paper, the launching (by the managers of contemporary art) of large promotional operations dubbed "neo-expressionism" in Germany; "Bad Painting" or "New Painting" in the US; "Trans-avant-garde" in Italy; "Free Representation" and the "New Fauvism" in France, and so on. Otherwise, it would be too easy for me to demonstrate that postmodernism is nothing but the last gasp of modernism; nothing, that is, but a reaction to and, in a certain way, a mirror of the formalist abuses and reductions of modernism from which, in the end, it is no different. No doubt there will emerge from these schools some authentic painters whose personal talent will protect them against the pernicious effects of this sort of fad that maintains itself by means of publicity. In any case, postmodernism will not be able to revive the creative phylum as it has claimed.

On the other hand, because it is better secured to the deeply reterritorializing tendencies of present capitalistic subjectivity, postmodern architecture seems to me less superficial and much more indicative of the place assigned to art by the dominant power formations.

Let me explain myself. From time immemorial, and regardless of which historical misadventure, the capitalist drive has always combined two fundamental components: the first, which I call deterritorialization, has to do with the destruction of social territories, collective identities, and systems of traditional values; the second, which I call the movement of reterritorialization, has to do with the recomposition, even by the most artificial means, of personologically individuated frameworks, schemata of power, and models of submission which are, if not formally similar to those this drive has destroyed, at least homothetical from a functional perspective.

As the deterritorializing revolutions, tied to the development of science, technology, and the arts, sweep aside everything before them, a compulsion toward subjective reterritorialization also emerges. And this antagonism is heightened even more with the phenomenal growth of the communications and computer fields, to the point where the latter concentrate their deterritorializing effects on such human faculties as memory, perception, understanding, imagination, etc. In this way, a certain formula of anthropological functioning, and a certain ancestral model of humanity, is appropriated from the inside. And I think that it is as a result of an incapacity to adequately confront this phenomenal mutation that collective subjectivity has abandoned itself to the absurd wave of conservatism that we are presently witnessing.

Let's return to our postmodern architects. Whereas in the domain of the plastic arts, young painters are required to submit to the prevalent conservatism of the market, failing which they find themselves condemned to vegetate on the margins, here adaptation to the values of the most retrograde neo-liberalism is made without hesitation. And while painting has never been for the ruling classes anything more than a matter of a "supplement of the spirit", a kind of currency of prestige, architecture has always occupied a major place in the making of territories of power, the fixing of its emblems, and the proclamation of its durability.

Are we not, then, at the center of what Jean-François Lyotard calls the postmodern condition, which I, unlike him, understand to be the paradigm of all submission and every sort of compromise with the existing status quo? For Lyotard, postmodernism represents the collapse of what he calls the grand narratives of legitimation (for example, the discourses of the Enlightenment, those of Hegel's accomplishment of the Spirit and the Marxist emancipation of the workers). It would always be wise, according to Lyotard, to be suspicious of the least desire for concerted social action. Any promotion of consensus as an ideal, Lyotard argues, is to be regarded as out-dated and suspect. Only little narratives of legitimation, in other words, the "pragmatics of linguistic particles" that are multiple, heterogeneous, and whose performativity would be only limited in time and space, can still save some aspects of justice and freedom. In this way, Lyotard joins other theorists, such as Jean Baudrillard, for whom the social and political have never been more than traps, or "semblances", for which it would be wise to lose one's fondness.

Whether they are painters, architects, or philosophers, the heroes of postmodernism have in common the belief that the crises experienced today in artistic and social practices can only lead to an irrevocable refusal of any large-scale social undertaking. So we ought to take care of our own backyards first and, preferably, in conformity with the habits and customs of our contemporaries. Don't rock the boat! Just drift with the currents of the marketplace of art and opinion that are modulated by publicity campaigns and surveys.

But where does the idea that the socius is reducible to the facts of language, and that these facts are in turn reducible to binarizable and "digitalizable" signifying chains, come from? On this point postmodernists have hardly said anything innovative! In fact, their views are directly in keeping with the modernist tradition of structuralism, whose influence on the human sciences appears to have been a carry-over from the worst aspects of Anglo-Saxon systematization. The secret link that binds these various doctrines, I believe, stems from a subterranean relationship – marked by reductionist conceptions, and conveyed immediately after the war by information theory and new cybernetic research. The references that everyone continually made to the new communications and computer technologies were so hastily developed, so poorly mastered, that they put us far behind the phenomenological research that had preceded them.

Here we must return to a basic truism, but one pregnant with implications; namely, that concrete social assemblages – not to be confused with the "primary group" of American sociology, which only reflects the economy of opinion polls – call into question much more than just linguistic performance: for example, ethological and ecological dimensions, as well as the economic semiotic components, aesthetic, corporeal and fantasmatic ones that are irreducible to the semiology of language, and the diverse incorporeal universes of reference which are not readily inscribed within the coordinates of the dominant empiricity . . . .

Postmodern philosophers flit around pragmatic research in vain. They remain loyal to a structuralist conception of speech and language that will never allow them to articulate the subjective facts in the formations of the unconscious, aesthetic and micro-political problematics. To say it in the clearest way possible, this view does not merit the name of philosophy, for it is only a prevalent state of mind, a "condition" of public opinion that pulls its truths out of the air. Why should it take the time to elaborate, for example, a serious speculative support for its theory regarding the inconsistency of the socius? Doesn't the present ubiquity of the mass media amply demonstrate that, in effect, any social link can stand in for, without any noticeable resistance, the desingularizing and infantilizing levelling of the capitalist production of signifiers? An old Lacanian adage, according to which "a signifer represents the subject for another signifier", could serve as an epigram for this new ethic of non-commitment. Because this is, in fact, what we have come to! Except, however, that there is nothing really to rejoice about, as the postmodernists seem to think. The question, rather, ought to be: how can we escape this dead end?

For their part, linguists concerned with theories of enunciation and speech acts have highlighted the fact that certain linguistic segments, parallel to their well-known classical functions of signification and denotation, can acquire a particular pragmatic effectiveness by crystallizing the respective positions of speaking subjects or by putting into place, de facto, certain situational frames. (The classical example being the president who declares "the session is open", and in so doing, really opens the session.) But these linguists have decided they must limit the significance of their discovery to the register of their specialization. Whereas in reality this third "existentializing" function, the one they emphasize, ought to imply, logically speaking, a definitive break with the structuralist corset within which they continue to constrain language.

It is not by right that the linguistic signifier occupies the royal place that capitalist subjectivation has afforded it, on account of constituting an essential support for its logic of generalized equivalence, and its politics of the capitalization of abstract values of power. Other regimes are capable of "running" the businesses of the world, and in this way deposing the signifier from its transcendent position with regard to the rhizomes woven by the realities and imaginaries of this symbolic-signifying imperium, in which the current hegemony of mass-mediated power is rooted. But they will certainly not be born through spontaneous generation. Rather, they are there to be constructed and brought within reach at the intersection of new analytic, aesthetic, and social practices; practices that no postmodernist spontaneity will be able to offer us on a platter.

Notes

"L'impasse post-moderne" appeared in *La Quinzaine littéraire* 456 (du 1er au 15 Fév. 1986): 21. It is an extract from a paper first delivered at a conference in Tokyo during November

1985, and repeated in Paris before the Collège de peinture of the Université européenne de philosophie on January 10, 1986. A slightly longer extract from Guattari's paper appeared as "The Postmodern Dead End", trans. Nancy Blake, *Flash Art* 128 (1986): 40–1. Guattari continues: "The emergence of these new practices of subjectivation in a postmedia era will be greatly facilitated by a concerted reappropriation of communications and data processing technologies, insofar as they will gradually make possible: 1) the promotion of new forms of collective agreement and interaction and, in the end, a re-invention of democracy; 2) through the miniaturization and personalization of machinery, a re-singularization of mechanically mediated means of expression; one can presume, in this connection, that the most surprising prospects will be afforded by the extension of data banks to network proportions; 3) the unlimited multiplication of the 'existential levers' that will make it possible to accede to changing creative realms.

Let us point out, finally, that the decentralization and subjective autonomization of postmedia operators will not correspond to a withdrawal or to a postmodernist type of release. The forthcoming postmedia revolution will have to be guided to an unprecedented degree by those minority groups that today are still the only ones who have realized the mortal risk for humanity of questions such as: the arms race; world famine; irreversible ecological degradation; mass-media pollution of collective subjectivity.

This, at least, is what I hope for, and it is what I humbly suggest you work for. If the future does not follow these paths, it is unlikely to endure longer than the end of the present millenium".

Translated by Todd Dufresne

10

Postmodernism and Ethical Abdication

An Interview by Nicholas Zurbrugg

NICHOLAS ZURBRUGG – To begin with, could I ask you how you became interested in performance poetry, particularly the work of Americans such as Ginsberg and Burroughs. What was it that you found most interesting in their work?

FÉLIX GUATTARI – I first got the know them through Jean-Jacques Lebel, the organizer of the *Polyphonix* festivals,[1] who had spent much of his early life among that generation of artists and writers in America. What interested me in these writers' work was the discovery of something very similar to my own concerns – above all in the realm of psychopathology, but also in the context of more political issues. This may seem a little paradoxical, because these are very different things, but I think there is a certain overlap or convergence between them. In terms of psychopathology, it's the problem of semiotic reintegration – that of gesture, the body, of spatial relations and so on.

Burroughs's cut-ups and semiotic inventions, for example, create new universes of mutated and mutating meanings. Then, at the same time, there's this sort of movement, which is not so much a traditional party or association, which is reappropriating and reinventing poetry – which, considered in ecological terms – is a disappearing species. That's why I suggest that the problem of "mental ecology" is so important – the problem of disappearing species, such as poetry. Because poetry is as important as vitamin C.

It's very important for children, for example, and is often very important for psychotic patients, whether as something written or as something declaimed. So it's this double project of untying the bonds of language and opening up new social, analytical and aesthetic practices which interested me in new forms of poetic performance. .

NZ – Your suggestion that poetry can be reinvented is very interesting given that many theorists of postmodern culture and mass-media practices tend to detect the neutralization of art, the death of the subject, the impossibility of originality and the loss of history. Would you consider the new mutational languages which you associate with the multi-media poets to offer some sort of advance towards a new kind of unity?

FG – When one considers the extent to which contemporary sensibility is agitated by the influences of academia, the mass-media, publicity and so on, it seems unlikely that there's any possibility of returning to the civilizations of the past. Whereas here in Québec, or doubtless in Australia, there's a privileged environment of open spaces in which one can more or less return to spatial respirations. The future which lies ahead is much more likely to be that of Bangladesh, Mexico, or Tokyo, where millions of inhabitants cluster together. In this respect, it is necessary to reinvent the body, to reinvent the mind and to reinvent language. Perhaps the new telematic, informational, and audio-visual technologies can help us to progress in this direction.

NZ – What would you say were the main examples of such new languages and technologies?

FG – Well, it already seems evident that informational "language" is evolving quite independently from traditional forms of language. Both in terms of its interactive and intertextual aspects it is combining communicative, perceptive, and sensitive dimensions in such a way that new modes of subjectivity are no longer restricted to past textual paradigms. We seem to be in the process of discovering a new realm of orality. We're not going to enter into dialogue with computers via digital systems, but by speaking directly to computers. Things will change considerably – we'll speak to machines, we'll speak to our cars, to people working twenty miles away – and we'll discover a new kind of sociality based upon quite different conventions. At present this is all embryonic – but things will probably change very rapidly in the years ahead, above all with the development of the interactive compact disc.

NZ – Have such technologies modified your ideas and practices significantly?

FG – I've not really changed my ideas since the sixties, when I developed the concept of *les machines désirantes* – the desiring machines – and the intersection of machines and subjectivity. That's exactly what is happening today, before our very eyes, so I've not really changed my ideas. As for the presentation of my ideas, I remain a member of my generation, and write with a ballpoint pen.

NZ – Are you optimistic regarding future developments?

FG – Well, there are a lot of problems and developments at present. The main question is the extent to which we are prisoners of dominant institutions such as academia, the media, and so on. Then, more generally, there's the problem of the way in which the West has cut itself off from the Third World.

NZ – Given such problems, what sort of role might one attribute to cultural avant-gardes such as the new forms of multi-media performance that we've been talking about? Do you think that the concept of the avant-garde still carries conviction?

FG – Avant-garde movements have often been rather dogmatic and have tried to impose this or that kind of program or world vision. I think that what is most significant in terms of sound poetry and performance poetry is the attempt to re-individualize subjectivity and creativity – a tendency that is not necessarily characteristic of some avant-garde movements. For example, an extremely individual artist like Antonin Artaud was rejected by the surrealist avant-garde precisely because of his individuality.

NZ – In this respect, the present sound poetry and performance poetry avant-gardes seem most interesting as open or fragmented coalitions of fellow artists, rather than as more systematic, programmatic movements.

FG – Exactly.

NZ – Do you have the same reservations regarding the programmatic and rather dogmatic ways in which the term "postmodern" has been used? How do you respond to this term?

FG – Very unfavourably.

NZ – Don't you think that the term has at least some validity as a concept distinguishing present work from that of the early twentieth century?

FG – Of course, but that doesn't mean that one would want to englobe everything in a kind of neo-liberal cultural market which only values the commercially viable. The prostitution of architecture in postmodern buildings, the prostitution of art in trans-avant-garde painting, and the virtual ethical and aesthetic abdication of postmodern thought leaves a kind of black stain upon history.

NZ – In many respects, aren't we witnessing a kind of cultural *Club Mediterranée*?

FG – Exactly.

NZ – What would you say were the most significant exceptions to these negative impulses in postmodern culture?

FG – I can't think of very many. There are certain inventive, intelligent advances in ecology, but even these tend to be rather dogmatic in character. No, there's not very much. In the Third World there are some political developments which I find very interesting, particularly union initiatives focussing upon women's issues, health issues, youth problems, the drugs problem and so on – lots of things – but nothing really offers a new polarity in opposition to the dominant forms of capitalism. Since the collapse of Eastern Europe we've witnessed a kind of triumph of dominant capitalist values. In the years ahead, I think new developments will occur on a vaster scale – on a more international scale.

NZ – Where does this leave the contemporary intellectual?

FG – So far as the organic intellectual is concerned, there are no more organs. It is no longer possible to exist organically. Accordingly, it is all the more necessary for the intellectual to be self-assertive, to be individual, to be brave, and to continue to work, resisting the fascination of academia, of the media, and of other such institutions.

Notes

This interview was published in the Australian arts magazine *photofile* 39 (July 1993): 11–13.

1 This interview was recorded in June 1991 at the *Oralités* Colloquium during the *Polyphonix* 16 performance poetry festival in Québec City. Another interview given by Guattari to Alain-Martin Richard and Richard Martel during this conference appeared as "Félix Guattari", *Inter* 55 (automne 1992 – hiver 1993): 11–13. In this interview Guattari cites several examples of promising inventive and experimental relations he witnessed in Chile that greatly pleased him involving a group of elderly persons who had an "ecology of retirement" in which they assisted one another in the reinvention and the eroticization of their lives and relations, as well as a group of architects who worked in the slums helping people to make and erect personalized signposts out of found materials (cardboard, plastic, and the like).

PART III

A Discursive Interlude

11

Institutional Practice and Politics

An Interview by Jacques Pain

JACQUES PAIN – [Guattari is invited to respond to the question of "institutional practice and politics".]
FÉLIX GUATTARI – What you call "institutional practice", as it has concerned me, has always been at the intersection of various domains which had to be in one way or another interconnected. In the 1950s, for me this essentially concerned:

(1) a militant practice in different youth and political organizations;

(2) a clinical practice with Jean Oury at La Borde;

(3) an analytic practice with psychotics, and later an analytic practice with clients.

The theoretical references relative to these diverse domains were rather discordant: Oury, Tosquelles, Lacan, Marxism, a personal attraction for philosophy . . . for a long time I travelled disparate paths. In the course of a day, or a week, I would change hats. As a militant, I was a Marxist inspired by Trotsky; when I worked I was a Freudo–Lacanian; when I reflected I was for the most part Sartrean, but all of that did not flow together very well.

It was in the course of discussions at the heart of GTPSI (Groupe de travail de psychologie et de sociologie institutionnelle), under the impulse of Tosquelles, who complained that one "walks with two legs" – one Marxist leg, and another Freudian leg – that I began to reflect on another possible analytic path, which I baptised at the time "institutional analysis", an expression that I did not really impose on that milieu, but which proliferated outside. It sought to make discernable a domain that was neither that of institutional therapy, nor institutional pedagogy, nor of the struggle for social emancipation, but which invoked an analytic method that could traverse these multiple fields (from which came the theme "transversality").

I came to consider the problems that we discussed at GTPSI (the "institutional transference" for example) as not specific to relations of mental illness, but as equally concerning the relations of the individual to the collectivity, the environment, economic relations, aesthetic productions, etc.

Unfortunately, the expression "institutional analysis" was taken up by people who certainly did not lack talent (such as Laureau, Labrot, Lapassade, etc.) but worked within a psycho-sociological perspective which was far too reductionistic for my taste. Gaining the field of the social and the micro-political, my intention had never been that the analysis would thereby lose on the side of the individual and pre-personal singularities, for example in the world of psychotics. Nothing was further from my intention than to propose a psycho-social model with the pretention of offering it as a global alternative to existing methods of analyzing the unconscious! Since that time my reflection has had as its axis problems of what I call *metamodelization*. That is, it has concerned something that does not found itself as an overcoding of existing modelizations, but more as a procedure of "automodelization", which appropriates all or part of existing models in order to construct its own cartographies, its own reference points, and thus its own analytic approach, its own analytic methodology. So, finally, when I saw the exploitation that had been wrought of "institutional analysis" (especially in Latin America) I expunged all that, and I tried to elaborate a method of analyzing the formations of the unconscious which was in no way simply a tributary to the individuation of subjectivity or to its incarnation in groups and institutions. What was being done at Saint-Alban and La Borde was to me already the beginning of such a decentering, allowing the disengagement of analysis from the personological and familialist frameworks to give an account of *assemblages of enunciation* of another sort (be it of a larger social size or an infra-individual size). From which came the ulterior problematic of *Capitalism and Schizophrenia*, in collaboration with Gilles Deleuze, which concerned the function of pre-personal subjectivity – prior to the totalities of the person and the individual – and supra-personal, that is, concerning phenomena of the group, social phenomena. Further, for us, the assemblages of enunciation must involve "machinic components", like the components of information systems . . .

In sum, what seemed important to me was to reappropriate the best of Freud and Marx with the knowledge that the subjective formations did not, should not, and could not coincide with the form of the individual. Minimally, subjectivity founds itself in a complex relation to the other, the alter ego, mother and father, relations of caste, class struggles, in short, to the entire context of social interaction. All this was more or less taken up by Lacan, with his decentering of the unconscious in language, but unfortunately was matched with a return to universals, structural "mathemes" which allowed subjective individuation which had been chased out the door of theoretical practice to re-enter by the window of theoretical phantasms. But I don't want to go into that right now.

Once one considers that subjectivity is not assimilable to a black box inserted in the cerebral circumvolutions, but works itself out through the entire social and "pre-personal" context, the analysis of the unconscious must take account of the "machinic circuits" and these assemblages of the production of subjectivity in no way reducible to interpersonal relations relevant to oedipal triangulation. For example: the subjectivity of the court produced at Versailles in the time of Louis XIV, or at Chambord in the time of François I, takes its bearings from a new type of "collective apparatus" promoted by the centralist system of national royalty. The subjectivity which the aristocrats saw themselves assuming has as its explicit object the production of a sort of "summons to residence" close by the royal power, without relation to the institutional "nomadism" of the ancient chevaliers. This genre of subjective assemblage engaged a series of ethnologico-architectural dimensions which it would be most interesting to study from the perspective of the later development of collective apparatuses of producers within capitalist subjectivity in the 19th and 20th centuries.

We teachers, shrinks, workers of the socius, we are thus at the same time products of collective apparatuses and producers of subjectivity. We are the workers at the tip of an industry, an industry that furnishes the primary subjective matter for all other industries and social activity. Indeed, this subjectivity has domains of individual application relative to individual enunciators, but it is not reducible to a simple plurality of speaking individuals; there exists a variety of entry points through which to construct subjectivity: political, social, ecological, etc. . . .

I do not know if I answered your question. I at least tried to address it in a general way.

JP – Could one say that you remain distinctly Marxist?

FG – Yes, to a certain extent. Moreover, one cannot change one's point of reference with respect to such subjects as one can change a shirt, in the manner of the ghastly *nouveaux philosophes*. Marx is an author of the first degree who profoundly marked his epoch. There are certainly many things that have come to pass since then. But I don't think this kind of question makes much sense.

JP – It has a sense for me inasmuch as I came to your texts by way of a militant practice, always with a demand: that of analysis. At that time I found in the formulations you employ throughout here and there – the "militant analytic function", the limits of analysis – themes that appear somewhat contradictory, but which effectively present a key. That was what led me forcefully into your method of work. One must ask oneself at the same time if this is not only a utopia and, at the limit, if it is nonsensical to analyze the militant life, limiting analysis to its purview.

FG – I repeat, I do not propose theories of reference. I do not pretend, and have never pretended, to engage in an analysis of a scientific character. All the same I came to think of a cartography of subjectivity in order to gain an analytic bearing, that is to say, in order to be processual; by definition it is necessary to have done with any scientific ideal. It seems to me that the phenomena of social struggles, as they are disentangled from the history of the world of work (and thus not only through the analysis of Marxist theorists), are processes that inscribe themselves in a genealogy of *subjective locations*. Thus they constitute, taken together, relations of objective force and enterprises of the production of subjectivity. One cannot understand the history of the workers' movement if one refuses to see that, in certain periods, institutions of the labor movement have produced new types of subjectivity and, to force the issue, I would even say different "human races". A certain type of worker of the Paris Commune thereby became so "mutant" that there was no other solution for the bourgeoisie than to exterminate this type. They are perceived as a diabolical menace, as insupportable. The Paris Commune was liquidated, as were, in another epoch, the reformers of Saint-Bartholomew. History also presents to us veritable *wars of subjectivity* which one cannot gain access to if one does not take into account the mutations at issue here. For example, Lenin posed explicitly the question of the invention of a new mode of subjectivity which would distinguish itself from the social-democratic subjectivity integrated with capitalism.

Today, the production of capitalist subjectivity on a grand scale, through collective apparatuses, media, rapid systems of communication, the production of information, telecommunications, robotics – which tend to organize the entire planet into quadrants – is of a nature radically different from that of "pre-capitalist" societies, founded on direct servitude or on an indirect symbolic allegiance, in relatively well circumscribed territories, or that of proto-capitalist societies, founded on a subjective affectation of caste or class, in the context of a general deterritorialization of flows (demographic, of work, exchange, culture . . .). Today, not only are economic and social territories deterritorialized, but also the modes of subjectivation, which tend to be only the result of a completely artificial production. The subjective territorialities of the Ego, the Super-Ego, the family, the primary group, etc., are fashioned by the productive machine. From all this results the paradoxical cocktail of *hyper-segregation* and *generalized communication*.

In this context, how can a de-alienated, de-serialized subject be reassembled, a subject I call "processual" because it produces its own existence across processes of singularization, because it engenders itself as *existential territory* to the extent that it constitutes itself as an analytic cartography? This is the sticky problem which I have circled for a couple of decades. Against the fashions and returns to orthodoxies, post-modernisms and neo-conservatisms, nothing appears to me more urgent!

JP – That is why you spoke earlier, before we began the interview, of the importance of responding to the Milner[1] operation. I have the same thoughts.

FG – Yes, because it is a cunning attempt at disfiguring and dissuasion with respect to any dissident pedagogical attempts and all singular processes of institutionalization in that dead universe of National Education. That sermon in favor of a return to training, civic instruction, and other throwbacks, is truly a crass stupidity, because it completely misunderstands the actual conditions of the production of subjectivity, which no longer have anything to do with those of the epoch of Jules Ferry.

JP – It redoubles Chevènement[2] perfectly.

FG – That says a lot – Chevènement has no idea: we offer him a model and he takes it as a gift package and nothing more! It's already what he did at the Ministère de la Recherche. But one must say that there the result was less catastrophic! Be that as it may, Chevènement does not have the intention of tormenting himself for a few small percentiles of maladapted children: that makes up part of "incidental expenses", like unemployment referred to as "structural" – it cannot be reduced. What counts, in the context of economic competition, is the selection of elites and, to that end, to shift to Japanese methods of formation. They are obsessed with Japan! They don't know anything else! But the Japanese, for their part, are beginning to seriously question themselves about the insolvency of their own education system, which has led to a rate in nervous breakdown, suicide and aggression towards teachers which is truly disturbing. But that does not matter – one wants to imitate Japan! This is clearly absurd, because there is no room on the planet for more Japan! So it suffices to make the children work under discipline without concern for their affective problems, their social relations, their creativity, etc. . . . . That's the new socialism! The socialism of the people of the ENA (École nationale d'administration) and the Normale Supérieure, who would like to have people working at the mother school as under a whip. In that context, there is nothing to discuss: such a regression! One is dealing with technocrats who have never had the slightest idea of education who then find themselves promoted to Minister of National Education! And they make their conservative perorations with an authority that former reactionary governments never had; they believe they have popular legitimacy, because a certain number of factions of the teacher's union, as you well know, support them.

JP – Could we return to a notion at once seductive, important, and not always easy to grasp: that of the machine. For it seems to me that this essential concept is related to what you have elaborated concerning subjectivity and what you call from time to time micro-political assemblages. Where are you with respect to this theory of machines defined as "desiring"?

FG – They are not only desiring! And note that I am not the only one who has expanded the use of the notion of machine: biologists and mathematicians have also done so. It is completely insufficient to only think of the machine in technical terms; before being technical, the machine is diagrammatic (in the sense of the semiotician Charles Sanders Peirce), which is to say, inhabited by diagrams, plans, equations, etc. The Concorde, for example, is not only made of steel, aluminum, electrical wires . . . if one only retains the weights of steel and aluminum, that does not get very far! In particular, that does not allow flight through economic space and the space of desire. . . . Besides, and in articulation with the technical, chemical and biological machines, it is necessary to admit the existence of machines that I call semiotic or diagrammatic, of theoretical and abstract machines, not to mention economic and political machines, etc. For example, think of the Apollo program inaugurated by President Kennedy; without the will and the political machine supporting that program, the engine would have never seen the light of day! Without the slightly crazy desire, not only of Kennedy, but of generations that had dreamt of going to the moon, the machine would never have taken off. All this is to say that a technical machine of that sort indeed engages machines that are semiotic, economic, political, institutional (the Air Force and the Army were not in accord with the delegation of this project to NASA). If one does not want to fall into a childish naturalism opposing nature and culture, infrastructure to superstructure, if one really wants to describe how historic mutations operate, it seems to me necessary to develop expanded concepts of the machine that account for what it is in all its aspects. There are visible synchronic dimensions, but also diachronic virtual dimensions: a machine is something that situates itself at the limit of a series of anterior machines and which throws out the evolutionary phylum for machines to come; it is thus a material and semiotic assemblage which has the virtue of traversing, not only time and space, but also extremely diverse levels of existence concerning as much the brain as biology, sentiments, collective investments. . . .

JP – Do you think that, today, this would be a work which would only try to locate, to some degree, the machinic structures, the machinic phylum? But where is one placed in that new kind of reading when one poses the question: how can one militate within the actual problematic as its stands today?

FG – Militate, or simply have a *social practice?* Many people try to persuade us otherwise. For example, for Baudrillard it is not even certain that the social has ever existed! In any case, it seems evident to him that there isn't one any longer, or only in the form of a lure. However, I don't believe this. The social exists more than ever. And even without making the infrastructure out of other forms of subjectivity, that remains a big piece! But it is true that different political and social enunciators have completely collapsed. However, that is not to say that there is no longer any social practice possible. All that one can conclude is that previous social practices, those of syndicalism and various grist of the parties of the left, have completely failed!

The consequence to be drawn from this is that one must air social practices that respond to very complex actual conditions. A militant practice precisely must not separate the social from the political and the economic. I think that, today, the existence of parties like the socialist party and the communist party has become a historical absurdity. One can no longer mistake in that way the interactions between the political level and everyday life, the inter-individual relations and the social relations on a greater scale. All that overlaps constantly. Today, one does not change National Education if one does not at the same time change the micro-social relations of the school, etc. – the mentalities, the relations of knowledge, the relations to bodies, to music. . . .

JP – That social practice of which you speak is a practice of intersection.

FG – These social practices can no longer circumscribe themselves into clearly delimited collections, as were the old social classes. New subjective territories correspond to them less and less (for example those of the conditions of women, of children, of those "without guarantee" from society, of ethnic transmigrations, of national aspirations – Irish, Basques, Corsican, etc.). They do not square well with national spaces, and rarely with regional spaces. Further, the "North–South" problems intersect, without coincidence, with relations of class. An entire transcultural society shows its profile (hence the rise in racism). These social practices must also take account of the aberrant relations of force along the axis of East–West: the cleavage between societies called socialist and societies called capitalist has become completely artificial, and we have not yet well grasped the major complicity that exists between American, Soviet, Chinese, European and others, to maintain the segregative pyramid on which planetary capitalism rests (I call it "Integrated World Capitalism"). In sum, one must no longer think of political practice in terms of East–West relations or North–South relations, but rather link it to social practices which it falls on us to invent in the transverse relations between the levels which I have just invoked. It seems particularly urgent to redefine the objectives of struggle relative to salaried labor; all the old corporate demands tend to be overtaken by the fact of the setting up of machinic networks for the production of information. It is no longer a question of agreeing on a base salary, but a *minimum* social *guarantee* which takes into account the irreversibly rising mass of the "non-guaranteed" of society: marginal workers, the unemployed, the future unemployed, the chronically marginalized, etc. An entire conception of work and of the nobility of professional work is completely falsified by the evolution of the relations of production. . . .

JP – I return to that notion of the machine. It seems to me that there has been a tendency, within intellectual opinion, to draw the *Anti-Oedipus* in the direction of a theory of desire precisely in opposition to a theory of the system, whereby, instead, desire defines itself within the actual system and only appears as something problematic, related in one way or another to the breaking down of that system. Is it not the case that the history of that desiring machine is firmly rooted in that system?

FG – For the most part, the intellectuals in question have not read, or do not want to understand, what was said in the post-68 period. Our conception of desire was completely contrary to some ode to spontaneity or an eulogy to some unruly liberation. It was precisely in order to underline the artificial, "constructivist" nature of desire that we defined it as "machinic", which is to say, articulated with the most actual, the most "urgent" machinic types. . . . That is to say, we are far from Reich, far from orgone energy. . . .

JP – Where do you stand now à propos everything you wrote with respect to that conception of desire as "constructed"?

FG – I have not changed, it is always a question of the same thing: that question really should be asked to others.

JP – Still within that conception, then. . . .

FG – People presented us as saying things that were completely ludicrous which they assumed in advance: complete liberty under the stars, outside any social regulation! This is a projection in keeping with prevalent ideas of that time.

JP – Don't you continue to some degree, but not in the same manner, in *The Molecular Revolution*: you end by bringing into relief that desire is on the side of minorities?

FG – Desire appears to me as a *process of singularization*, as a point of proliferation and of possible creation at the heart of a constituted system. These processes can pass through stages of marginality, of becomings that are "becoming-minor" which disengage the nucleus of singularity. What can all this say about an institution like La Borde? In a period of time in which everyone was very unhappy, an event sprang forth which, without being able to know precisely why, changed the atmosphere. An unexpected process led to the secretion of different universes of reference; one sees things otherwise. Not only does the subjectivity change, but equally the fields of possibility change, the life projects. For example, a cook, originally from the Ivory Coast, decided to return there. However, he had no means to establish himself again in his village. He worked at La Borde for a number of years and was much loved. A group formed to help him, which transformed itself into an association in accord with the law of 1901[3]: "La Borde-Ivoire". They collected twenty thousand francs to assist him in his move. Later a doctor and a nurse went to visit him. Then, in turn, a kind of village came to visit La Borde for three months. Now there is a group of six patients who are going there for three weeks of vacation. Here we have a *process of institutional singularization*. Is this psychotherapy? Good works? Militancy? In each case the local subjectivity was profoundly modified, especially its latent racism (indeed, something frequently present in psychotics). Desire is always like that: someone falls in love with something in a universe that appears closed and, in a flash, other possibilities are opened. Love, sexuality, are only means of semiotization of these mutations of desire, modes of inscription as we used to say. Desire is the fact that where the world was closed there arises a process which secretes other systems of reference which authorize – but which never guarantee – the opening of new degrees of liberty.

JP – One of your important propositions speaks of desire within "molecular revolution", that is, desire as being intergrated with, or making up a part of, or situated in, the infrastructure.

FG – To say of desire that it makes up part of the infrastructure amounts to saying that subjectivity produces reality. Subjectivity is not an ideological superstructure. The old structures of the base, the old territories of reference, ecological and anthropological, with their intrinsic systems of modelization, have been deterritorialized by the capitalist economy and subjectivity. At present it is not, as in archaic societies, that one becomes someone or something at the end of some deterritorialized course [*cursus*], of a local "initiation". It is only universities that still believe that. Today most people don't know where they are or what they are. A huge phylum of machinic systems affects them at a certain place – good or bad is not the question. It is necessary to see that individuated subjectivity has become the object of a sort of industrial production. Take the following historical example to situate what I am trying to say. Two countries came out of the Second World War completely destroyed: Germany and Japan. They were not only physically crushed under the bombs, like Bremen, they were socially and psychologically devastated and, beyond that, cruelly occupied. From that two economic "miracles" resulted. And, paradoxically, these countries had practically no raw materials or capital reserves. But they reconstituted a prodigious "capital of subjectivity" (capital of knowledge, of collective intelligence, of will to survive). In fact, they invented new types of subjectivity out of that same devastation. The Japanese in particular recovered archaic elements of their subjectivity and converted them into the most "advanced" forms of social and material production. One can see clearly that this mode of the production of subjectivity was infrastructural, if I may say so (because, I repeat, it is not any more "infra" than "supra" – these are lame concepts, and it is somewhat of a provocation that I say that). There is a sort of complex of subjectivity production which allowed the release of a multitude of creative processes, some of which are hyper-alienating. Such examples show that there is not a biological, energetic [*pulsionnelle*], economic, geopolitical base on which is established, necessarily, a super-structural subjectivity. Subjectivity can find itself at the base of the assemblages in question. It is these forms of subjectivity that most governments run up against today. Nationalist questions infect the capitalist system in the West and the East. These go under the names of the Palestinian problem, the Basque problem, the Black problem, the Polish problem, the Jewish problem, Afganistan . . . Governments, in theory, have all the means to bring to these problems rational solutions. But that implies neutralizing the resistance of a collective subjectivity, to convert it into a "subjectivity of equivalence", in which each individual, each function, each thought, each sentiment is standardized as in a set of Lego. And there are places where that does not work, because subjectivity is not only produced by capitalist machines, but also by you and I, in our institutions, in the family, sometimes alone. It is inscribed in a desire, a novel, a voyage, etc. . . . It is the main event [*grande affaire*]   !

JP – It is the main thing [*grande chose*] which also changes labor.

FG – Yes, it transforms all perspectives. As soon as one takes account of that singularization of desire as an essential component of the present crisis, one can no longer view things in the same way as the "current managers" of the economy. In the name of crisis, one intimates the order for arranging the cloakroom of the problems of our schools, of urban life, of social changes, etc. One would, thereby, solve the economic problem! . . . The problem of desire is never for today . . . The theme of 68: "We desire everything, now" was certainly poorly formulated, confused, or whatever you want to call it. But one must say that, on many points, it remains absolutely relevant. We want everything – that is another way of saying that it is urgent that we take account of the economy of desire. It is now, without delay, that we must construct a multi-racial society in France, and another form of sociality and citizenship. There will be needed ten million more immigrants in France to meet the future. I'm not the only one saying this, it is serious people, demographers. Without such an "importation" (and I apologize for the ugliness of the expression) in twenty years France will be a power of the tenth order. But what is it that resists understanding that? What is it that engenders the collective stupidity of a Le Pen? The fact that all the factors of alterity, all the factors of singularization, are systematically extinguished, falling back on social "normality" and the conformity of standard models. A small child sees a person of black or yellow skin in the street. That "interpellates" the child as they say? But how does he manage that singularity which is constituted in him? With the assistance of whom? In what context? There will be a massive rejection if he has been conditioned to negate anything that is different, anything that exceeds the norm. So, this becomes a problem that is not only that of black or yellow skin, but more generally of the type who limps, who has a strange nose or a strangely shaped mouth, or is old. A racism against the old has developed in our societies. Normal people – they are what we see on television (for example women announcers – but it is no longer necessary that they are beautiful!). It is necessary to keep alterity in its place [*créneau*]: the place of average infantilization. But infants, precisely they are the ones who are able to assume difference and singularity. It is the dominant adulthood that constitutes the royal road of puerilisation.

JP – Precisely the desire to do what you propose is a certain kind of decoding, an act of becoming aware [*prise de conscience*] in the Sartrean sense. Have you ever had the desire to generalize this type of machinic militantism, this type of work on singularization?

FG – From 1964 to 1968 there was an effort to expand with the revue *Recherches* and the FGERI (*Fédération des groupes d'études et de recherches institutionnelles*). It was a pleasant surprise to discover at which point people whom we did not know – economists, architects, educators – were interested in these thematics. We discussed institutional pedagogy, institutional psychology, the question of women, the media, etc. Then there was 1968, and everything overflowed. There was nothing to analyze and to manage in any precise way in all of that. We were carried along by events, the slogans that were coined, and the splinter groups. But as the song says, "Je ne regrette rien"! I learned more things in two months than in twenty years. Since, conservatives of every kind believe they have re-established control of the situation. It is relatively true in most of the developed nations. However, in Latin America and in Africa nothing is played out. We have entered into a kind of masked war [*guerre larvée*] between the North and the South. What is in question is the final principle of development; how is one going to manage life on the planet, and not only material life, but social life, the desire to live, the desire to create . . . History is not linear, that's all you can say. One can expect the worst as well as the most surprising recurrences . . .

JP – As relevant as ever . . .

FG – That is my conviction. But someone seems like they're cracked when they say such things!

JP – That brings to mind a question: is schizoanalysis a method? Where would you place it in relation to what you have just said?

FG – What seems important to me is the introduction of a certain number of fundamental dimensions relative to singularities, to processes of singularization. If you do not introduce that analytic dimension concerning the invention of subjectivity at the heart of social practice, whether it concerns political or union struggles, or everyday struggles, ecological or other struggles, then there is failure and guaranteed demoralization. Happily, there are people who have begun to realize this. Note the strength of the Greens in Germany who now have acquired important arbitrating power in certain relations of political power.

There is, perhaps, a new alliance in the process of formation among those who refuse to see the forests destroyed, immigrants treated as cattle, huge amounts of money devoured by military budgets, which is to say, among the Greens, and other alternative parties, and the revolutionaries. In my opinion, it is the only hope of escaping the present impasse.

With respect to schizoanalysis in all that, it is clear that it cannot pose itself as a general method which would embrace the ensemble of problems and new social practices. It is more a matter of a theoretico-practical reflection concerned above all, for now, with institutional fields, shrinks, and others. Without pretending to promote a didactic program, it is a matter of constituting networks and rhizomes in order to escape the systems of modelization in which we are entangled and which are in the process of completely polluting us, head and heart. The old psychoanalytic references (mechanistic and/or structuralist), the systemic references that spread like an epidemic, the residues of dogmatic Marxism, continue to obstruct our ability to develop new analytic-militant cartographies. The debates around quelling all these "maladies" of theory are not a light affair!

At base, schizoanalysis only poses one question: "how does one model oneself"? You are psychotic and you construct idiosyncratic references; you are attached as with a ball and chain to a familial-oedipal territory; you stick to the collective apparatus – for instance, National Education – as if it concerned your ethnicity . . . Each time the scene changes, so do the protagonists and the myths of reference. One day, instead of going to the office, you stay in bed and turn yourself into a beetle. Perhaps you have some genius and you write *The Metamorphosis*! Sometimes life changes because of something very simple, a mini-revolution. Other times it requires a hyper-sophisticated disposition. Everything is possible! Nothing is mechanical, structural, but nothing is guaranteed:

no interpretation, no analytic qualification – like the "cure-type" – supplies the ticket to change life and liberate desire!

Schizoanalysis, I repeat, is not an alternative modelization. It is a meta-modelization. It tries to understand how it is that you got where you are? "What is your model to you"? It does not work? – Then, I don't know, one tries to work together. One must see if one can make a graft of other models. It will be perhaps better, perhaps worse. We will see. There is no question of posing a standard model. And the criterion of truth in this comes precisely when the meta-modelization transforms itself into auto-modelization, or auto-gestation, if you prefer.

JP – So, at the limit, that would be a practice like the one Tosquelles evokes in a text: doctor-workers who establish points of connection, working with this and that [*bricolent*] . . .

FG – Yes, indeed. But when you say these kinds of things in the distinguished world of psychoanalysis, they call you a social assistant: "That is not analysis"! – "Indeed, you make them a gift of it"! But this is unfortunate. For an analysis of the formations of the unconscious that has done with the reductionist traps of familialism and logocentrism and which opens itself to all possible forms of exploration, to all the arbitrary points of semiotic conjunction, is not bad at all. Don't you agree?

Moreover, this implies theoretical approaches that are complex enough to take account of transferences of subjectivity from one domain to another and transformations of systems of sense among diverse semiotic components. For instance, how can an economic relation influence an obsessional syndrome? It is not simple. Partial objects and the signifier are not sufficient. It is necessary to try to register, through a concrete cartography of the assemblages of enunciation, how the phenomena of the planes of consistency are jumped, what are the semiotic systems that allow passage from the world of recognized significations to the world of a-signifying *ritornellos* constitutive of new existential territories? It is also necessary to be suspicious of master concepts, like that of sexuality. The sexuality of puberty is not of the same nature as the sexuality of an adult. No general category of libido traverses them. They constitute themselves as radically different modes of composition, the one and the other, and they never communicate by any pathways of direct causality.

JP – But then, doesn't one arrive at some sort of idea of a technician who, effectively, through certain competencies, would be a schizoanalyst?

FG – The ideology of 68 would require that it is necessary for the "therapy" technicians to abandon all responsibility. But things being as they are, and the production of subjectivity being what it is, it is evident that one cannot imagine that the "users" could reappropriate that responsibility without some other process. Social workers exist, teachers, care givers, etc. The question is not to eliminate them, but to rearrange their position in such a way that their knowledge capital and their transferential potentialities are not manifest to the credit of perverse functions of power. Is it that one must only direct and apply a scientific knowledge, or is it, on the contrary, that one must refute any scientific qualification of this knowledge, which in reality is only efficacious in the singular procedures of analytic cartography? And, I repeat, the analytic map can no longer be distinguished from the *existential territory* that it engenders. The object of knowledge and the subject of enunciation coincide in this kind of assemblage. That notion of scientificity, and the use that is made of it in the so-called human sciences, must be examined in the light of the work of Kuhn on the relativity of the paradigms of knowledge in the realm of "hard" sciences. Theoreticians, technicians, creative people, recipients of welfare, and the agents of the state are so many components of the assemblages of production of subjectivity. Each of these poses the question of the micro-political – *and thus not at all scientific* – character of their practical options. If it is true that the production of subjectivity has become the great issue of our time, then it is these people in society who hold the privileged position of the potential decision makers with respect to a number of choices of our society – a place which was earlier occupied by the classes of industrial workers and before that by the urban bourgeoisie and secular clergy.

JP – The circle closes – but I still have one question. Don't you think, precisely in light of the extremely dialectical manner in which all this is described, that there is something very complex here with all these references to abstract machines? Don't you think that all these conceptions of "therapy" are somewhat imprisoned in a formalism? This semiotic scaffolding, the machinic unconscious, through all this vocabulary that isn't always easy to navigate, is it possible to get to the heart of the subject, outside this formalization, or is it necessary to pass through all these apparatuses?

FG – Certainly not – when I call this scaffolding, I really mean scaffolding.

JP – What is this scaffolding?

FG – It could be – sadly it isn't – like a work of art. What is best in Freud is his literary dimension.

JP – There isn't a search for the fundamental machine or the fundamental equation?

FG – In what concerns me, absolutely not!

JP – One can at certain moments – I have felt it, being myself from time to time pursued by that intoxication – come to discover the matrix, the transversal matrix, which allows one to operate within the different fields that you have mentioned.

FG – That was my own cartographic problem when I was young – I was caught up by the different fields. I said to myself, I must try to reconnect everything somewhat. But that did not become "The Five Lessons of Schizoanalysis", or "The Three Essays on Desiring Machines". Certainly not!

JP – Do you still maintain an analytic practice now?

FG – Yes, I pursue an analytic practice on an individual basis and with myself. But I do not separate that practice from my intervention in a number of groups and institutions.

JP – Do you think that today – and it is something that can be asked of the present as it was asked in 68 – one can still work within institutions?

FG – One does not have a choice! Not to work in institutions – what would that mean? An analyst who received patients in his office is in an institution, a splintered institution, but an institution that has strong links in the "public" mind, in the mind of doctors, in the mind of the media; it is still a particularly formidable form of institution. . . .

JP – I am convinced of that.

FG – At base, the individual is nothing but the intersection of institutional components. Even dreams are institutional, branching into films and televisual sequences; all of this is institutional!

JP – It is for this reason that you react in relation to Milner as you do. You have always defended active methods and social innovations. . . . Today nobody gives a damn. And it is true that such work does not reach the point of developing itself, that it remains within that order of being parceled out, of being splintered.

FG – There are two ways of thinking of innovative experiments like those of Freinet, Fernand Oury, Gaby Cohn-Bendit. Either one considers them uniquely in their contingency, either their partial consequences, their often limited discourses, their restricted range, or one considers them as problematics which are forever taken up again, forever reworked. That is an abstract machinic phylum. If a true mutation appears, if a new way of discerning a problem establishes itself – for example, the necessity of receiving, in an analytic mode, an individual or collective symptom in a school class – then the muddlings of Chevènement mean nothing, the new truth will exert its own pressure. One day, even if in China, it will re-emerge. I say that because a popular student from China just made a request for a residency at La Borde.

JP – That is perhaps how it must come to pass. It cannot happen otherwise because each time there is a displacement which is within the order of desire. But I want to return to a question: what are the pragmatic ends [*finalités*] of this technician of schizoanalysis?

FG – There could never be a technician of schizoanalysis – that is a contradiction in terms. If schizoanalysis must exist, it is because it exists everywhere, and not only in schizophrenics, but in the schizzes, the lines of flight, the processual ruptures that are taken up by a cartographic self-mending. Its end? One can say that there isn't one, because it is no longer the end that matters but the "milieu", the process becoming processual [*le processus en train de se processualiser*]. This implies a sort of blind confidence in the process of deterritorialization. When you engage in a project, for example, an institutional project, or a film or novel, you can internalize a pre-existing model (the Stendhalian novel or film of Marcel Lherbier). One aims at a consummate object against which one can measure the ends and the means. With schizoanalysis it is the inverse. One no longer wants to make a definite object. One does not want to enter into a pre-established program. One tries to live the field of the possible that is carried along by the assemblages of enunciation. You begin a novel, but you do not know how it is going to finish; perhaps it will not even be called a novel. But precisely that would be an analytic process; you throw yourself into an analysis without knowing what you are going to find. It is precisely that notion of process that to me is fundamental. One abandons the idea that one must seek to master an object or a subject – I am no longer "either master of myself or master of the universe".

One introduces into analytic research a dimension of finitude, of singularity, of existential delimitation, of precariousness in relation to time and values. When one has filled one's head with the notion that one is immortal in some manner, that one can fix objects and hold them – that is at bottom a folly, a folly that is often murderous. Ethical decentering and micro-politics imply a complete reversal in relation to the existing system of education. This is not to say that the ends are effaced by the means, because the formula itself is broken: there are no longer either ends or means, there are only processes, processes of auto-construction of life, auto-construction of the world, with mutant effects that are new, unexpected, unheard of. If everything is inscribed in advance, so it is immediately destroyed! There is no point in seeing the end of the film – you know it already!

JP – What is strange is that one would place one's belief paradoxically in something idealist; while that changes perspectives, I believe there is something very materialist in what you have said, but that is not evident for our frame of mind.

FG – What is idealist – in the good sense of idealist – is to believe that one can effect the course of things by virtue of an ideal engagement. There is no destiny inscribed in the infrastructure. Capitalist societies construct a society, secrete a subjectivity which is in no way natural or necessary. Certainly one could do something else. What is insupportable to me is the idea of an inevitable programmatic necessity. One thinks that history is programmed like a computer. Mitterand had the same economic politics as Barre because he believed, at bottom, that it was the only politics possible. That is a horror! The system programs itself on its own by systematically deforming all singularities, all the things of life, all that which, in appearance, is of no use for anything. Whether you are happy, whether you stutter, whether you are afraid of death or of old age – all this counts for nothing. That is modern capitalism: desire, madness, gratuitousness – all this counts for nothing! On the contrary, it inconveniences. It makes too much "noise" in the sense of information theory.

JP – Concretely, how does one organize institutional practices given this?

FG – Trick question par excellence! I have just been trying to explain to you that there is no protocol, no model, and you ask me for a method of application. Offer me a concrete situation, tell me how it is constructed, what relations of "incarnation" you maintain with it. Inasmuch as I would be hooked by your proposal, that I would want to interest myself a little more in it, and – why not – go along with it, the question changes its nature. It consists in marking the indicative elements, the experienced sequences of non-sense as a symptom, as institutional lapses which, instead of being pushed to the side, marginalized, will see themselves confer a field of expressions, a gamut of possibilities that they did not have before. From that, and in association with the diverse interlocutors concerned, another processual cartography of unconscious formations of this field of subjectivity perhaps becomes possible. There, where there exists a univocal expression, a polyphony of enunciation will affirm itself. For me, that is to "work the unconscious". It is not simply to discover it, but first and before all else to lead it to produce its own lines of singularity, its own cartography, in fact, its own existence. In brief, there is no recipe!

JP – Between us, one could say that one falls back on classical institutional practices.

FG – Believe me that I have never claimed anything to the contrary! But one must add that current institutional practice – non-analytic – often lacks the interpretation of singularities. There is often an overlap of collective assemblages and group practices. For me this is quite different. The silence of a catatonic can make up a part, perhaps even constitute the masterpiece, of an institutional assemblage of enunciation! All of the pre-personal dimension of singularities is too often separated from the group dimensions. What is interesting in the theoretico-practical developments of Oury and Tosquelles is that they always endeavoured to make a place for non-sense, for institutional signifiance, for the empty word [*la parole vide*] or for what Lacan saw with his generalized theory of the partial object (*objet a*).

Notes

This unedited interview was published in Jean Oury, Félix Guattari, François Tosquelles, *Pratique de l'institutionnel et politique*. Collection proposé par Jacques Pain (Vigneux: Matrice, 1985), pp 45–83. Jacques Pain teaches at Université de Paris X, at Nanterre.

1 The linguist Jean-Claude Milner wrote a widely read and controversial book entitled *De l'École* (Paris: Seuil, 1984).

2 Jean-Pierre Chevènement was Minister of [National] Education from 1984–86.

3 The law of 1 juillet 1901 permits anyone, including psychiatric inmates, to form an association in order to accomplish a social goal.

Translated by Lang Baker

PART IV

Polysemiosis

12

Semiological Subjection, Semiotic Enslavement[1]

What is the crystallization of power in the field of linguistics? One will understand nothing of this question if power is represented exclusively as an ideological superstructure. Power is not something that only concerns well defined social wholes or groups. A power formation binds more than "human communication". It implicates as well an entire complex of "extra-human" semiotic machines. It is also the power of the ego and the power of the super-ego, that which makes one stammer from fear, that which generates somatic reactions, neuroses, suicides, etc. The stability of a "state of language" corresponds to an equilibrium between these diverse levels of power. But each level does not situate itself in relation to the others in any old way. Here, again, we are not dealing with amorphous matter. One cannot account for the stabilization of a "stratum of competence" except by articulating the precise make-up of domains as different as these:

— individual, human acts of semiotization (from internal perceptions all the way to mass media communications);

— semiotic operations relative to social machines, economic machines, technical machines, scientific machines, etc.;

— machinic indices and abstract machines (concerning the machinic phylum and the plane of consistency);

— systems that allow correspondences amongst the preceding domains (deterritorializing lines of flight, components of passage, etc.).

We have seen that a clear-cut opposition between competence-performance, apart from neutralizing the foundations of language, squeezes[2] the collective assemblages of enunciation – that is to say, the true parties of creation as far as language is concerned – for the benefit of an alternative: individualized subjectivity or universal subjectivity. But one can agree with the position of psycholinguists such as T.G. Bever who consider judgements of grammaticality "comportments like any other"[3] without, however, succumbing to the shortcomings of a systematic "psychologization" of linguistics. The point is not to deny the systemic characteristics of the modes of signifying grammaticalization that have assured themselves, for example, an overall control of capitalist pragmatic fields, but only to reject the abstract categorizations upon which some pretend to found them. We are, in fact, in the presence of the same type of retroactive universalizing process used by all power formations that have wanted to give themselves the appearance of a divine legitimacy, and, in particular, those that have sought to "justify" the expansionism of capitalism. From the fact that performances, of the monetary, linguistic, and musical types, for example, can always be "structuralized", made discursive and binary, one comes, then, to consider them as having *always and already been there* in full force, to believe that their elements carry *in their seeds* the creation of the form of Capital, of the Signifier, of Music, etc. But the real processes of power and the machinic mutations that have fixed and stabilized a form, developed and delimited a set of creative potentialities or metastable equilibria amongst assemblages, are themselves *absolutely indestructible*. Abstract machines can always be complicated but they can never be broken down without losing their mutational specificity. So one must take them in their entirety. It is impossible to reach them piece by piece, through learning or conditioning. They cling to each other, every part of them becoming a process. They assimilate themselves into an assemblage and change its "destiny". Or they silence themselves and return to a plane of pure machinic virtuality.

Pragmatic fields of power formations, prior to their stabilization under the forms of language, dialectics, etc., must first be "experimented on" in the name of collective performance: all the intermediaries, all the degrees of fluidity, are thus conceivable in the course of an individual semiotic performance, be it marginal or even delirious, up to the completely sclerotic encodings of the standard dictionary, academic grammar, religious or political credos, etc. Their efficiency depends on the dominant type of semiotization which they put into place and, in particular, on whether or not the diagrammatic components activate certain abstract machines (financial, scientific, artistic, etc.). Pragmatic micropolitics concerns semiotic assemblages overflowing from all sides – from the side of the "infra" towards corporeal intensities, and from the side of the "supra" towards the *socius* – personological linguistics.[4] The crystallization of signifying powers corresponds to a particular mode of the libido's overcoding:

— through semiological subjection at the heart of fields of resonance;

— through semiotic enslavement at the heart of fields of interaction amongst machinic redundancies.

The abstract machinic level of a signifying assemblage is specified by the fact that it assures the congruence of its two types of encoding and that it directs the instauration of:

— the imperatives of the *dominant grammaticality* of expression (the redundancy of a-signifying figures of expression);

— "ideological" assemblages of semiological *subjection* at the level of content (redundancies of resonance);

— diagrammatical assemblages of *enslavement* of decoded capitalist flows at the level of the "referent": the flow of abstract labor as the essence of exchange value; the flow of monetary signs as the expressive substance of Capital; the flow of syntagmatic and para-digmatic linguistic signs adapted to standardized interpersonal communications, etc.

The normatized agents of production are set in motion before the transformation of each individual into a speaker-listener capable of adopting a linguistic comportment compatible with the modes of competence that assign to one a particular position in society and in production. The components of semiotic enslavement constitute, in reality, the fundamental tools that permit the dominant classes their assurance of power over the agents of production. The "miracle" of capitalism is that it manages to direct language, as it is spoken, as it is taught, as it is televised, as it dreams, etc., in such a way that it remains perfectly adapted to its own evolution. Furthermore, this operation always appears to be self-evident: the syntagms of power, its presuppositions, its threats, its modes of intimidation, of seduction and of submission, are conveyed at an unconscious level, a little like the "clandestine" images that advertisers insert into a film. If there is an urgency that compels a febrile search for a new model of the unconscious, such a phenomenon must be accounted for! Reject the idea that the syntactic markers of capitalist languages express the fundamental requirements of the human condition; consider these markers, on the contrary, to be the result of a field of semiological transformations established by a system of power less and less tolerant of modes of intrinsic coding. These seemingly harmless moves singularly exceed the traditional scope of linguistics and semiotics!

The totality of machines, be they social, technical, desiring, etc., can no longer escape from the overcoding of the signifying machines of the

State. In fact, the signifying power of national languages and the multi-form power of States and of the network of collective assemblages tend to coincide. The molecular links of expression substitute for the ancient segmentary structures of the socius to constitute a homogeneous plane of content that conveys at the same time the categorical imperative of the Kantian moral law, the "necessities" of class conscience, the demands of custom and the repressive habits of the majoritarian consensus, and, on top of this, the persecuting themes of the ambient super-ego. It is by the exhaustion of this plane that the intensities of desire detach from their ancient territories and receive their subject-object polarities. Mediatized and controlled, they become social need, demand, necessity and sub-mission. They exist no longer except to the degree that their expression resonates with mass-mediatized significations. Or they withdraw into themselves, translate themselves, that is to say, renounce their character of nomadic flux.

There is no doubt that the threat of a seizure of power by a decoded flux exists prior to capitalism and already in the most "primitive" so-cieties (in this regard it is appropriate to distinguish, amongst these latter, between what Pierre Clastres called societies with a State and societies without a State, as they do not share the same attitude to the "defense" against an eventual accumulation of power in a State appara-tus[5]). There is no doubt that ancient societies were already traversed, strictly speaking, by the capitalist flows that they were trying so hard to master! But one must admit that a series of causes, circumstances, and accidents peculiar to the Middle Ages and the Western "Renaissance" resulted in the social structures losing definitively a certain type of control of the decoded flows and engaging in a kind of generalized Baroque style – economic, political, religious, aesthetic, scientific, etc. – leading to capitalist societies in the proper sense.

The semiotic and machinic enslavement of desiring flows and the semiological subjection on which capitalist societies rest are established in reaction to an uncontrollable dispersion of territorialized codes. They are the correlatives of the installation of new types of divisions between the sexes, the generations, the divisions of labor, the relations of social segmentarities, etc. A new use of languages, signs, and icons leads to a state of affairs in which the least effect of meaning – even the most intimate, the most unconscious – falls under the control of social hierar-chies. Capitalist powers never cease "rethinking" in detail each significa-tive relation, differentiating and specifying each semiological "allocation". During the course of an apprenticeship in language, a child will be called upon, for example, to model its first infinitive intensives[6] in such a way as to put them into the service of pragmatic predicatives and fundamental deictic strategies of power (encodings of hierarchical position, role permutability, sexual division, etc.). "Becoming sexed-body" will be fixed in its relation with "becoming social-body" by the regime of pronominality and the genres which axiomatize the subjective positions of feminine alienation. Despite appearances, in a pragmatic capitalist field the different social categories of an identical linguistic community – men, women,[7] children, the elderly, people in rural areas, immigrants, etc. – *do not speak the same language.*

National languages, those which are spoken at the Académie française or on television, are metalanguages. Their "distance" in relation to the languages of the land, the arbitrary forcefulness of their overcoding, are the guarantors of their efficiency and, paradoxically, of their degree of interiorization. This semiological economy of power and its implications for modes of generation, of the transformation of syntactic components, lexicals, morpho-phonological and prosodic elements of language, is the foundation for even the pragmatic fields of enunciation, which Oswald Ducrot designated as the "polemical value" (in the etymological sense) of language.

To Return, or To Detour, By Way of Hjelmslev?

The systematic ignorance of society and politics characteristic of current linguistics and semiotics can only be smashed by calling into question or dismembering their basic categories. From this point of view, a return to Louis Hjelmslev, or perhaps a detour by way of Hjelmslev, will be useful. The issue is not to recapture or resume his project of a radical axiomatization of language but to start up again from those categories which appear to be the result of a truly rigorous examination of the totality of the semiotic problematic. This means drawing out in particular all the consequences of his calling into question of the status of content and expression. "The terms *expression plane* and *content plane* and, for that matter, *expression* and *content* are chosen in conformity with established notions and are quite arbitrary. Their functional definition provides no justification for calling one, and not the other, of these entities *expression*, or one, and not the other, *content*. They are defined only by their mutual solidarity, and neither of them can be identified otherwise. They are each defined only oppositively, as mutually opposed functives of one and the same function".[8]

It is regrettable that the Hjelmslevian expression-content pair coincides in fact with the Saussurian signifier-signified couple, which has in effect made the totality of semiotics fall back upon a dependency on linguistics.[9] Be that as it may, at the most essential level of what glossematicians call the "semiotic function", the form of expression and the form of content contract themselves to constitute a "solidarity" that radically relativizes the classic opposition between signifier-signified.[10] This opposition only recovers its law at the level of substances, in knowing the *sens* [purport] of content and the *sens* [purport] of expression. This must lead us, of course, to give up envisaging the existence of forms, except as they are manifested or put into action by particular substances. This point is paramount because, as I have tried to show, it is only by starting from non-linguistic – or non-signifying linguistic – semiotic assemblages, that these substances may be produced: in other words, "before" the constitution of significative redundancies and without that which would confer to them a status of priority or hierarchical superiority vis-a-vis other semiotic productions (symbolic, diagrammatic, etc.).

By semiotizing the most diverse base matter this solidarity or congruence of forms – which coincides here with the abstract machinism of language[11] – constitutes substances of expression and content. In this way the formalism of substances rises in tiers upon the matter which must be, as Hjelmslev emphasizes, "scientifically formed" – at least to a sufficient degree – to allow these substances to be "semiotically formed".[12] Finally, let us remember that the distinction this author established between the system and the process of syntagmatization does not imply that this latter remains captive to autonomous form. No form can subsist by itself independently of its process of formation. We do not have to think of this process in terms of universal codes, sealed off but indissociable, on the one hand, from the assemblages that they support and, on the other, from the base matter that is put into play (which Christian Metz has called, following Hjelmslev, the *pertinent traits of matters of expression*[13]).

We meet again here the problem of the genesis of formalism. What confers a creative function on a semiotic component and what removes it? Languages, as such, do not have any privilege in this domain; in the name of encodings of normalization they can even slow down or block all semiotic proliferation, and it often comes back to the non-linguistic components to catalyze mutations and to break the conformist shell of dominant linguistic significations. It is neither at the level of formal unities of content nor at that of the distinctive elementary traits that we will be able to seize the spring of semiotic creativity, but at the pragmatic level of assemblages of enunciation and at that of the molecularity of matters of expression, of abstract machines that they put into place. The operation of linguistic overcoding of semiotic processes "in a free state", which tends to reduce them to the state of signifying components or the dependency of language, consists essentially in the extraction from each of them of the traits and redundancies recuperable by power formations and in neutralizing, repressing and "structuralizing" the others. This permanent selection, this systematic politics of "good semiotic choice", assumes not only the existence of the assemblages that produce it but also the components that manufacture the signs, symbols, indices, and icons on which it rests.

Notes

This article, "Assujettissement sémiologique, asservissement sémiotique", is an excerpt from Chapter 2, "Sortir de la langue", pp. 34–42, of Guattari's *L'Inconscient machinique*.

1 The notion of "enslavement" must be understood here in a cybernetic sense.

2 This term appears in English in the original text.

3 T.G. Bever, *Hypothèses* (Change, 1972), p. 203.

4 From this perspective, pragmatics must, contrary to the Anglo – American tradition, cease to be considered as a suburb of syntax and semantics and, contrary to the Franco –European tradition, as a subset of linguistics. It is, on the contrary, signifying semiologies that become special cases of a much more general pragmatics.

5 Pierre Clastres, *La Société contre l'Etat* (Paris: Minuit, 1974). [Society Against the State, trans. Robert Hurley (New York: Zone, 1987)].

6 The first verbal expressions of a child are, for the past, the past participles ("parti", "tombé") and for the future the infinitives. The development of periphrases comes later ("je vais aller") and lastly, the inflections. Cf. E. Traugott, "Le changement linguistique et sa relation à l'inquisition de la langue maternelle", *Langages* 32 (1973), p. 47.

7 Cf. Robin Lakoff, *Language and Woman's Place* (New York: Harper & Row, 1975).

8 Louis Hjelmslev, *Prolégomènes à une théorie du langage* (Paris: Minuit, 1968), p. 85. [Prolegomena To a Theory of Language, trans. Francis J. Whitfield (Madison: University of Wisconsin Press, 1961 and 1969), p. 60]

9 Hjelmslev defines language as a "semiotic into which all other semiotics may be translated – both all other languages, and all other semiotic structures", *Prolégomènes*, p. 138; *Prolegomena*, p. 109.

10 As René Lindekens writes: ". . . the semiotic relation of absolute interdependence characterizes the bond between the planes of expression and content – from which proceeds the denotative power of sign systems –, and which Hjelmslev calls the relation of solidarity, must be considered as contracted exclusively by the two forms, from one sign plane to the other". *Hjelmslev* (Paris: Hatier, 1975).

11 This expression of the linguistic "abstract machine" comes from Chomsky. Cf. *Dictionnaire encyclopédique des sciences du langage*, Oswald Ducrot and Tzvetan Todorov, p. 59.

12 Hjelmslev, *Essais linguistiques* (Paris: Minuit, 1971), p. 59.

13 Christian Metz, *Essai sur la signification au cinéma* (Paris: Klincksieck, 1967); *Langage et cinéma* (Paris: Larousse, 1971).

Translated by Peter Trnka, with the assistance of Fadi Abou-Rihan

13

The Place of the Signifier in the Institution

The categories of Louis Hjelmslev will only be taken up here in the effort to clarify the position of the signifier in the institution. This position was not identifiable from the classic analytical perspective. Recall that Hjelmslev's distinction between expression and content is intersected by a tripartition between matter, substance and form. We will essentially emphasize the opposition he established between matter (matter of expression, matter of content) and the formation of semiotic substances.

What I would like to establish here is that semiologies of signification function in the four squares of expression and of content that are intersected by substance and form. On the other hand, the semiotics with which we are confronted, in an institutional context, bring into play two additional dimensions of non-semiotically formed matter: that is, *sens* [purport][1], as matter of expression, and the continuum of material fluxes as matter of content. This mobilizes the six squares of our table [see below].

For Hjelmslev a substance is semiotically formed when form is projected onto matter or *sens* [purport], "just as an open net casts its shadow down on an undivided surface".[2] It is well known that the signifying chains put into play, at the level of the substance of expression, finished batteries of signs rendered discrete and digitalized whose formal compositions are linked to the formalization of signified contents. It seems to me that linguists have too hastily equated Hjelmslev's distinction between expression and content with that of Saussure's between signifier and signified. Indeed, the separation between non-semiotically formed matter and semiotically formed substance, insofar as it is established independently of the relations of expression and content, opens the way to the study of semiotics independent of signifying semiologies, that is to say, of semiotics which, to be precise, would not be based on the bipolarity of signifier-signifed. Our concern not to crush institutional semiotics under the weight of signifying semiologies leads us to distinguish between them, and to hold them both at a distance from what we call a-semiotic encodings.

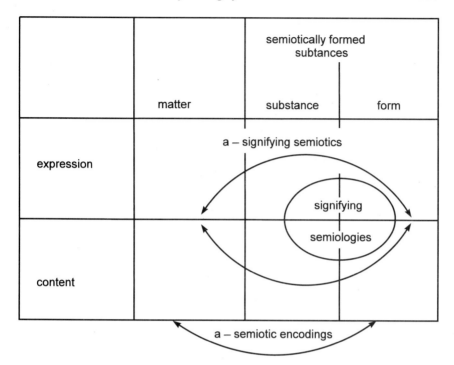

Let's summarize again the classification that we have proposed else-where on this subject. We will distinguish:

1   *A-semiotic encodings*: For example: genetic encoding or any type of so-called natural encoding which functions independently of the constitution of a semiotic substance. These modes of encoding formalize the field of material intensities without recourse to an autonomous and translatable "écriture". Do not succumb to the semiotic illusion of projecting an *écriture* onto the natural field. There is no genetic writing. The second vertical column of our table is therefore not involved.[3]

2   *Signifying semiologies*: These are based upon sign systems, on semi-otically formed substances which enter into relations of formaliza-tion on the double plane of content and expression. One can distinguish two types of signifying semiologies: symbolic semio-logies and the semiologies of signification:

a   *Symbolic semiologies*: These put into play several types of substan-ces. For example, in archaic societies: a gestural semiotics, a semiotics of sign language, a postural semiotics, a semiotics of inscriptions on the body, a ritual semiotics, etc. The constitution of the "world" of childhood or the "world" of madness equally put into play several decentered semiotic circles which are never completely translatable into a system of universal signification. Semiotic substance therefore retains a certain autonomous territoriality which will correspond to a certain type of specific *jouissance*.

b *Semiologies of signification*: By contrast, all their substances of expression (sonorous, visual, etc.) are centered on a single signifying substance. This is the "dictatorship of the signifier". The reference substance can be understood as *archi-écriture*, but not in the Derridean way: it is not a matter of an *écriture* which would "orginate" all the semiotic organizations, but of the sudden, historically dated appearance of writing machines, which is to say of a fundamental instrument of the great despotic empires.

Writing machines are essentially tied to the institution of the machines of State power. From the instant when they are put into place, all the other polycentered semiotic substances become subordinate to the specific stratum of the signifier. The totalitarian character of this dependency is such that, by an imaginary retrospective effect, it seems "to originate" all other semiotics from a basis in the signifier. From that moment, the insistence of the letter in the unconscious becomes fundamental, not because it returns to an archetypal *écriture*, but because it manifests the permanence of a despotic *signifiance* which, although it emerges in specific historical conditions, continues to produce effects and develop under other conditions as well.

c *A-signifying semiotics*: These must be distinguished from semiologies of signification; it is a question, in short, of post-signifying semiotics. Examples of a-signifying semiotics would be: a machine of mathematical signs which lacks the vocation of producing significations; or an artistic, musical, economic, scientific technico-semiotic complex; or again, a revolutionary analytic machine. These a-signifying machines continue to rely on signifying semiotics, but they only use them as a tool, as an instrument of semiotic deterritorialization allowing semiotic fluxes to establish new connections with the most deterritorialized material fluxes. These connections function independently of whether they signify something for someone or not. In one respect, Emile Benveniste is correct to consider that all semiotics depend upon a signifying language in order to come into existence. But this correlation does not at all imply a relation of hierarchization and subjection. It is not the concern of a physico-chemical theory to propose a mental representation of the atom or electricity, even though, in order to express itself, it must continue to have recourse to a language of significations and icons. It can do without this kind of crutch, but most of what it brings into play is a certain type of *sign machine* which acts as support for abstract machines setting up an assemblage of experimental complexes and theoretical complexes. One reaches a point where the very distinction between sign machine and techno-scientific machine ceases to be pertinent; the invention of a new type of chemical chain or the updating of a microphysical particle is, as it were, pre-formed by a semiotic production which determines not only their spatio-temporal coordinates but also their conditions of existence. With a-signifying semiotics, then, the relations of production and of reciprocal engenderment between the semiotic machine and material fluxes are radically reorganized.

The signifying machine was based on the system of representation, that is, on a production of semiotic redundancy constituting a world of quasi-objects, icons, analogon, and schema, acting as substitutes for intensities and real multiplicities. The signification-effect which results from the conjunction of the two formalisms of signifier and signified is itself caught in a veritable vicious circle in that the semiotic fluxes and the material fluxes cancel each other out in the field of representation. A world of dominant signification installs itself on the signifying reterritorializations which result from the self-mutilation of the semiotic machines constituted by their mono-centering on the signifying machine – a machine of simulacra and powerlessness. The signifier is deployed on an autonomous stratum, and it no longer refers to the signified, while the real is radically separated from semiotic fluxes. A subjectivity individuates itself in the structures of this signifying machine, following the Lacanian formula that "a signifier represents the subject for another signifier". It is an ambiguous, duplicitous subjectivity: on its unconscious side it participates in a process of semiotic deterritorialization which "works" the linguistic machines and prepares to transform them into a-signifying semiotic machines, while, on its conscious side, it rests on reterritorializations of signifiance and interpretance.

This position of the subject changes radically with the foregrounding of a-signifying semiotics. The world of mental representation (which Frege opposed to concepts and objects; also called "reference", positioned between the symbol and the referent at the summit of Ogden and Richards' triangle) loses, then, its function of centering and of semiotic overcoding. Signs "work" things prior to representation. Signs and things combine with one another independently of the subjective "hold" that the agents of individuated enunciation claim to have over them.

A collective assemblage of enunciation is, then, in a position to relieve speech of its role as the imaginary support of the cosmos. It substitutes for it a collective saying [*dire collectif*] that brings together machinic elements of every kind: human, semiotic, technical, scientific, etc. The illusion of an enunciation specific to the human subject vanishes, revealing that it was only an effect adjacent to statements produced and manipulated by politico-economic systems.

It is generally considered that children, the mad and primitive peoples, fail to acquire mastery of signifying semiotics, and are forced to express themselves by "secondary" means such as bodily and gestural expressions, cries, etc. The major disadvantage of these means lies in the fact that they do not allow the messages which they carry to be translated in a univocal manner into a linguistic code, generating dominant significations. This relative untranslatability of diverse semiotic compositions is attributed either to a deficit, or a fixation at the pre-genital stage, or a refusal of the law, or a cultural deficiency, or a combination of several of these elements. This entire perspective of interpretive analysis must be thoroughly reshaped into another type of analysis of the unconscious the aim of which would be to foreground a-signifying semiotic components.

But before evoking one such possibility, it is necessary to try to show that an analysis of institutions or an institutional analysis which did not define itself as a micro-politics of desire would be incapable of moving beyond the classical Freudian analysis.

Dual analysis and institutional analysis, whatever their theoretical arguments, essentially differ as a result of the different range of semiotic means that one and the other bring into play. The semiotic components of institutional psychotherapy are much more numerous; they make it difficult to respect the sacrosanct principle of "analytic neutrality". That can "put things right" but it can also make them a lot worse. The institution sometimes succeeds in bringing into play a-signifying machines working toward the liberation of desire, as do certain literary, artistic, scientific machines, etc. Consequently, the question of the analyst's or the analytic group's micro-political choices is more ambiguous and sometimes much more "open" in institutional analysis than in "consulting room" analyses. By force of circumstance, classical psychoanalysis almost never gets to the point of – assuming it ever intended to! – abandoning its role as normalizer of the libido and behavior. The status of subjectivation and of transference is completely different in an institution.

A-signifying diagrammatic effects, just as well as the effects of signifiance and interpretance, can assume much greater proportions than in a dual analysis, and eat away at the smallest nooks and crannies of everyday life. The mania of interpretation, the continuous surveillance of alleged "slips" of the unconscious, may go so far that one could call it a "paradigmatic institutional perversion". It can happen that the blackmail of analysis, and the anguish which accompanies it, reinforces the mechanisms of identification with and even mimicry of the gurus of analysis. This is the way in which a new type of psychoanalytic despotism has established itself, these last years, in most of the institutions for children that are "interested in analysis".

Schizoanalysis intends to radically dissociate itself from these so-called "institutional analyses". In schizoanalysis what counts is precisely not a centering on the signifier and on the analytic leaders. It intends to favor a semiotic polycentrism by furthering the formation of relatively autonomous and untranslatable semiotic substances, by accommodating the sense and non-sense of desire as they are, by not attempting to adapt the modes of subjectivation to signification and to dominant social laws. Its objective is not at all to recuperate facts and acts that are outside the norm; on the contrary, it is to make a place for the singularity traits of subjects who, for one reason or another, escape the common law. How will these collective assemblages be able to counter the effects of this sort of analytic scabies, which has become particularly virulent since private radio stations have deemed it one of their prerogatives to assure its proliferation? At the very least, by laughter, by humor, by a mockery which deflates blow by blow the pseudo-scientific pretensions of psychoanalysts of all stripes. This will lead to "semiotically formed", but also socially organized, packets of resistance not only to the ravages of psychoanalysis but also to the diverse techniques of intimidation that work toward the alignment of the population on family-centered models and on the hierarchies of the system. Let it be understood that if we condemn psychoanalysis, it is in the name of another practice of analysis, of a micropolitical analysis which never cuts itself off – in any case, never deliberately cuts itself off – from the real and the social field. In short, we condemn psychoanalysis in the name of a *genuine practice of analysis*. The principle reproach that we have to address to psychoanalysts is, in effect, that *they do not engage in analysis*. They take refuge in their offices and hide behind transference so that the treatment unfolds in isolation, so that nothing from the outside creeps in. They have turned analysis into an exercise of the pure contemplation of sliding signifiers, accompanied by a few interpretations which are, most often, only games of seduction without consequence.

Let's return for a moment to a problem that has already been touched upon: that of psychopharmacology. Besides its use as a means of immobilization, until now it has been in the service of a despotic signifying semiology, of an interpretation tying problems back to closed categories. This led the anti-psychiatrists to condemn it along with psychopathological semiology as a whole. Psychopharmacological interventions are, in fact, coded as much by repressive and police categories as by medical ones. Making noise and disturbing the peace become something abnormal: a drug is the answer. But does this repressive use of drugs constitute a sufficient reason to condemn every use of drugs? In certain experiments in institutional psychotherapy, attempts have been made to reorient psychopharmacology toward collective experimentation. The administration of drugs no longer depends exclusively on the doctor–patient relation, but is determined by groups bringing together care-givers and cared-for. The reference ceases to be the laboratory, becoming – at least this would be the ideal – a collective taking up of corporeal intensities and subjective effects.

The separation between drugs subject to police repression and those utilized to quiet "agitation in the hospital" is not written in their molecules. The distinction between certain drugs in the modern pharmacopoeia and certain illegal drugs is at times only based on side-effects, which perhaps will be eliminated in the future. It suffices to evoke the role played by mescaline in the work of Henri Michaux in order to understand that drugs can participate in a system of intensity semiotically formed in an a-signifying mode. But today psychopharmacology is above all utilized by psychiatry for repressive ends. Classical nosographies have deteriorated, and with the passage of time psychiatrists have resorted to lumping everyone together. In the United States, for example, most problems are fit into the holdall category of schizophrenia. And as soon as one is labelled schizophrenic, one graduates to very high dosages of neuroleptics. Nevertheless, psychopharmacology could just as well orient itself toward the constitution of an a-signifying semiotic – freed from medical overcoding, the State, power, multinationals, etc. Instead of suppressing all the richness of expression and every opening onto the real and the socius, it would help individuals to regain their potential.

An objection that, personally, I find rather paradoxical has been raised against analytic collective assemblages. They are seen as running the risk of suppressing the singularities of desire, as threatening to develop into a new type of despotism. Without a doubt what I have proposed in this regard has been understood only in terms of what is known about the analysis of groups, or the analysis of institutions. I repeat, for me it is not at all a matter of substituting for the individual analysis the techniques of the group – which can in fact end up bringing individual singularities to heel. When I speak of assemblages, I am not necessarily speaking of groups. Assemblages may involve individuals, but also functions, machines, diverse semiotic systems. It is only by taking desiring machines all the way back to the molecular order – that is, to a point prior to the group and the individual (on the side of what Lacan called *l'objet a*) – that we will succeed in disarticulating mass-produced institutional structures, and in giving marginal positions of desire the possibility of freeing themselves from neurotic impasses. The slope of the individuation of desire always leads in the direction of paranoia and particularism. The problem is thus one of finding collective means to escape from the tyranny of systems based on identification and individuation. It's true that the effects of groups easily lead to systems of closure, to fixations on certain kinds of particulars, to xenophobic and phallocratic attitudes, etc. But these reterritorializations, if they are taken back by creative assemblages, can open onto other perspectives. In fact, we should carefully distinguish between the neurotic encircling of subjectivity engaged in a process of personological *individuation*, and the *idiosyncracies* of groups which conceal possibilities of recomposition and transformation.

Consider a final example, that of a psychotic child who bangs his head against a wall day after day. A machine of self-destructive *jouissance* operates here for itself, outside of every influence. How can the desiring energy to "bang-one's-head-against-the-wall" connect with a collective assemblage? It's not a question of transposing this activity, of sublimating it, but rather of making it operate on a semiotic register connectable to a certain number of other a-signifying systems. It's not a question of curbing desire, of switching its objects, but of expanding the field of *jouissance*, of opening it to new possibilities. It will be difficult, however, to outmaneuver adaptive and repressive attitudes, unless it is emphasized that *jouissance* centered on the self always leads to the temptation of its extreme expression: powerlessness and abolition.

For a subject, the exit from destructive narcissism does not require its repression in the real or its castration in phantasy: it requires, on the contrary, a supplementary strength and a neutralization of the powers which alienate it. Thus it is essentially a matter of taking power over the real, and never one of pure manipulation of the imaginary or symbolic. Fernand Deligny neither represses nor interprets; he helps the mentally challenged persons with whom he lives to succeed in *experiencing* other objects, other persons, managing to construct another world.

Readaptive analysis develops a politics of signifiance; it tends to reduce the horizon of desire to the control of the other; to the appropriation of bodies and organs; it seeks to regain a pure becoming-conscious of the awareness of self. Schizoanalysis renounces the "will to identity" and personologically coordinated signifiers, in particular those of familialism. It turns away from strategies of power, in favor of a body without organs which disindividuates desire and accepts seeing identity swept up in a-semiotic cosmic fluxes and a-signifying socio-historic fluxes.

In the traditional analytic approach, each time one goes from a pre-signifying semiotic to a signifying semiotic, a loss of *jouissance* occurs, and a field of culpabilization and a figure of the superego impose themselves. Playing with one's shit is participating in a kind of "matter" (you've said it!). When an analytic intervention attempts to transform this pleasure, to transform this matter into a translatable semiotic substance, subject to interpretation according to the dominant code, it ends up mutilating or abolishing it by fixing it on a "signifying semiotic semblance" which will substitute itself for the body without organs. Normative institutions have always devoted themselves to programming individuals, conditioning them to an indefinite translatability of their desires. Far from changing this state of affairs, psychoanalysis has only brought about technological improvements in this same type of project.

It remains to be determined what grants consistency to the psychoanalytic politics of the emasculation of desire. Why does psychoanalysis emerge at this point as a sort of alternative religion? To whom do its problems belong, in the last instance? They essentially belong to formations of power which have an interest in every praxis becoming transmissible, indefinitely transposable in terms of the economy of decoded fluxes. They essentially belong to capitalism (and perhaps, tomorrow, to bureaucratic socialism) inasmuch as it is based on laws which establish the equivalence and general translatability of all semiotic expressions. Certainly, access to *jouissance* is still possible in such a system, but on the condition that the libido submit to the dominant norms. New and quite specific types of perverts develop under these conditions. For example, bureaucratic perverts, whose mode of *jouissance* has been wonderfully explored by Kafka. The insistence of the bureaucratic letter develops like a canker in the tissue of industrial societies, to the benefit of "elites" who have access to its *jouissance*. But since spaces are expensive and rare, and require much preparation and training, there are countless castaway from desire. For them, the *jouissance* of the capitalist letter amounts to little more than playing the horses and the joys of watching Sunday football on tv. But add to this the fact that losers at the races and football matches are also countless, and much of the population ends up in psychiatric hospitals, rehabilitation programs, prisons, etc.

In short, major choices in the economy of desire can be reduced to two types:

— either a guilty *jouissance*, constituted in such a way that everything always refers to everything else – desire having no outlet other than to invest in its own flight, and in a system of indefinite translatability which constitutes the most deterritorialized modality. Rather than opening themselves to desire, the world and history shrivel up, closing onto a black hole-effect which absorbs everything.

— or a collective economy of desire which tends to scatter the miasmas and signifying simulacra on the basis of which this principle of universal debt is instituted. It reabsorbs the points of individuation of the libidinal economy, the points of guilty responsibilization, the exclusive transferences which fold desire back onto persons, roles, hierarchy, and everything that is organized around points of power. Its objective is to prevent a-signifying semiotic components from falling under the sway of the signifying semiology.

Notes

This selection, "La Place du signifiant dans l'institution", is taken from Guattari's *La Révolution moléculaire*, Fontenay-sous-Bois: Recherches, 1977, pp. 277–90. I would like to thank Brian Massumi for his advice on the finer points of this translation.

1 The French *le sens* or *matière-sens* is usually rendered as purport, a technical term in Hjelmslev's vocabulary meaning unformed matter.
2 L. Hjelmslev, *Prolegomena to a Theory of Language*, trans. F. J. Whitfield, Madison: The University of Wisconsin Press, 1963, p. 57.
3 To know whether there exist strata in a-semiotic encodings which correspond to those of expression and content is a question that we cannot address here. Let's say simply that there certainly exist complex systems of articulation, if only in genetic encoding.

Translated by Gary Genosko

14

Ritornellos and Existential Affects

"If one is afraid of robbers in a dream, the robbers, it is true, are imaginary – but the fear is real", notes Freud in *The Interpretation of Dreams*.[1] The content of an oneiric message can be transformed, adorned with makeup, or mutilated, but not its affective dimension, its thymic component. Affect sticks to subjectivity, it is a glischroid matter, to pick up a qualifier used by Minkowski to describe epilepsy.[2] Only, an affect sticks just as well to the subjectivity of the one who is its utterer as it does to the one who is its addressee; and, in so doing, it disqualifies the enunciative dichotomy between speaker and listener. Spinoza perfectly pin-points this transitivist character of affect ("from the fact of conceiving a thing like ourselves to be affected with any emotion, we are ourselves to be affected with a like emotion") and from which results what he calls "an emulation of desire" and the deployment of multi-polar affective compositions. Thus, the sadness we feel through the sadness of another becomes commiseration, while "he who conceives another as effected with hatred, will thereupon be affected himself with hatred; he who hates a man will endeavour to remove or destroy him".[3] Affect is thus essentially a pre-personal category, installed "before" the circum-scription of identities, and manifested by unlocatable transferences, un-locatable with regard to their origin as well as with regard to their destination. Somewhere, there is hatred, in the same way that, in animist societies, beneficent or nocuous influences circulate through the spirit of ancestors, and, concurrently, of totemic animals, or through the "mana" of a consecrated place, the power of a ritual tattooing, a ceremonial dance, the recounting of a myth, etc. There is thus a polyvocity of the components of semiotization, which nonetheless are still awaiting their existential completion [*parachèvement existentiel*]. As the color of the human soul as well as the color of animal becomings and of cosmic magics, affect remains hazy, atmospheric,[4] and nevertheless perfectly apprehensible to the extent that it is characterized by the existence of threshold effects and reversals in polarity. The difficulty here lies in that the delimitation of an affect is not discursive, that is to say, not founded upon systems of distinctive oppositions inflected according to sequences of linear intelligibility and capitalized in memory banks that are mutually compatible. Assimilable in this regard to the Bergsonian concept of duration, an affect does not arise from existential categories, which are able to be numbered, but from intensive and intentional categories, which correspond to an existential self-positioning. As soon as one decides to quantify an affect, one loses its qualitative dimensions and its power of singularization, of heterogenesis, in other words, its eventful compositions, the *"haecceities"* that it promulgates. This is what happened to Freud when he wanted to turn affect into the qualitative expression of a quantity of cathecting energy (the libido) and its variations. Affect is a process of existential appropriation through the continual creation of heterogeneous durations of being and, given this, we would certainly be better advised to cease treating it under the aegis of scientific paradigms and to deliberately turn ourselves toward ethical and aesthetic paradigms.

This is, it seems to me, what Mikhail Bakhtin invites us to do when, in order to specify aesthetic enunciation in its relation to the ethical evaluation of objective knowledge, he emphasizes that enunciation's characteristic of "externally encompassing the content" of its "value bearing", and the fact that it leads to reckoning with oneself as a "creator of form".[5] In thus drawing affect towards the aesthetic object (which is what I wish to underscore), Bakhtin in no way turns affect into the passive correlative of enunciation, but into its engine, a bit paradoxically it is true, since affect is non-discursive and entails no expense of energy – which is what has led us elsewhere to characterize it as a deterritorialized machine.

Finitude, completion, the existential singularizing of the person in his or her relation to him/herself, just as much as the circumscription of his or her domain of alterity, are not self-evident, are given neither by right nor by fact, but result from complex processes in the production of subjectivity. And, in very particular historical conditions, artistic creation has represented an extraordinary excrescence and exacerbation of this production. Thus, instead of reducing subjectivity, as the structuralists wish, to the result of signifying operations (structuralists are still, in this regard, under the spell of Lacan's famous formula whereby a signifier is supposed to represent the subject for another signifier), we would prefer to chart the various components of subjectivization in their fundamental heterogeneity. Even in the case of the composition of a literary form which seems nonetheless wholly tributary to language, Bakhtin underscores how reductive it would be, in accounting for that composition, to cling to nothing but the raw material of the signifier. By opposing the creative personality, organized from within (to which he assimilates the contemplator of the work of art), to the passive personality of the character, organized from without as the object of a literary vision, Bakhtin is led to distinguish five "facets" of linguistic material in order to disengage

an ultimate level of verbal affect that assumes the sentiment of engendering all at once sound, sense, syntagmatic liaisons, and phatic valorization on the emotional and volitional order (74). The verbal activity of
engendering a signifying sound is thus correlated with an appropriation
of rhythm, intonation, the motor elements of mimicry, articulatory tension, the internal gesticulations of narration (which are creative of movement), the figurative activity of metaphor, and the entire internal impetus
of the person "actively occupying, by means of the word and of the
utterance, a certain axiological and semantic position" (74). But Bakhtin
insists that this sentiment cannot be reduced to that of a brute organic
movement engendering the psychical reality of the word, but that it is
also the semiotic movement that engenders meaning and appreciation –
"in other words, the feeling of a movement, of a taking of position which
would concern the whole man, a movement in which are drawn
together all at once the organism and its semantic activity, for what is
engendered is at once the flesh and the soul of the word, in their concrete
unity"(74).

   This active potency of affect is no less complex for being non-discursive, and I would even qualify it as hyper-complex, wishing to mark
that it is an instance of the engendering of the complex, a processuality
in the throes of birth, a place for mutational becomings. Along with
affect is thus raised the question of a dis-position of enunciation on the
basis of the modular components of proto-enunciation. An affect speaks
to me, or at the very least it speaks through me. The somber red color of
my curtain enters into an existential constellation with nightfall,
with twilight, in order to engender an uncanny effect that devalues the
self-evidences and urgencies which were impressing themselves on
me only a few moments ago by letting the world sink into an apparently irremediable void. On the other hand, other scenes, other existential
territories could become canvases for highly differentiated affects. For
example, the leitmotifs of the *Rheingold* will induce in me countless sentimental, mythical, historical, and social references, or, the evo-
cation of some humanitarian problematic will trigger a complex feeling of
repulsion, revolt, and compassion. As soon as such scenic or territorializing dispositions – all the while persisting to exist on their own account
and in their own quadrants – begin to protrude beyond my immediate
environment and to engage memory and cognitive procedures, I find
myself tributary to a multi-headed enunciative lay-out [*agencement*]: the
individualized subjectivizing which, in me, is authorized to speak in
the first person is no more in fact than the fluctuating intersection,
and the consciousness "terminal", of these diverse components of
temporalization. Along with the curtain and the late hour, an affect
which one calls sensory is given as being immediately there, where-

as with problematic objects, an affect's spatio-temporal congruence dissolves and its elucidating procedures threaten to fly off in all directions.

My idea, however, is that problematic affects are at the basis of sensory affects and not vice versa. In such a case, the complex ceases to be propped upon the elementary (as in the conception that prevails in scientific paradigms) and organizes, at the whim of its own economy, synchronic distributions and diachronic becomings.

Let us go back over these two aspects, one after the other. As the precarious result of a composition of modules of heterogeneous semiotization, its identity permanently comprised by the proliferating phylums of problematization which work it over, an affect, in its "rich" version, is forever seeking to repossess itself. Moreover, it is essentially from this ontological flight "in retreat", consecutive upon an infinite movement of virtual fractalization,[6] that its existential power of self-affirmation results. On the phenomenological plane, this question of a crossing of a threshold by an affect, with a view toward attaining a sufficient consistency, is raised for us by the majority of psychopathological syndromes. Below such a threshold, it is the sphere of "pathic time" – to use the fortunate term of Von Gebsattel[7] – which is threatened. One will also recall here Binswanger's repercussive chiasmus relative to autism, which would be characterized less by an empty time – in the genre of ennui – than by an emptiness of time.[8] Psychopathological syndromes reveal, no doubt better than any other lay-out, what I would call the inchoate dimensions inherent in affect, some of which literally begin to work on their own account. All of which in no way means that one ought to characterize normality as a harmonious equilibrium between the modular components of temporalization. Normality can be just as "disordered [*déréglée*] as the other tableaux! (Certain phenomenologists have even taken note of a syndrome of hyper-normality in melancholia.[9]) Discordance in the ways of keeping time – what I call its *ritornellizations* – is not specific to an abnormal subjectivization. What would characterize the latter, rather, is that one mode of temporalizing, either temporarily or definitively, takes precedence over the others, whereas a normal psyche would always be more or less on the point of crossing from one to the other. As Robert Musil so superbly put it: "the sane person is full of countless insanities, and the insane person is possessed by only one".[10] The exploration of the expressive levels of pathic temporalizations has not yet been seriously undertaken. It seems to me, however, that the fallout one could bank on from this exploration would extend well beyond the narrow field of psychopathology and would be particularly significant in the domain of linguistics. I imagine that the analysis of the modal and aspectual consequences of the obsessive, or of the melancholic, retention of time would lead to the formulation of a more general function of the inhibition of enunciation; and symmetrically, that the analysis of the crazy maniacal acceleration [*Ideenflush*] would lead to a function of liquefaction. ("The maniac is continually seized by an infinite fanning out of referrals, which are always current, fleeting, and interchangeable." His or her temporalization is "reduced to an absolute momentaneization" which ignores all duration and disappears like the melancholic temporalization.[11]) Also imagine what the semioticians could take from a study, undoubtedly much more arduous, of the gap between the mute expression of the catatonic and the fantastic "internal gesticulation" – to pick up once again Bakhtin's expression – whose mask it is. In a more general way, it would have to be admitted that the disordering of the myths of enunciation and the resulting semiotic discordances cannot be grasped in a homogeneous register of the production of meaning. They always refer to the seizures of power by extra-linguistic components: somatic, ethological, mythographical, institutional, economic, aesthetic, etc. This business is less visible during the "normal" use of speech, on account of the fact that existential affects are more disciplined there, subjugated as they are to a law of generalized homogenization and equivalence.

Under the generic term of ritornello, I would place reiterative discursive sequences that are closed in upon themselves and whose function is an extrinsic catalyzing of existential affects. Ritornellos can find substance in rhythmic and plastic forms, in prosodic segments, in facial traits, in the emblems of recognition, in leitmotifs, signatures, proper names or their invocational equivalents; they can just as well be found transversally between different substances – this is the case with Proust's "ritornellos of times past", which are constantly entering into correspondence with each other.[12] They can just as well be of a sensory order (the madeleine dipped in the cup of tea, the uneven paving stones in the courtyard of the Guermantes's Hotel, the "bit of phrase" of Vinteuil, the plastic compositions around the belltower of Martinville) as of a problematic order (the ambiance in the salon of the Verdurins), as of a facial order (Odette's face). In order to situate the intersectional position of ritornellos between the sensory and the problematic dimensions of enunciation, I propose to "frame" the significational relation: f (sign) (that is, the relation of reciprocal presupposition, or of solidarity, according to Hjelmslev's terminology, between the form of an Expression and the form of its Content), of four semiotic functions relating to the Referent and to Enunciation. Thus, we would have:

1   a denotative function: f (den), corresponding to the relations between the form of the Content and the Referent;

2   a diagrammatic function: f (diag), corresponding to the relations between the matter of the Expression and the Referent;

3   a function of sensory affect (ritornello), corresponding to the relations between Enunciation and the form of the Expression;

4   a function of problematic affect (abstract machine), corresponding to the relations between Enunciation and the form of the Content.

Note that, inasmuch as it is possible to conceive of keeping the significational, denotative, and diagrammatic functions within the traditional framework of the semantic and syntactic domains, there is no question here of enclosing the two existential affect functions within a third compartment that would be labeled: pragmatics. As Hjelmslev has forcefully underscored, linguistics cannot (anymore than the other semiotic systems) arise from an autonomous axiomatization.[13] And it is along this slope formed by the concatenations of partial enunciative territories that there occurs a generalized flight of the systems of expression towards the social, the "pre-personal", the ethical, and the aesthetical.

What can one expect from our ritornello-abstract machine dyad? Essentially a pinpointing and a deciphering of the practical existential operators installed at the intersection of Expression and Content. An intersection where, I insist, nothing is ever played out within a perfect structuralist synchrony, where everything is always an affair of contingent lay-outs, of heterogenesis, of irreversibility, of singularization. With Hjelmslev, we learned that the fundamental reversibility between the

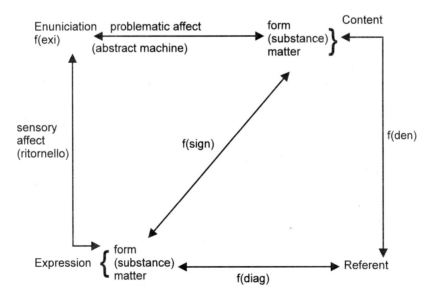

form of the Expression and the form of the Content arches over the
heterogeneity of the substances and matters which are its support. But,
with Bakhtin, we learned to read the foliatedness of enunciation, its
polyphony and its multi-centeredness. How can it be understood, for
example, that the heterogeneous voices of delirium and of creation are
able to cooperate in the lay-out of sense productions beyond common
sense which, far from establishing themselves in a deficit position from
the cognitive point of view, sometimes allow access to highly enriching
existential truths? For too long, linguists have refused to face up to
enunciation, having only wanted to take it into account as a breaking and
entering into the structural woof of semantic-syntactic processes. In fact,
enunciation is in no way a faraway suburb of language. It constitutes the
active kernel of linguistic and semiotic creativity. And, were they truly
disposed to greet its singularizing function, it seems to me that linguists
would be advised, if not to substitute proper names for the categorical
symbols that dominate the syntagmatic and semantic trees they have
inherited from the Chomskyans and the post-Chomskyans, then at least
to graft them onto the rhizomes of ritornellos clinging to those proper
names. We must re-learn ritornello games which fix the existential ordering of the sensory environment and which prop up the meta-modelizing
scenes of the most abstract problematic affects. Let's survey a few examples. Marcel Duchamp's *Bottle Rack* functions as the trigger for a constellation of referential universes engaging both intimate reminiscences (the
cellar of the house, a certain winter, the rays of light upon spider webs,
adolescent solitude) and connotations of a cultural or economic order –
the time when bottles were still washed with the aid of a bottle
brush . . . The Benjaminian *aura*[14] or Barthes's *punctum*[15] arise equally
from this genre of singularizing ritornellization. It is the latter too which
confers the sense of scale onto architectural lay-outs.[16] Onto what details,
perhaps miniscule, does the perception of a child alight while traversing
the bleak pathways of an HLM ensemble?[17] How, on the basis of some
distressing seriality, does he/she succeed in gracing his/her discovering
with the world of magic halos? Without this aura, without this ritornelliz-
ing of the sensory world – which is established, moreover, in the deterritorialized prolongation of ethological[18] and archaic[19] ritornellos – the
surrounding objects would lose their "air" of familiarity and would
collapse into an anguishing and uncanny strangeness.

Ritornellos of Expression take the lead in sensory affects: the intonation, for example, of an actor will fix the melodramatic turn of an action,
or the "deep voice" of the father will trigger the thunderbolts of the Super
Ego. (Some American researchers have even succeeded in demonstrating
that the most constrained smile will entail, in the manner of a Pavlovian
reflex, some anti-depressing bio-somatic effects!) On the other hand, the

prevalence of Content ritornellos, or abstract machines, is affirmed by problematic affects, which operate just as well in the sense of an individuation as of a social serialization. (Moreover, the two procedures are not antagonistic; the existential options, in this register, are not mutually exclusive, but entertain relations of segmentarity, of substitution and of agglomeration.) For example, the primary purposiveness of an Icon of the Orthodox Church is not to represent a Saint, but to open an enunciative territory for the faithful, allowing them to enter into direct communication with the Saint.[20] The facial ritornello then derives its intensity from its intervening as a shifter – in the sense of a "scene changer" – in the heart of a palimpsest superimposing the existential territories of the proper body upon those of personological, conjugal, domestic, ethnic, and other identities. In a wholly other register, the signature posed upon a banking slip functions too as a ritornello of capitalist normalization: what is behind this scratch? Not just the person it denotes, but also the assonances of power that it triggers in the society of "well placed" people.

The human sciences, especially psychoanalysis, have for too long accustomed us to think of affect in terms of an elementary entity. But there also exist complex affects, inaugural of irreversible diachronic ruptures that would have to be called: the Christic affect, the Debussy affect, the Leninist affect . . . So it is that for decades, a constellation of existential ritornellos gave access to a "Lenin-language" engaging specific procedures which could just as well be of a rhetorical and lexical order as of a phonological, prosodic, facial, or other order. The threshold crossing – or initiation – that legitimates a relation of full existential belonging to a group-subject depends upon a certain concatenation and becoming consistent of these components, which are thereby ritornellized. I have previously tried to show, for example, that Trotsky never truly succeeded in crossing the threshold of consistency for the collective apparatus that was the Bolshevik Party.[21]

Enunciation is like an orchestra conductor who on occasion accepts a loss of control over the musicians: at certain moments, it is articulatory pleasure or rhythm, or it is an inflated style that begins to play a solo and to impose it upon the others. Let us underscore that if an enunciative lay-out can entail multiple social voices, it also engages pre-personal voices susceptible of inducing an aesthetic ecstasy, a mystical effusion, or an ethological panic – such as an agoraphobic syndrome – as well as an ethical imperative. It can be seen that every concerting emancipation is conceivable. A good conductor does not strive despotically to overcode the ensemble of these components but attends to the collective crossing of the aethetic object's completion threshold as designated by the proper name inscribed at the head of the musical score. "There you go!"

Tempo, accent, phrasing, equilibrium of the parts, harmonies, rhythms, and tone: everything conspires to the reinvention of the work and to its propulsion into new orbits of deterritorialized sensibility . . . .

An affect is therefore not, as the "shrinks" commonly wish to represent it, a passively endured state. It is a complex, subjective territoriality of proto-enunciation, the site of a work, of a potential praxis, bearing upon two conjoined dimensions:

1   a process of extrinsic dissymmetricalization which polarizes an intentionality towards fields of non-discursive value (or Universes of reference); such an "ethicalization" of subjectivity being correlative of an historicizing and a singularizing of its existential trajectory;

2   a process of intrinsic symmetricalization, evoking not only Bakhtin's aesthetic completion but also Benoit Mandelbrot's fractalization[22] and which consists in conferring to affect the consistency of a deterritorialized object and the taking of a self-existentializing enunciative autonomy.

Let us listen again to Bakhtin: "By its own forces, the word translates the completing form into content: thus, in poetry, imploration, aesthetically organized, begins to suffice in and of itself and has no more need to be satisfied, being in some way satisfied by the very form of its expression; prayer has no more need of a god who would hear it; the plea has no more need of help; the repentance no more need of pardon, etc. With the help of matter alone, the form fulfills the event, and every ethical tension, up to its full accomplishment. With the help of matter alone, the author adopts a creative attitude, productive in relation to its content, that is to say, in relation to cognitive and ethical values. It is as if the author entered into the event isolated and became there a creator without being a participant" (73–74). The function of completion as disjunction of content – in the sense that a circuit breaker may trip or disjunct – and this self-generation of enunciation seem altogether satisfying to me. But the other traits by which Bakhtin characterizes the aesthetically signifying form, namely unification, individuation, totalization, and isolation, seem to me to call forth certain elaborations. Isolation: yes, but an active one, going in the direction of what I have elsewhere called a processual putting into a-significance. Unification, individuation, totalization: certainly! but open and "multiplicatory". It is here that I would like to introduce another idea, that of a fractal setting of consistency. The unity of the object is, in reality, but a subjectivizing movement. Nothing is given in and of itself. Consistency is only attained through a perpetual flight in advance of inwardness, which conquers an existential territory in the very time that it loses it, and wherein, however, it strives to retain a stroboscopic memory. Reference is no longer there except as the canvas for a reiterative ritornello. What matters is the cut, the gap, which turns reference around on itself and which engenders not only a feeling of being – a sensory affect – but also an active way of being – a problematic affect.

This deterritorializing reiteration is effected equally along two axes (synchronic and diachronic), not separated this time into the autonomy of extrinsic coordinates, but woven together into intensive ordinates:

1   Some of these are intentional, whereby each affect territory is the object of a fractalization – which one can illustrate by the mathematical operation called "the Baker transformation" which develops relations of internal symmetry.[23] By this I understand that it is through an inchoate tension, a permanent "work in progress", that an affect's "taking of being" is renewed and takes its consistency; none of its partitions, be they infinitesimal, escape the existential procedures of homothetic replication deployed outside the registers of discursive extensivity by sensory and problematic ritornellos. Not only do all the spatio-temporal angles of approach turn out to be thereby explored and subsumed, but so also does the set (or the integer) of the points of view of scale – to return again to that fundamental category of architecturology.

2   A trans-monadic axis, one of transversality, which confers its transitivist character onto enunciation, making it constantly drift from one existential territorialization to another, and generating, on the basis of this territorialization, datings and singularizing durations. (Once again, a primal example here would be that of the Proustian ritornellos.)

Subjectivization straddles both actual and virtual enunciative points of view. It wants to be everything without exception and is in fact nothing, or almost nothing, because it is irremediably fragmentary, in a perpetual lag [*décalage*] vis-à-vis its pomp and its works . . . Finitude and existential completion, result from a crossing of threshold which is in no way a fencing in, a circumscription. Self and other are agglomerated in the heart of ethical intentionality and of the aesthetic promotion of an end. What completely falsifies the reading of psychoanalytic authors when they discuss the ego is that, literally, one does not know what they are talking about because they have not given themselves the means to understand that the ego is not a discursive ensemble entertaining gestalt relations with a referent. So one cannot accept the validity of the divisions they propose. Of course, it's always posible to make out of all this a "displaced" representation, to construct a meta-modeled scene and to decree that the ego is precisely identified with that scene. In any of the ways one looks at the ego, one scarcely has other means to talk, to draw, to write something about it. It does not remain any the less for that matter that the ego is the whole wide world: I am all that [*Je suis tout ça*]! No more than to the cosmos do I recognize any limit to myself. If, by chance, it were otherwise, if I had to "fall back" onto my body, then there is a malaise. The ego arises from a logic of all or nothing. There always exists a part of myself that poorly tolerates anyone's declaring that beyond this territory, it is no longer me. No! Beyond, it will always be me, even if another kind of territory claims to impose itself on me; unless the question of the ego ceases to be raised and that every possibility of self-enunciation is abolished; a horrifying and unnamable perspective, which one would prefer not to look too fully in the face, and which generally leads us to talk about something else . . .

It is because affect is not a massively elementary energy but the deterritorialized matter of enunciation, an integer of highly differentiated insight and "outsight", that we have something to do with it, that we can work it out. Not in the manner of traditional psychoanalysis, that is, under the force of modeling identifications and symbolic integrations, but by deploying its ethico-aesthetic dimensions through the mediation of ritornellos. (On this point, I rejoin Emmanuel Lévinas, when he draws an intrinsic association between faceness and ethics.[24]) Consider, for example, the symptomatic ritornellos inhabiting Pierre Janet's psychological automatisms, Karl Jasper's primary delirious experiences, or Freud's fantasmatic unconscious. There are two possible attitudes: those which make of these an immovable state of fact and those, on the contrary, which begin from the idea that nothing is played out in advance, that analytico-aesthetic and ethico-social practices are susceptible of opening up new fields of possibility. In its origins, Freudianism truly was a mutation in the lay-out of enunciation. Its interpretive techniques, its interventions within oneiric and psychopathological ritornellos bore in appearance only upon semantic contents – the illusory revelation of a "latent content". In fact, the whole of Freud's art consisted in making ritornellos play in unprecedented scenes of affect: free association, suggestion, tranference . . . – all so many new ways to speak and to see things! But what psychoanalysis has missed, in the course of its historical development, is the heterogenesis of the semiotic components of its enunciation. At its origin, the Freudian unconscious still took into account two matters of expression, linguistic and iconic; but with its structuralizing, psychoanalysis claimed to reduce everything to the term of the signifier, indeed, to that of the "matheme". Everything leads me to think, on the other hand, that it would be preferable for psychoanalysis to multiply and differentiate, to the extent possible, the expressive components that it puts into play. And that its own enunciative lay-outs be no longer necessarily disposed adjacent to the couch and in a way that radically forecloses the dialectics of the gaze. Analysis has everything to gain from enlarging its means of intervention; it can work with words, but just as well with modeling clay (as does Gisela Pankow) or with videos, movies, the theatre, institutional structures, familial interactions, etc., in short, everything that would allow it to sharpen the a-significant facets of the ritornellos it meets and in such a way that it would be in a better position to engage their catalyzing functions in the crystallization of new universes of reference (the function of fractalization). Under these conditions, analysis will no longer rest upon the interpretation of phantasms and the displacement of affects, but it will strive to make each of them operational, to give them a new "stave" in the musical sense of the word. Its basic work would consist in detecting encysted singularities (what goes around in circles, what insists on nothing, what stubbornly refuses the dominant evidence, what puts itself in opposition to its manifest interest . . .), and in exploiting their pragmatic virtualities.

What can account for the reductionist slope of signification along which psychoanalytic affect has not ceased to slide, with its increasingly empty transferences, its increasingly stereotypical asepticized exchanges? This slope is inseparable, it seems to me, from the much more general curvature of capitalist universes towards an entropy of significational equivalences. This would be a world in which everything is worth everything else, where every existential singularity is methodically devalued, where in particular affects of contingency relative to old age, sickness, madness, and death are emptied of their existential syntagms and will henceforth arise only from abstract paradigms that are managed by a network of help and care outfitters – all of this steeped in an ineffable but omnipresent atmosphere of anxiety and unconscious guilt.[25] Is this a Weberian disenchantment, correlative, we remember, of a devaluation, of a "sacramental anti-magic",[26] or is it the all-directional re-enchantment of the productions of subjectivity, through the depolarizing of collective universes of reference with regard to the values of a generalized equivalencing and to the profit of an infinite gearing down of the existential *takings of valence*? Although the current inflation of informational and communicational logics scarcely seems to be moving in this direction, it seems to me that it is indeed upon the promotion of analytical, social, and aesthetic practices which are preparing the arrival of such a post-media era that our future depends, at whatever level one considers it.

Notes

This translation was published in *Discourse* 12/2 (1990): 68–88. It has also appeared as "Ritournelles et affects existentiels" in *Chimères* 7 (1989) and *Cartographies schizoanalytiques* (Paris: Galilée, 1989), pp. 251–68.

1 Sigmund Freud, *L'interprétation des rêves* (Paris: PUF, 1967). [In the *SE*, the line is marked as a quotation from a certain S. Stricker.]

2 [On epilepsy as "glischroidy", see Eugène Minkowski, *Lived Time: Phenomenological and Psychological Studies*, trans. Nancy Metzel (Evanston: Northwestern University Press, 1970), pp. 102–11.]

3 Benedict de Spinoza, *The Ethics*, ed. and trans. R.H.M. Elwes (New York: Dover, 1951), pp. 148, 156–7, vol. 2 of *Chief Works*.

4 With regard to schizophrenic alienation, phenomenological psychiatry advocates a diagnostic based upon a precocious lived experience (Rümke) or upon a feeling (Binswanger) or an intuition (Weitbrecht). Tellenbach envisages an "atmospheric diagnostic" as ascertaining the dissonance between the atmospheres proper to each of the two "partners", without seeking to amalgamate isolated symptoms. Cf. Arthur Tatossian, *Phénoménologie des psychoses* (Paris: Masson, 1980).

5 Mikhail Bakhtin: "In order to become compositional and to bring about form in the aesthetic object, every verbal syntactic liaison must be penetrated by the unity of the unique feeling of a liaison-making activity, which aims at the unity (brought about by it) of objective and semantic liaisons with a cognitive or ethical character, over and above the unity of the feeling of tensions and formative encompassing of the external encompassing of the theoretical and ethical content". "Le problème du contenu, du matériau et de la forme dans l'oeuvre littéraire", *Esthétique et théorie du roman* (Paris: Gallimard, 1978), p. 78. Guattari's further references to this volume are embedded in his essay.

6 Here, virtuality is correlative of a fractal deterritorialization, which is at once of infinite speed upon the temporal plane and generative of infinitesimal deviations upon the spatial plane. See my text, "Le Cycle des agencements".

7 Quoted in Tatossian, p. 169.

8 Tatossian, p. 117.

9 Tatossian, p. 103.

10 Robert Musil, *L'Homme sans qualité* (Paris: Le Seuil, 1956), Tome II, p. 400. *The Man Without Qualities*, trans. Eithne Wilkins and Ernst Kaiser, re. ed. (London: Pan, 1979), Vol. iii, pp. 421–22.]

11 Tatossian, p. 186.

12 See the chapter on "Les Ritornelles du temps perdu" in my *L'Inconscient machinique* (Paris: Recherches, 1979), pp. 239–336.

13 Louis Hjelmslev, *Nouveaux essais*, ed. François Rastier (Paris: PUF, 1985), pp. 74–75.

14 Walter Benjamin, *Essais* (Paris: Denoël-Gonthier, 1983) ["The Work of Art in the Age of Mechanical Reproduction", in *Illuminations*, ed. Hannah Arendt, trans. Harry Zohn (New York: Schocken, 1969.]

15 Roland Barthes, *La chambre claire* (Paris: Le Seuil, 1980) [*Camera Lucida: Reflections on Photography*, trans. Richard Howard (New York: Hill and Wang, 1981.]

16 Christian Girard, *Architecture et concepts nomades* (Brussels: Mardaga, 1986). Philippe Bouton, in *La Ville de Richelieu* (Paris: AREA, 1972), distinguishes twenty types of scales that are considered as the space of reference for architectural conceptualizing: technical, functional, formal symbolic, the dimensional symbolic of a model, semantic, sociocultural, environmental, optical visibility, apportionmental, geographical, from the point of view of extensiveness, cartographical, from the point of view of repre-

sentation, geometrical, the levels of conceptualization, human, global, economic. Other classifications and regroupings can be conceived, but what matters here is respect for the heterogeneity of the points of view.

17 [*Habitation à loyer modéré* . . . a large, usually state-run, housing project for low-income renters.]

18 See my chapter on "L'Ethologie des ritornelles sonores, visuelles et comportementales dans le monde animal", *L'Inconscient machinique*, pp. 117–53.

19 In *La Pensée chinoise* (Paris: Albin Michel, 1980), Marcel Granet shows the complementarity between the ritornellos of social demarcation in ancient China and the affects, or virtues as he calls them, borne along by vocables, graphisms, emblems, etc.: "the specific virtue of a lordly race was expressed by a song and dance (with either an animal or a vegetable motif). Without a doubt, it is appropriate to recognize for the old family names the value of a kind of musical motto – which translates graphically into a kind of coat of arms – the entire efficacity of the dance and the chants lying just as much in the graphic emblem as in the vocal emblem" (pp. 50–1).

20 This is only true for those icons, whose fabrication is staggered between the ninth and the sixteenth centuries, that are centered upon a mystic, almost sacramental, faceness. Afterwards, the icons become weighed down with vestimentary details, their characters multiply, and they are covered over with metallic sheathings (*oklads*). Cf. the article "Icônes", by Jean Blankoff and Olivier Clément, *Encyclopedia Universalis*, Tome 9 (1984), pp. 739–42.

21 See my chapter, "La Coupure léniniste", in *Psychanalyse et transversalité*, 2nd ed. (Paris: Maspero, 1974), 183–95.

22 Benoit Mandelbrot, *Les objets fractals* (Paris: Flammarion, 1984) *Fractals: Form, Chance and Dimension* (San Francisco: Freeman, 1977).]; "Les Fractals", *Encyclopedia Universalis*, Symposium, pp. 319–23.

23 Ilya Prigogine and Isabelle Stengers, *La Nouvelle alliance* (Paris: Gallimard, 1979) [*Order Out Of Chaos: Man's New Dialogue With Nature* (Boulder: New Science Library, 1984).]; Ivan Ekelard, *Le Calcul, l'imprévu* (Paris: Le Seuil, 1984).

24 Emmanuel Lévinas: "I think that access to the face is in and of itself ethical" (*Ethique et infini*. Paris: Fayard, 1982, p. 89). Lévinas: "The signification of the face is not a kind for which designation or symbolism would be the genre" (*Heidegger ou la question de Dieu*. Paris: Grasset, 1981, p. 243). Lévinas: "The responsibility for the other is not an accident happening to a subject, but in that subject precedes Essence and engagement on behalf of others" (*Humanisme de l'autre homme*. Paris: Fata Morgana, 1972).

25 Cf. Jean Delumeau, *Le Péché et la peur: La culpabilisation en Occident* (Paris; Fayard, 1983).

26 Max Weber associated the idea of a disenchatment (*Entzauberung*) of the world to a devaluation (*Entwertung*) of the sacraments as the message of salvation and to a loss of sacramental magic consecutive to the rise of the capitalist subjectivity (*L'éthique protestante et l'esprit du capitalisme*. Paris: Plon, 1967) [*The Protestant Ethic and the Spirit of Capitalism*, trans. Talcott Parsons (New York: Scribner's, 1958).]

Translated by Juliana Schiesari and Georges Van Den Abbeele

15

Microphysics of Power /
Micropolitics of Desire

(Milan, May 31, 1985)

The following abbreviations are used to cite Michel Foucault's work. The original pagination is cited first, followed by the available English translation.

A.S. *L'Archéologie du savoir* (Paris: Gallimard, 1969); *The Archaeology of Knowledge*, trans. A.M. Sheridan Smith (New York: Pantheon Books, 1972).

H.F. *Histoire de la folie à l'âge classique* (Paris: Gallimard, 1976); *Madness and Civilization*, trans. Richard Howard (New York: Random House, 1973).

H.S. *Histoire de la sexualité*, Vol. 1. *La Volonté de savoir* (Paris: Gallimard, 1976), Vol. 2. *L'Usage des plaisirs* (Paris: Gallimard, 1984); *The History of Sexuality*, trans. Robert Hurley (New York: Random House, 1978); Vol. 2. *The Use of Pleasure*, trans. Robert Hurley (New York: Random House, 1985).

M.C. *Les Mots et les choses* (Paris: Gallimard, 1966); *The Order of Things* (New York: Random House, 1970).

M.F. Hubert Dreyfus and Paul Rabinow, *Michel Foucault. Un Parcours philosophique*, trans. Fabienne Durand-Bogaert (Paris: Gallimard, 1984); *Michel Foucault: Beyond Structuralism and Hermeneutics* (Chicago: University of Chicago Press, 1983).

O.D. *L'Ordre du discours* (Paris: Gallimard, 1971); "The Discourse on Language", in *The Archaeology of Knowledge*.

P. "L'Oeil du pouvoir", in Jeremy Bentham, *Le Panoptique* (Paris: Belfond, 1977); "The Eye of Power", in *Power/Knowledge: Selected Interviews and Other Writings 1972–1977*, ed. C. Gordin (New York: Pantheon Books, 1980).

R.R. *Raymond Roussel* (Paris: Gallimard, 1963); *Death and the Labyrinth: The World of Raymond Roussel*, trans. Charles Ruas (New York: Doubelday and Co., 1986).

S.P. *Surveiller et punir* (Paris: Gallimard, 1975); *Discipline and Punish: The Birth of the Prison*, trans. Alan Sheridan (New York: Vintage Books, 1977).

Having had the privilege of seeing Michel Foucault take up my suggestion – expressed somewhat provocatively – that concepts were after all nothing but tools and that theories were equivalent to the boxes that contained them (their power scarcely able to surpass the services that they rendered in circumscribed fields, that is, at the time of historical sequences that were inevitably delimited), you ought not as a result be surprised in seeing me today rummaging through Foucault's conceptual tool shop so that I might borrow some of his own instruments and, if need be, alter them to suit my own purposes.

Moreover, I am convinced that it was precisely in this manner that Foucault intended that we make use of his contribution.

It is not by means of an exegetical practice that one could hope to keep alive the thought of a great thinker who has passed away. Rather, such a thought can only be kept alive through its renewal, by putting it back into action, reopening its questioning, and by preserving its distinct uncertainties – with all the risks that this entails for those who make the attempt.

I leave it to you to relate this initial banality to the somewhat tired genre of the posthumous homage! In one of his last essays, which dealt with the economy of power relations, Foucault entreated his reader not to be repelled by the banality of the facts that he mentioned: "the fact [that] they're banal does not mean they don't exist. What we have to do with banal facts is to discover – or try to discover – which specific and perhaps original problem is connected with them" (M.F. 299/210). In this way, I believe that what is quite exceptional and perhaps now ready to be discovered, in the manner which Foucault's thought is destined to survive him, is that this thought traces out, better than any other, the most urgent problematics of our societies. And to date, nothing has shown itself to be as elaborate as this thought, certainly not the already outmoded approaches of "postmodernisms" and "postpoliticalisms", which in the face of these same problematics have all run aground.

The most crucial aspect of Foucault's intellectual development consists in having moved away from both a starting point that was leading him towards a hermeneutic interpretation of social discourse and from a final goal that would have entailed a closed structuralist reading of this same discourse. It is in *The Archaeology of Knowledge* that he supposedly carried out this two-fold conspiracy. Whereas in fact it is here that he explicitly freed himself from this perspective, initially employed in *Madness and Civilization*, by announcing that for him it was no longer a question of "interpreting discourse with a view to writing a history of the referent". Rather, his stated intention was to henceforth "substitute for the enigmatic treasure of 'things' anterior to discourse, the regular formation of objects that emerge only in discourse" (A.S. 64–67/47–49).

This refusal to make reference to the "foundation of things", as well as the renunciation of the profound depths of meaning, is parallel and symmetrical to the Deleuzian position that rejects the lofty objects [*objet des hauteurs*] as well as any transcendental position of representation. With Foucault and Deleuze, horizontalness – a certain *transversality* accompanied by a new principle of contiguity-discontinuity – is presented in opposition to the traditional vertical stance of thought. It should be noted that it was around this same turbulent period that oppressive hierarchies of power were being put into question. It was also a period marked by the discovery of new lived dimensions of spatiality; as seen, for example, in the somersaults of the astronauts, the innovative experiments in the field of dance and, in particular, the flourishing of the Japanese Buto.

Foucault's new programme was now spelled out: to renounce the "question of origins",[1] to leave for analysis "a blank, indifferent space, lacking in both interiority and promise" (A.S. 54/39) without, however, falling into the trap of a flat reading of the signifier.

It was in this respect that during his inaugural talk in 1970 at the Collège de France, Foucault issued a kind of solemn warning: "[d]iscourse thus nullifies itself, in reality, in placing itself at the disposal of the signifier" (O.D. 51/228).

Indeed, after a period of initial hesitation, Foucault came to consider as pernicious any structuralist endeavor to "treat discourse as groups of signs (signifying elements referring to contents or representations)". Instead, he wished to apprehend these discourses from the perspective of "*practices* that systematically form the objects of which they speak". "Of course", Foucault continues, "discourses are composed of signs; but what they do is more than use these signs to designate things. It is this *more* that renders them irreducible to language [*langue*] and to speech" (A.S. 66–67/49) [t.m.]. In this way, Foucault left the ghetto of the signifier and the asserted will in order to take into account the productive dimension of the enunciation. But of what is this "more" (that is here in question) constituted? Is it a matter of a simple subjective illusion? Does this "more" go in search of an "already there", or a process that is being deployed? There is probably no universal answer to these questions. Each regional or global cartography, depending on whether it is inclined towards aesthetic or scientific ideological claims, defines its own field of pragmatic efficiency. And it is quite evident that a renunciation – of the sort proposed by Foucault – of the reductive myths that are generally in fashion in the human sciences would not be without its effect on the political and micropolitical stakes of, for example, the care giver–cared for relationship, the role of specialists in psychology, the positions occupied by these specialists within the university, the preoccupations of the mass media, the hierarchies existing between the different levels of the state, and so forth. Having successfully devalued the imaginary component of the real, to the exclusive benefit of its symbolic component, the French structuralists of the sixties in effect established a kind of religious trinity comprised of the Symbolic, Real, and Imaginary – its missionaries and converts disseminating and preaching the new good tidings just about everywhere, attempting brutally, or sometimes quite subtly, to invalidate any view that did not mesh with their own hegemonic will. But we know quite well that no Trinity – whether it be of the overwhelming sort that is the Hegelian accomplishment, or that of a Charles Sanders Pierce, whose richness still remains largely unexplored – has been, nor will ever be, able to take into account, for example, the singular being of an ordinary sliver in desiring flesh. And upon a moment's reflection, we can very well understand why this is so: these trinities are constituted precisely as a way to conjure away the random ruptures or rare occurrences which Foucault has shown us to be the essential thread of any existential affirmation. "Rarity and affirmation; rarity in the last resort of affirmation – certainly not any continuous outpouring of meaning, and certainly not any monarchy of the signifier" (O.D. 72/234).[2] In a word, the reality of history and desire, the productions of the soul, body, and sex, do not pass through this kind of tripartition, which is ultimately quite simplistic.[3] These involve a completely other categorical reduction [*démultiplication catégorielle*] of the semiotic components opening onto imaginary scenes or in the form of symbolic diagrams. Both the rupturing of the portmanteau-concept of the signifier, as well as the critique of the Lacanian adage that only the signifier can represent the subject for another signifier, go hand in hand with the radical questioning of the philosophical tradition of the "founding subject". Foucault challenges the conception of the subject that supposedly "animates the empty forms of language with its objectives" (O.D. 49/227) [t.m]. Instead, Foucault commits himself to describing the actual agents that engender the discursivity of social groups and institutions – which in turn leads him to the discovery of a vast domain of forms of collective production and technical modalities of the construction of subjectivity, virtually unrecognized until then. This is not to be understood in the sense of a causal determination, but rather, as the *rarefaction* and/or *proliferation* of the semiotic components at the intersection from which they arise. Behind the obvious "logophilia" of the dominant culture, he analyses a profound "logophobia", a ferocious will to master and control "the great proliferation of discourses, in such a way as to relieve the richness of its most dangerous elements; as well as to organize its disorder so as to elude its most uncontrollable aspects" and a mute fear against the sudden appearance of statements, of events, and against "everything that could possibly be violent, discontinuous, querulous, disordered even and perilous in it, of the incessant, disorderly buzzing of discourse" (O.D. 52–53/228–29) [t.m].

We can distinguish two ways in which Foucault considers how the subjectivity which he explores eludes the reductionistic approaches that have taken root virtually everywhere:

1 that of a reterritorialization leading to an updating of subjectivity's institutional components of semiotization, and what charges it with history and factual contingency – it is at this level that it distinguishes itself from all variations of structuralism;

2 that of a deterritorialization that shows subjectivity to be, according to an expression put forth in *Discipline and Punish*, a creator of a "real, non-corporeal soul". It is also implied in this humorous warning: "It would be wrong to say that the soul is an illusion, or an ideological effect. On the contrary, it exists, it has a reality, it is produced permanently around, on, within the body . . ." (S.P. 34/29). We are here in the register of an "incorporeal materialism" (O.D. 60/231) that is as far removed from the rigid forms of hermeneutical interpretations as it is from the lures of a certain currently fashionable "non-materialism".

It is a matter, henceforth, of escaping from, by way of an analytic practice – what Foucault calls a "discourse as practice" – the agents of subjugation whatever may be their level of institution. In an interview – that seems to constitute a kind of testament – with Hubert Dreyfus and Paul Rabinow, Foucault continues to aver that "we need to promote new forms of subjectivities by renouncing the type of individuality that was imposed upon us over several centuries" (M.F. 301–302) [my trans.]. Furthermore, he takes care to list the conditions that permit an advancement towards a new economy of power relations. The struggles for the transformation of subjectivity, Foucault explains, are not ordinary forms of opposition to authority. Rather, they are characterized by the following aspects:

1 they are "transversal" (for Foucault this means that these struggles are to be understood as emerging from the particular context of the country in question);

2   they are opposed to all categories of power effects, and not just those that pertain to "visible" social struggles; for example, those effects that are exercised over people's bodies and their health;

3   they are immediate, in the sense that these struggles are aimed at the forms of power that are closest to those engaged in the struggle, and because they do not yield to any predetermined resolution, such as we find in the programmes of political parties;

4   they put into question the status of the normalized individual and assert a fundamental right to difference (which is, moreover, not in the least incompatible with community choices);

5   they are opposed to the privileges of knowledge and their mystifying function;

6   they involve a refusal of the economic and ideological violence of the State, and of all its forms of scientific and administrative inquisition.

Across these various prescriptions, we see that the decoding of "the political technologies of the body", the "microphysics of power" (S.P. 31/26) and of the "discursive 'policy'" (O.D. 37/224), proposed by Foucault does not consist of a simple contemplative point of reference, but rather involves what I have called *micropolitics*, that is, a molecular analysis that allows us to move from forms of power to investments of desire.

When Foucault speaks of desire, which he does repeatedly in his work, he always means it in a sense that is far more restricted than the way Deleuze and I employ this term. We can, nevertheless, note that his quite distinct notion of power has, if I may say so, the effect of "pulling" this concept in the direction of desire. It is in this way that he deals with power as a matter that has to do with an investment and not with an "all or nothing" law. Throughout his entire life, Foucault refused to conceive of power as a reified entity. For him, relations of power and, by consequence, strategic struggles, never amount to being mere objective relations of force. Rather, these relations involve the processes of subjectification in their most essential and irreducible singularity. And within them, we will always find "the obstinacy of the will and the intransitivity of freedom" (M.F. 312–315) [my trans.].

As such, power is not exercised "simply as an obligation or a prohibition on those who 'do not have it'; it invests them, is transmitted by them and through them; it exerts pressure upon them, just as they themselves, in their struggle against it, resist the grip it has on them" (S.P. 31–32/27). To this I would add that despite our different points of view, let us say of our "framing of the field", it seems to me that our problematics of analytic singularity overlap.

But before settling on this point, I would like to make a more general remark regarding our shared dispute against Lacanian and related theories in order to underline the fact that our dispute was never accompanied by a neopositivist or Marxist negation of the problem of the unconscious. The *History of Sexuality* brought to the fore the decisive nature of the break that Freudianism carried out with respect to what Foucault called the "series composed of perversion-heredity-degenerescence", that is, the solid nucleus of the technologies of sex at the turn of the last century (H.S. vol. I. 157/118–119, 197–198/149–150). As Deleuze and myself are concerned, one must recall that we were rebelling against the attempt to reconstruct a particular form of analysis, namely, the Lacanian pretension of erecting a universal logic of the signifier that would account for not only the economy of subjectivity and of the affects but also of all the other discursive forms relating to art, knowledge, and power.

Let us now return to the feature that aligns us, perhaps more than any other, with Foucault, namely, a common refusal to expel those dimensions of singularity of the analytic object and its procedures of elucidation: "The theme of universal mediation", Foucault writes, "is yet another manner of eliding the reality of discourse. And this despite appearances. At first sight it would seem that, to discover the movement of a logos everywhere elevating singularities into concepts, finally enabling immediate consciousness to deploy all the rationality in the world, is certainly to place discourse at the center of speculation. But, in truth, this logos is really only another discourse already in operation, or rather, it is things and events themselves which insensibly become discourse in the unfolding of the essential secrets" (O.D. 50–1/228). This return to singularity rests, in Foucault, on his very distinct conception of the statement as no longer representing a unity of the same sort as the sentence, the proposition, or the speech-act. Consequently, the statement, for Foucault, no longer functions on the authority of a segment of a universal logos leveling out existential contingencies. Its proper domain is therefore no longer simply that of a relation of signification, articulating the relationship between signifier and signified, nor of the relation of the denotation of a referent. For it is also a capacity of *existential production* (which, to use my terminology, I call a *diagrammatic function*). In its mode of being singular, the Foucauldian statement is neither quite linguistic, nor exclusively material. It is, nevertheless, crucial that we be able to state whether or not we are dealing with a sentence, proposition, or speech act. "The statement is not therefore a structure . . . it is a function of existence that properly belongs to signs and on the basis of which one may then decide, through analysis or intuition, whether or not they 'make sense' . . ." (A.S. 115/86).

Is not this intersection between the semiotic function of meaning, the denotative function, and this pragmatic function of *mise en existence* precisely on that which all psychoanalytic experience turns – with its symptomatic indexes, witticisms, its lapses, its "dream navels" [*ombilics du rêve*], failed actions, its fantastical training and behavioralism clutching as it is onto its own existential repetition that is empty of meaning, or at the very least, empty in a pragmatic sense in the coordinates of dominant meanings? Whether he was traversing the "discourses" of collective instruments (for example, that of hospitals or prisons), the marking of bodies and of sexuality, the history of the emergence of the figures of reason and madness, or even the mechanical worlds of a Raymond Roussel (R.R. 120/93), Foucault's primary research was always concerned with the rifts of discourse, that is, the ruptures of meaning of ordinary language or of scientific discursivity. Foucault's objective was always that of carrying out a mapping of large groups of statements as a "series of interwining lacunas and interplays of differences, distances, substitutions, and transformations". He never accepted as self-evident the view that these groups of statements are to be characterized as "full, tightly packed, continuous, [and] geographically well-defined" (A.S. 52/37) [t.m.]. When following Foucault on this terrain, one senses at times a connection with the dissident logic of the Freudian primary processes.[4] While this is true, Foucault's concept of singularity, whose importance I have already underlined, nevertheless differs profoundly from this logic in two ways.

First, one must never forget that Foucault undertook, indeed, in every way possible, to dismantle the false appearance of the individuation of subjectivity. I have already mentioned the subjugating function of social individuation – what Foucault calls "government of individualization" – which at once individualizes and totalizes (M.F. 302/212–13), and which, by means of a faceless gaze "transforms the whole social body into a field of perception: thousands of eyes posted everywhere, mobile attentions ever on the alert, a long, hierarchized network . . ." (S.P. 216/214). But this function is not necessarily exercised by a clearly defined rational social operator such as a caste in control of a state or by the executive administration of a political party. It may involve an *intentionality without subject* (H.S. vol. I. 124–25/94–95) proceeding from "collective surfaces and inscriptions" (A.S. 56/41). Panoptic control, for example, leads to the subjectification of those who observe as much as those who are observed. It is an apparatus wherein no one has exclusive authority, and where "everyone is caught, those who exercise power just as much an those over whom it is exercised" (P. 156). In a more general way, we

need to keep in mind that there exists no statement – in the Foucauldian
sense – that would be free, neutral, and independent. Statements are
always an integral part of an associated field; it is only because they are
immersed in an enunciative field that they can emerge in their singularity
(A.S. 130/99).

This perspective also led Foucault to reconsider the status of the
author at the level of the most basic procedures of the delimitation and
control of discourse. For Foucault, the author is not to be identified with
the speaking individual who has delivered or written a text, but as a
"unifying principle of discourse" – which on my part, I have called a
"collective assemblage of enunciation" – that gives this discourse its
unity, its gesture, its meaning, as the seat of its coherence (O.D. 28/221)
[t.m.].

Secondly, the way Foucault positions the question of the existential
singularities also constitutes a potential, but decisive, departure from the
Freudian manner of approaching the forms of the unconscious, or "un-
thought" [*impensée*] to use a term inspired by the work of Blanchot. The
individual as ruptured is no longer synonymous with singularity, and can
no longer be conceived of as an irreducible point of escape from the
systems of relations and representation. Even the cogito has lost its
character of apodictic certainty to become, in a way, processual; it is now
understood as "a ceaseless task constantly to be undertaken afresh"
(M.C. 335/324). Singularity is formed or undone according to the hold
of the subjective strength of the collective and/or individual discursivity.
Let us say, by way of returning to the context of our particular categories,
that singularity has to do with a *process of singularization* in so far as it
comes to exist as a collective assemblage of enunciation. With this aim in
view, singularity can just as well embody itself through a collective
discourse as it can lose itself in a serialized individuation. And even when
it concerns an individual entity, it might very well continue to be a matter
of processual multiplicities. This is not to say, however, that in becoming
fragmented, precarious, and in freeing itself from its identitarian fetters a
singularity is necessarily led to impoverish or weaken itself. On the
contrary: it affirms itself. At least that is the orientation proposed by
Foucault's micropolitics of the "analytic of finitude", breaking completely as it does with the analytic of representations issuing from the Kantian
tradition. It would therefore be a serious misinterpretation to restrict his
perspective to one type of global intervention of the subjectification of
the social body. For Foucault's perspective is also, and above all, a
micropolitics of existence and desire. Finitude, in this perspective, is not
something that one resignedly endures as a loss, a deficiency, a mutilation, or castration. Rather, finitude entails existential affirmation and
commitment.[5] All the themes that we might call Foucauldian existential-

ism converge on this pivotal point between semiotic representation and the pragmatics of "existentialization", and, in this way, places the micropolitics of desire alongside the microphysics of power according to specific procedures. Each of these themes demands to be reinvented, one at a time, and case by case, in a process akin to artistic creation. Foucault's immense contribution lies in its exploration of the fundamentally political fields of subjectification, as well as the guiding light of a micropolitics that frees us from the pseudo-universals of Freudianism or the Lacanian mathemes of the unconscious. As a result of the methods he articulated, the lessons we can derive from his intellectual and personal development, as well as from the aesthetic character of his work, Foucault has left us with a number of invaluable instruments for an analytic cartography.

Notes

This conference paper, "Microphysique des pouvoirs et micropolitique des désirs", presented in Milan at a colloquium devoted to the work of Foucault, was published in *Les Années d'hiver* 1980–1985 (Paris: Bernard Barrault, 1986), pp. 207–222.

1 See also the theme of the "labyrinth of origins" in the work of Raymond Roussel (R.R. 204/162).
2 We were on our part fighting, during this very period, against what we called the "imperialism of the signifier". Were our positions separated here by slightly different nuances? Or is there perhaps a prevalence in Foucault of the role played by the "classical age" in this hold of power of the signifier over power in general – whereas Deleuze and I emphasized the dimensions of the signifier as they related to advanced capitalism?
3 For the production of the domains of objects, see O.D. 71/234; for that of events: O.D. 61/231; of the soul: S.P. 34/29; that of sex: H.S. vol. I. 151/114, etc.
4 If one is to take seriously the assertion that struggle is at the heart of power relations, then one must realize that the good old "logic of contradiction is no longer sufficient, far from it, for the unraveling of actual processes", P. 30/164.

Translated by John Caruana

PART V

Queer/Subjectivities

16

Three Billion Perverts on the Stand

1 Prefatory Note

The object of this file – homosexualities, today, in France – cannot be approached without questioning again the standard methods of research in the social sciences where, under a pretext of objectivity, all care is taken to maximize the distance between the researcher and the object of study. To arrive at the radical decentering of scientific enunciation that is required for the analysis of such a phenomenon, it is not sufficient to "*give voice*" to the subjects concerned – which at times amounts to a formal, even Jesuitical, intervention. Rather, it is necessary to create the conditions for a total, indeed a paroxysmic, exercise of that enunciation. Science should have nothing to do with just measures and compromises for the sake of good taste! It is not readily apparent how to break through the barriers of established knowledge, in fact of dominant power. At least three sorts of censure must be thwarted:

— that of the pseudo-objectivity of *social surveys*, in the manner, for example, of the Kinsey Report transposed onto the "*sexual behaviour of the French*" – which contain a priori all possible responses, and in such a way as not to reveal to the public anything that does not accord with what the observer and the director of the study wish to hear;

— that of *psychoanalytic prejudices* which pre-organize a psychological, topical and economic "*comprehension*" – in fact a recuperation – of homosexuality, such that, with the persistence of the most traditional sexology, will continue to be held within a clinical framework of perversion, which implicitly justifies all the forms of repression it has suffered. Here, then, there will be no question of "fixation" at the pre-genital, pre-oedipal, pre-symbolic or pre-anything stages, which would define the homosexual as lacking something – at the very least normality and morality. Far from depending on an "*identification with the same-sex parent*", homosexual maneuvering effects a break with all possible adequation to a prominent parental pole. Far from resolving itself by fixation on the Same, it is an opening into Difference. For the homosexual, refusal of castration does not indicate a shrinking from his or her social responsibilities, but rather, at least potentially, indicates an attempt to expunge all normalizing, identificatory processes – processes which are, fundamentally, no more than the remnants of the most archaic rituals of submission;

— that, finally, of *traditional militant homosexuality*. Likewise, in this domain, the period of the "Case of Uncle Tom" has passed. Here, the defense of the legitimate and unassailable claims of oppressed minorities will no longer be at issue; and no question, either, of a quasi-ethnographic   exploration   of   a   mysterious   *"third sex"*. . . . Homosexuals speak for us all – speak in the name of the silent majority – by putting into question all forms, whatever thay may be, of desiring-production. Nothing in the order of artistic creation or of revolution can be accomplished in ignorance of their questioning. The era of homosexual geniuses, who set about separating and diverting their creativity from their homosexuality, forcing themselves to conceal that their creative spirit originated in that very break with the established order, has now passed.

Incidentally, for the deaf: the gay, no more than the shizo, is not *of himself* a revolutionary – the revolutionary of modern times! We are simply saying that, among others, he *could* be, *could* become, a site for an important libidinal disruption in society – a point of emergence for revolutionary, desiring-energy from which classical militantism remains cut off. We do not lose sight, insofar as it also exists, of an infinitely unfortunate commitment to asylums, or an indefinitely shameful and miserable oedipal homosexuality. And yet, even with these cases of extreme repression, one should stay in touch.

May '68 taught us to read the writing on the walls, and, since then, we have begun to decipher the graffiti in prisons, asylums, and now in urinals. There is a *"new scientific spirit"* to recapture!

2 A Letter to the Court

In recent years, the position of homosexuals in society has greatly evolved. In this area, as in many others, one observes a discrepancy between reality and psychiatric theory, medical-legal and juridical practice. Homosexuality is less and less felt to be a shameful malady, a monstrous deviance, a crime. This evolution has become increasingly pronounced since May '68, when the forces of social struggle took on previously neglected causes, such as life in prisons and in asylums, the condition of women, the question of abortion, of quality of life, etc. There has been, moreover, a homosexual political movement which, considering homosexuals to be a marginal minority, has defended their human dignity and demanded their rights. Some of these movements, in the United States for example, have joined forces with other protest groups: movements against the Vietnam War, civil rights movements for Blacks, Porto Ricans, feminist movements, and so on.

In France, this evolution has been different. The revolutionary movement, the FHAR [*Front homosexuel d'action révolutionnaire*], was launched with a political agenda right from the start. There was no conjunction of marginal homosexual movements with political movements: the problems of homosexuality were immediately posed as political questions. This spontaneist Maoist movement, formed around the journal *Tout* – the product of May '68 – refused not only to accept that homosexuality was an illness or a perversion, but advanced the view that it concerned all normal sexual life. Similarly, the women's liberation movement, the MLF [*Mouvement de libération des femmes*], argued that feminine homosexuality was not only a form of struggle against male chauvinism, but also a radical questioning of all dominant forms of sexuality.

Homosexuality would be, thus, not only an element in the life of each and everyone, but involved in any number of social phenomena, such as hierarchy, bureaucracy, etc. The question has thus been shifted: homosexual men and women refuse the status of an oppressed minority, and intend to lead a political offensive against the enslavement of all forms of sexuality to a system of reproduction, and to the values of bureaucratic capitalist and socialist societies. This is, in fact, more about transsexuality than homosexuality: at issue is the definition of what sexuality would be in a society freed from capitalist exploitation and the alienation it engenders on all levels of social organization. From this perspective, the struggle for the liberty of homosexuality becomes an integral part of the struggle for social liberation.

The ideas arising from this line of thought were explored in the issue of *Recherches* for which I have been charged – as the director of the publication – for "affronting public decency". In fact, the problems raised by this issue of *Recherches* are fundamentally, and only, political. The charge of pornography is merely a pretext, all too easily invoked in this particular domain; the main thing is suppression for the sake of "an example".

Recherches, in addition to a number of current publications, endeavors to break with the practice common to radio, television, and most print media of selecting information according to reigning prejudices, of making themselves the judges of decency and indecency, of transposing the voice of those concerned by a particular problem into a language deemed acceptable, in short, of substituting themselves. On the situation in prisons, for example, one would solicit commentary from a judge, a policeman, a former prisoner (one of exceptional character – one, for example, who had committed a crime of passion), but never from an average prisoner. The same applies for mental illness. At a push, one might bring forward an insane genius, but never would one seek out actual witnesses to the miserable life of a psychiatric hospital.

We wanted, therefore, to give direct voice to homosexuals. And the result? We are reproached for our impropriety. But of what nature is this impropriety, if it is not political? In fact, what is said in this issue of *Recherches*, and in the manner in which it is said, is clearly less than what can be found not only in publications for sex-shops – our goal was hardly to compete! – but also in scientific publications. The originality of the issue – that which shocks, and for which we are charged – lies in that for perhaps the first time, homosexuals and non-homosexuals speak of these problems for themselves and in an entirely free manner.

3 17th Magistrate's Court

(Notes for the trial)

— I will not repeat the terms of my letter to the court; it seems, as Mr. Kiejman has advised me, that this would have a negative effect,

— I am summoned as the director of the journal *Recherches* for its special issue on homosexuality: "Three Billion Perverts: An Encyclopedia of Homosexualities",

— what does the fact that I am held responsible for this issue signify?

- *Recherches* is the expression of a group
- this issue, in particular, was collectively produced
- all of its participants asked to be charged

— what does the fact of holding someone responsible for something signify?

- I am responsible, I represent *Recherches*
- you represent the law

- members of Parliament represent the people

- the President of the Republic: France

- universities: knowledge

- gays: perversion

— *Recherches* wishes to have done with this sort of representation, with all the bad theatre to which officials and institutions resort.

What we want is to give voice to those who never manage to be heard.

— At CERFI [*Centre d'études, de recherches et de formations institutionnelles*], we are often questioned on the issues surrounding these problems. It is, undoubtedly, for those who are interested to seek answers themselves! Sometimes, however, we cannot restrain ourselves from expressing our own ideas.

— Recently, the Minister of Justice asked us if we would agree to study what the "spatial disposition of a Law Court" could be.

There is at least one comment that I could make at the moment: that is that judges should be in the room, and that speakers, whoever they may be, should *face the public.*

— Can one speak seriously in a Court?

- when I was a young militant, I would have refused to participate in this "masquerade",

- I would have said to you: "So, now, to express myself freely in a journal, one must pay. Fine. Write up the bill and we won't waste any more time". And I would have thrown you a fistful of bills or change for the bailiffs to pick up.

Then you would have sentenced me with contempt of court and everyone would have been satisfied!

- now I think a bit differently. I know that things go on everywhere, even in the magistrature, even in the police, even in the prefecture,

- finally, then, this trial interests me: I would like to know if everything was played out in advance, if everything was already inscribed in the "pharmacopoeia" of laws. . . . In this case, then, I grant you, in advance, that this issue of *Recherches* is indefensible. (Even though, I am sure, Mr. Merleau-Ponty, Mr. Kiejman and Mr. Domenach would know how to prove otherwise!)

— What purposes do texts serve: whether it be a text of law or a text of *Recherches*? Are they not inseparable from the social relations that underlie them, and from what linguists call the context, the implicit? Isn't the important thing to look at life itself, at the evolution of what one could call the "jurisprudence of everyday life"? One would see that homosexuality has evolved in recent years – at the very least, its "customary law" – and it is of that which we must speak.

— But before continuing, I would like to ask you two things, Your Honour, for the enrichment of our proceedings:

1   have all the witnesses, up to the present, enter together,

2   give free voice to everyone in the room who asks to speak.

This affair has two sides:
— a ridiculous side,
— a serious side.

The ridiculous side: In April of 1973, I was in Canada participating in an extremely interesting conference. Unfortunately, I could not delay my return to France because of consultations that I could not reschedule. Arriving home in Paris, suitcases in hand, I found several people with whom I had appointments sitting in the stairway, in front of my padlocked door.

It took me a moment to realize that the padlock, roughly screwed on the door (which cost me 150 francs to repair), had been put there by the police after searching the premises. The two statutory witnesses to this search had been, in my absence, my upstairs neighbours and . . . the locksmith! All of my papers and my clothes had been gone through, and the bathroom turned upside down. During this time, ten police officers had undertaken a similar search of the clinic of La Borde where I work. *Dozens* of search warrants had been issued. . . . To what end? It defies belief! To find copies of the seized issue of *Recherches*, while that same issue was on sale in bookstores, and had been for weeks!

When I protested these proceedings to the examining judge, I must say that he remained largely perplexed. I thought then that there had been a mistake and that the case would be adjourned *sine die*.

The serious side: What exactly caused such a commotion? The content or the form?

a) *The content of the issue*

The content is certainly exceptionally rich, particularly insofar as it involved:
— the position of the homosexual in society,
— the way in which different immigrant groups from North Africa live their homosexuality,
— the sexual misery of young people,

— the racist fantasies which are sometimes invoked in relations of sexual dependence, etc.

— masturbation: some extremely interesting accounts of this relatively unknown subject were brought together. But it would require at least three hours for the witnesses summoned today to deal with these different subjects.

b) *The form of the issue*

It is the form that was the target of repression, undoubtedly because the issue doesn't fit into any pre-established category:

— it's not an "art" book,

— nor is it a porno magazine,

— nor an erotic novel for the elite,

— and nor is it a text that austerely presents itself as a scientific communication.

We dispensed here with the notions of an author and a work. When the examining judge asked me, for example, who had written this or that article, supposing I would even answer, I was not able to do so. More often than not, the articles were, in effect, made up of reports, discussions, and montages of text, which makes it impossible to determine individual responsibility! Even the layout was done collectively, and certain sentences were taken directly from graffiti! How can the law determine who is responsible! Rather than asking questions regarding the substance, one has opted for the ease of holding responsible: the legal director!

— Is it irresponsible to allow people to speak, without precautions, without supporting documentation, and without a pseudo-scientific screen? (Even though scientific research, at a second level, works with documents as up to date).

How otherwise to conceive of a study, whether it be in psychiatry, pedagogy, or in areas that concern justice?

Is it really dangerous to let people speak of things as they feel them, and with their language, their passions, their excesses?

Must we institute a police for dreams and fantasies? For what good do we suppress the public expression of popular spontaneity on the walls – or in the subways, as in New York . . .?

How can we not understand that to forbid expression, on this level, is to favor a transition to actions that will present undoubtedly larger inconveniences to the social organization?

We think that the expression of desire is synonymous with disorder and irrationality.

But the neurotic order that forces desire to conform to dominant models perhaps constitutes the real disorder, the real irrationality.

It is repression that makes sexuality shameful and sometimes aggressive.

Desire that can open itself up to the world ceases to be destructive and can even become creative.

This trial is political. It makes a cause of a new approach to daily life, to desire, and the new forms of expression that have irrupted since 1968.

Will we finally allow people to express themselves without having recourse to "representatives"? Will we allow them to produce their own journals, their own literature, theatre, cinema, etc.?

Violence engenders violence.

If we repress the new forms of expression of social desire, we will head for absolute revolt, desperate reactions, even, indeed, for forms of collective suicide (as was, in certain respects, Hitlerian fascism).

Thus, it's for the judges to choose as well. Do they situate themselves, a priori, on the side of the dominant order?

Or are they capable of giving a hearing to another order that seeks to build another world?

Notes

"Trois milliards de pervers à la barre" appeared in Guattari's *La révolution moléculaire* (Fontenay-sous-Bois: Encres/Recherches, 1977), pp. 110–119. A note is added to the effect that: "The March issue of *Recherches*, 'Three Billion Perverts: An Encyclopedia of Homosexualities', had been seized, and Félix Guattari, as the publications director, was fined 600 francs for affronting public decency. No. 12 of *Recherches* was judged to constitute a 'detailed display of turpitude and sexual deviation', the 'libidinous exhibition of a minority of perverts'. All copies of the issue were ordered to be destroyed".

Translated by Sophie Thomas

17

Subjectivities: for Better and for Worse

My professional activities in the areas of psychopathology and psychotherapy, along with my political and cultural engagements, have led me to place an increasing emphasis on subjectivity insofar as it is produced by individual, collective and institutional factors.

To consider subjectivity from the perspective of its production in no way implies, I suggest, a return to traditional systems of determination involving a material infrastructure and an ideological superstructure. The different semiotic registers that contribute to the engendering of subjectivity do not maintain obligatory, hierarchical relations that are fixed once and for all. It could happen, for example, that economic semiotization becomes dependent on collective psychological factors, as one sees with the sensitivity of stock market indexes to fluctuations of opinion. In fact, subjectivity is plural – *polyphonic*, to borrow a term preferred by Mikhail Bakhtin. It is not constituted by a dominant, determining factor that directs other factors according to a univocal causality.

Three considerations lead us to enlarge the definition of subjectivity in such a way as to bypass the classical opposition between the individual subject and society, and thereby to revise the models of the Unconscious that currently obtain: the irruption of subjective factors into the foreground of historical events, the massive development of machinic productions of subjectivity and, finally, the recent focus on ethologic and ecologic factors in human subjectivity.

Over the course of history, subjective factors have always held an important place. Now, however, since their global diffusion through the mass media, it seems they are coming to play a dominant role. We will retain here, in summary fashion, only two examples. The immense movement unleashed by Chinese students evidently had political democratization as its goal. But it is equally certain that its contagious, affective burden went beyond simple ideological demands. At issue were other factors: a whole lifestyle, a whole conception of social relations, and a collective ethic. And, ultimately, the tanks achieved nothing. As in

Hungary or in Poland, a collective, existential mutation will have the last word! But large movements for subjectivation do not necessarily move in an emancipatory direction. The immense subjective revolution that has mobilized the Iranian people for more than a decade has, as its focal point, religious archaisms and globally conservative social attitudes – particularly with respect to the condition of women. In a general way, one could say that contemporary history is increasingly dominated by the escalation of claims that are singularly subjective: linguistic quarrels, demands for autonomy, questions of nation and nationalist . . . . One must admit that a certain universalist respresentation of subjectivity, as it had been embodied by the capitalistic colonialism of the West and the East, is now bankrupt, and we are unable to measure fully the consequences of such a failure.

Must we keep the semiotic productions of the mass media, of computers, of telecommunications, robotics, etc., outside of psychological subjectivity? I don't think so. In the same way as the social machines that we classify under the general rubric of "collective apparatuses", technological machines for information and communication operate at the heart of human subjectivity – not only within its memories and intelligence, but also within its sensibilities, affects, and unconscious fantasies. Taking into account these machinic components of subjectivation brings us to insist, in our redefinition, on the heterogeneity of the components converging to produce subjectivity. These components contain signifying semiological dimensions, but also a-signifying semiotic dimensions, which escape properly linguistic axiomatics. It was a serious error on the part of structuralist thinking to claim to bring together everything concerning the psyche under the sole direction of the linguistic signifier! Machinic transformations of subjectivity constrain us to take into account a *heterogenesis*, rather than a universalizing and reductionist homogenization, of subjectivity. So it is that "computer assistance" leads to the production of images or, again, to the resolution of mathematical problems that would have been unimaginable only a few decades ago. But there, too, one must guard against all mechanistic causal thought. The machinic production of subjectivity can work for the better as for the worse. At best, it is creation – the invention of new universes of reference; and at its worst, it is the mind-numbing mass mediatization to which billions of individuals today are condemned. Technological evolutions, combined with social experimentation in these new areas, will perhaps be able to lead us out of the oppressive present moment and into a "post-media" era, which would be characterized by a reappropriation and a re-singularization of the use of the media (access to data bases, videotheques, interactivity between protagonists, etc.).

In this same train of thought, where subjectivity is understood as polyphonic and heterogeneous, we find that its ethological and ecological aspects are accounted for. Daniel Stern, in *The Interpersonal World of the Infant*, explored in a remarkable fashion the pre-verbal subjective formulations of the infant.[1] He demonstrates that it is not at all a question of stages, in the Freudian sense, but rather levels of subjectivation which are sustained in a parallel formation throughout life. He thus renounces Freudian complexes, which had been presented as structural "universals" of subjectivity, as overrated in psychogenesis. On the other hand, he emphasizes the initially trans-subjective character of the early experiences of the infant, who does not dissociate a sense of self from a sense of other. It is a dialectic between "sharable affects" and "non-sharable affects" that so structures *emergent subjectivity*. Subjectivity, that is, in its nascent state that we continually recover in dream, delirium, creative elation, feelings of love . . . .

Social ecology and mental ecology have found privileged sites for exploration in the experiments of institutional psychotherapy. I am thinking in particular of La Borde, the clinic where I have worked for a long time, and where everything has been done so that the mentally ill can live in a climate of activity and of responsibility on all levels (which involves a permanent mobilization of staff). In such a context, one perceives that the most heterogeneous dimensions contribute to the positive development of a patient: relations to architectural space, economic relations, co-management by the patient and care giver of the different vectors of treatment, the seizing of all opportunities of exposure to the outside, and the processual development of factual "singularities" – finally, everything that can contribute to the creation of an authentic relation to the other. To each of these components of the institution of care corresponds a necessary *practice*. That is, one is not before a subjectivity that is given, such as the *en soi*, but rather facing a process of assuming autonomy, or of autopoesis, in the sense given the term by Francisco Varela.[2]

I will take as a final example the way family psychotherapy has taken advantage of the ethological capacity of the psyche, particularly in the body of thought developing around the work of Mony Elkaïm, which attempts to free itself from the grip of the systemist theories which are currently in use in Anglo-Saxon countries and in Italy.[3]

The inventiveness of treatments for family therapy, as they are conceived here, distance us from scientistic paradigms and draw near instead to ethico-aesthetic paradigms. The therapist is engaged, takes risks, and doesn't hesitate to weigh in with his or her own fantasies, and to create an atmosphere that is, paradoxically, one of existential authenticity which nevertheless allows for freedom of play. Another remarkable point is the fact that during the training of family therapists, the simulated situations become, in a way, more real than life, which demonstrates the "creationist" character that has taken the stage of family therapy.

Whether we turn to contemporary history, to machinic semiotic production, or to social ecology or mental ecology, we find the same questioning of individuation, of a subjectivity that is only, in sum, a configuration of *collective assemblages* of *enunciation*. From where we are now, the most inclusive provisional definition of subjectivity that I would propose is: "the set of conditions that make it possible for individual and/or collective factors to emerge as a sui-referential *existential territory*, adjacent or in a determining position to an alterity that is itself subjective". In this way, in certain social and semiological contexts, subjectivity individuates itself; a person, held as responsible for him- or herself, positions him- or herself among relations of alterity that are governed by the family, by local customs, by law . . . . Under other conditions, subjectivity is collectively formed, which does not mean that it becomes, for all that, exclusively social. In fact, the term "collective" should be understood here in the sense of a multiplicity that develops beyond the individual, on the side of the *socius*, as well as on this side (so to speak) of the person, that is, on the side of pre-verbal intensities that arise more from a logic of the affects than from a well-circumscribed, comprehensive logic.

The conditions of production evoked in my sketch of a definition thus jointly implicate intersubjective human factors manifested in language, and suggestive or identificatory factors arising from ethology, from machinic mechanisms such as those having recourse to computer assistance, from different institutions, from universes of non-corporeal reference, such as the world of music, that of the plastic arts . . . .

Returning to the question of the unconscious . . . . Freud postulated the existence of a continent hidden from the psyche, within which the essential workings of drives, affects, and cognitions was to be found. Today, one cannot dissociate theories of the unconscious from psychoanalytic, psychotherapeutic, institutional, literary (and so on) practices, which make reference to it. The unconscious has become an institution, a "collective assemblage" in the broadest sense. The unconscious is imposed upon us as soon as we dream, or are delirious, or commit an *acte manqué*, or a *lapsus* . . . . Undoubtedly, Freudian discoveries – which I prefer to qualify as inventions – have increased the angles from which one can approach the psyche today. And it is not at all in a pejorative sense that I speak of invention! In the same way that Christians invented a new formula for subjectivation, as did courtly chivalry, or romanticism, or Bolshevism, various Freudian groups have generated a new way to feel, to live, to produce hysteria, infantile neurosis, psychosis, family conduct, a reading of myths, etc. The Freudian unconscious has itself evolved over the course of its history: it has lost the ebullient richness and disturbing atheism of its orgins, and has been recentered on the analysis of the self, the adaptation of society or, in its structuralist versions, conformity to the signifying order.

From my own perspective, which is guided by a shift of human and social sciences from "scientistic" paradigms to ethico-aesthetic ones, the question is no longer one of knowing if the Freudian unconscious or the Lacanian unconscious offers scientific solutions to the problems of the psyche. The models will only be considered as one among others for the production of subjectivity, inseparable from the technical and institutional mechanisms that support them, and from their impact on psychiatry, on university teaching, the mass media . . . . In a more general way, one will have to admit that each individual, each social group, conveys its own system of modelling unconscious subjectivity, that is, a certain cartography made up of reference points that are cognitive, but also mythic, ritualistic, and symptomatological, and on the basis of which it positions itself in relation to its affects, its anxieties, and attempts to manage its various inhibitions and drives. Moreover, today, our question is not only of a speculative order, but has practical implications: do the models of the unconscious that are offered us on the "market" of psychoanalysis meet current conditions for the production of subjectivity? Is it necessary to transform them, or to invent new ones? What processes are set in motion in the awareness of an inhabitual shock? How do modifications to a mode of thinking, to an aptitude for the apprehension of a changing external world, take effect? How do representations of the external world change as it changes? The Freudian unconscious is inseparable from a society that is attached to its past, to its phallocratic traditions, and its subjective variants. Contemporary upheavals undoubtedly call for a modelization turned more toward the future and to the emergence of new social and aesthetic practices in all areas. On the one hand, the devaluation of the meaning of life provokes the fragmentation of self-image: representations of self become confused and contradictory while, on the other hand, the conservative forces of resistance oppose themselves to all change, which is experienced by a secure, ossified, and dogmatic consciousness as an attempt at destabilization.

Gilles Deleuze and I have similarly refused the Conscious-Unconscious dualism of Freudian issues, and all the Manicheanist oppositions that follow on the level of oedipal triangulation, castration complex, etc. We opted for an unconscious of superimposed, multiple strata of subjectivations, heterogeneous strata of development with greater and lesser consistency. An unconscious, thus, that is more "schizo", liberated from familialist yokes, and turned more toward current praxis than toward fixations and regressions on the past. An unconscious of flux and abstract machines, more than an unconscious of structure and language. Nevertheless, we do not propose our "schizoanalytic cartographies" as scientific doctrines. Just as an artist borrows elements that suit him from his precursors and contemporaries, we invite our readers to freely take and leave the concepts we advance. The important thing is not the final result, but the fact that the cartographic method coexists with the process of subjectivation, and that a reappropriation, an autopoesis of the means of production of subjectivity, are made possible.

It must be clear that we are not assimilating psychosis to a work of art, and the analyst to an artist! We are only stating that their way of assuming their existence engages a dimension of autonomy that is of an aesthetic order. Therein lies a crucial ethical choice: either we objectify, we reify, we "scientifize" subjectivity, or else we attempt to seize it in its dimension of processual creativity. Kant emphasized that the judgement of taste engaged subjectivity and its relation to others in a certain modality of "disinterestedness".[4] But it is not enough to designate these categories of liberty and disinterestedness as essential dimensions of the aesthetic unconscious; one must still account for their effective mode of insertion into the psyche. How do certain semiotic segments acquire their autonomy, putting themselves to work to generate new fields of reference? It is on the basis of such a rupture that an existential singularization, consecutive to the genesis of new coefficients of freedom, will become possible. Such a detachment of a "partial object" from the field of dominant significations corresponds at the same time to the promotion of a mutant desire and to the consummation of a certain disinterestedness. Here, we find the terms used by Bakhtin in his first theoretical essay of 1924,[5] where he placed in luminous relief the function of enunciative appropriation of aesthetic form by the *isolation* or *detachment* of the cognitive and ethical content, and the *consummation* of that content in the aesthetic object, which I would qualify as a partial enunciator. Bakhtin describes a transfer of subjectivation that operates between the author-creator and the contemplator of a work – the "onlooker" of Marcel Duchamp. For him, the recipient becomes, to some extent, a co-creator in this movement. Aesthetic form doesn't arrive at this end only by means of the functions of isolation or detachment, of a sort that renders the expressive matter formally creative. The content of the work detaches itself from its cognitive as much as its ethical connotations: "isolation or detachment relates not to the material, not to the work as a thing, but to its significance, to its content, which is freed from certain necessary connections with the unity of nature and the unity of the ethical event of being" (306). It is, thus, a certain segment of content that takes hold of the author-creator, that engenders a certain mode of aesthetic utterance. Bakhtin reminds us that in music, for example, "isolation and constructedness cannot be axiologically related to the material: it is not the sound of acoustics that is isolated and not the mathematical number of the compositional order that is made up. What is detached and fictively irreversible is the event of striving, the axiological tensions, which actualizes itself thanks to that without any impediment, and becomes consummated" (307).

Creative subjectivity in poetry, in order to detach itself, to become autonomous, and in order to be consummated, will preferably seize upon:

1   the phonic side of a word, its musical aspect;

2   its material significations, with their nuances and variations;

3   its qualities of verbal connection or interrelation;

4   its intonational aspects, both emotional and volitional;

5   the feeling of verbal activity in the active generation of a signifying sound that involves motor elements of articulation, gesture, mimicry – a feeling of movement that draws in the whole organism, the activity and the soul of a word in their concrete unity.

Evidently, this last aspect encompasses the others.[6]

These ingenious analyses of Bakhtin, which I can only skim over here, lead me to enlarge his approach with respect to partial subjectivation. It is not only in music and poetry that we see such fragments of content detached from the work which, in a general way, I would place in the category of *existential refrains*. The polyphony of modes of subjectivation in fact corresponds to a multiplicity of ways to "beat time". Other rhythmics are also brought to crystallize what I will call existential enunciations, which they incarnate and singularize. A complex refrain – short of those of music and poetry – marks the intersection of heterogeneous modes of subjectivation. Time has long been considered a universal and univocal category, while in reality, we have none other than particular and multivocal apprehensions of it. Universal time is just a hypothetical projection of modes of temporalization which arise from modules of intensity-refrains – which operate simultaneously in several registers: biologic, socio-cultural, machinic, cosmic, etc.

To illustrate this mode of production of polyphonic subjectivity where the refrain-intersection plays a dominating role, we might consider the example of televisual consumption. As soon as I watch television, I exist simultaneously in a relation of perceptive fascination to the luminous center of the apparatus which verges on hypnotism,[7] and in a relation of captivity to the narrative content of the program, associated at the same time with a lateral vigilance with regard to surrounding events (water boiling on the stove, a child's cry, a telephone . . .), and, behind it all, the fantasies inhabiting my reverie, etc. This means that, in spite of the diversity of the subjectivation components that traverse me, I am one, it is this refrain-ing [*ritournellisation*] that fixes me in front of the screen, which is from then on constituted as a projective *existential territory*. Like Bakhtin, I would say that the refrain does not rest on the elements of form, material, or ordinary signification, but on the detachment of an existential "motif" (or leitmotif) instituted as an "attractor" in the midst of sensible and significational chaos.

The most simple cases of refrains for the delimitation of existential territory can be found in the ethology of several species of birds, where specific song sequences serve different purposes: the seduction of a sexual partner, the distancing of intruders, and the announcement of the arrival of predators.[8] In each case, a precise functional space must be defined. In archaic societies, it is on the basis of rhythms, songs, dances, masks, inscriptions on the body, on the ground, on totems, rituals and mythic references that other kinds of collective existential territories are circumscribed.[9] These kinds of refrains are found in Greek antiquity, with "nomes" which constitute, in some way, "acoustic indicators", and flags and seals for professional corporations. But we are all familiar with such crossings of the thresholds of subjective states by the activity of a subjective, catalyzing, temporal module that plunges us into sadness, or else into a state of gaiety and animation. With our concept of the refrain, we aim not only at such massive effects, but at hypercomplex problematics. Take, for example, the entry into the incorporeal worlds of music or mathematics. These are not cases, we suggest, of universes of reference "in general", but of singular universes, historically marked at the intersection of diverse lines of virtuality. In this type of register, time ceases to be subjected: it is acted, oriented, polarized, the object of qualitative mutations. Analysis is no longer the interpretation of symptoms according to a pre-existent, latent content, but the invention of new catalytic centers susceptible of bifurcating experience. A singularity, a rupture in sense, a cut, fragmentation, the detachment of semiotic content – for example, in a dadaist or surrealist fashion – can be at the origin of mutant centers of subjectivation. Just as chemistry had to begin by purifying complex mixtures in order to extract homogeneous atomic and molecular matter, and then to create from them an infinite array of chemical entities that had not existed previously, the "extraction" and "separation" of aesthetic subjectivites or partial objects, in the psychoanalytic sense, facilitates an immense complexification of subjectivity, of new and unprecedented existential harmonies, polyphonies, rhythms and orchestration.

In this way, the primacy of the machinically-generated information flow has led to a generalized dissolution of ancient territorialities. In the early phases of industrialized societies, the "demonic" continued to appear everywhere, but henceforth mystery became an increasingly rare commodity. It is sufficient here to evoke the desperate quest of a Witkiewicz to seize an ultimate "mysteriousness of existence" that seemed literally to slip between his fingers.[10]

In these conditions, it falls especially to the poetic function to reconstruct universes of subjectivation that are artificially rarified and re-singularized. However, it is not for that function to transmit messages, to invest in images as support for identification, or in formal patterns as props for modelization procedures, but to catalyze the existential operators capable of acquiring consistency and persistency within the current mass-media chaos.

This poetico-existential catalysis, found in action amid its scriptural, vocal, musical or plastic discursivities, engages quasi-synchronically the enunciative recrystallization of the creator, the interpreter, and the consumer of the work of art. Its efficiency resides essentially in its capacity to promote active or processual ruptures within semiotically structured significational and denotational fabric, from which it produces new universes of reference.

When it is effectively released into a given enunciative zone – situated, that is to say, from a historical and geopolitical point of view – such a poetic function is thus instituted as a mutant center of auto-referentiation and auto-valorization. This is why it must always be considered from two perspectives: as a molecular rupture, an imperceptible bifurcation, capable of overturning the framework of dominant redundancies, the organization of the "already classified" or, if one prefers, the order of the classical, and secondly as it selects certain segments of these very lines of redundancy, in order to confer upon them the existential, a-signifying function that I have just evoked, to render them "refrains", to make of them virulent fragments of partial enunciation which work to "shift" subjectivation. The quality of the base material is unimportant here, as it is with repetitive music or Buto dance which, as Marcel Duchamp has it, are completely turned toward the "onlooker". Of primordial importance, however, is the mutant, rhythmic trajectory of a temporalization that is capable of holding together the heterogeneous components of a new existential structure.

Beyond the poetic function lies the question of the mechanisms of subjectivation, and, more precisely, what characterizes these mechanisms so that they move out of seriality – in Sartre's sense[11] – and into processes of singularization, which restore to existence what one might call its auto-essentialization. We are entering an epoch where, the antagonisms of the cold war having receded, there appear even more distinctly the major threats that our productivist societies have imposed upon the human species, whose survival on this planet is threatened not only by environmental deterioration, but also by the degeneration of social solidarities and modes of psychic life that will literally have to be reinvented. The remaking of politics must pass through aesthetic dimensions that are implicated in the three ecologies of the environment, the socius, and the psyche. A response to the poisoning of the atmosphere, and global warming due to the greenhouse effect, is inconceivable without a mutation of mentalities, without the advancement of a new art of living. International cooperation in this area is inconceivable without finding solutions for the problems of famine in the world, and hyper-inflation in the Third World. We cannot conceive of a restructuring of the mass media toward a collective reappropriation of their use, that is not consequent upon a re-singularization of subjectivity, a new way of conceiving political and economic democracy, in the area of cultural differences. We cannot hope for an amelioration in the living conditions of the human species without considerable effort to advance the condition of women. The division of labor, its modes of valorization and its purposes must be rethought. Production for the sake of production, obsession with the growth rate, whether it be on the capitalist market or in socialist economies, leads to monstrous absurdities. The only acceptable end result of human activity is the production of subjectivity such that its relation to the world is sustained and enriched. The mechanisms of the production of subjectivity can be on the scale of the megalopolis as well as on that of the language games of a poet. To apprehend the inner workings of this production, its fundamental ruptures of the meanings of existence, poetry, today, has perhaps more to teach us than the economic and human sciences put together.

Notes

This article was published as a "Colloque" under the title of "Les subjectivités, pour le meilleur et pour le pire", *Chimères* 8 (1990): 23–37. The journal *Chimères* was founded by Gilles Deleuze and Félix Guattari in 1987.

1 Daniel Stern, *Le Monde interpersonnel du nourrisson* (P.U.F., 1985). [*The Interpersonal World of the Infant: A View from Psychoanalysis and Developmental Psychology* (New York: Basic Books, 1985).]

2 F. Varela, *Autonomie et connaissance* (Paris: Le Seuil, 1989).

3 Mony Elkaïm, *Si tu m'aimes, ne m'aime pas* (Paris: Le Seuil, 1989). [*If You Love Me, Don't Love Me: Constructions of Reality and Change in Family Therapy*], trans. Hendon Chubb (New York: Basic Books, 1990); See Guattari's review of this book, "La famille selon Elkaïm", *Le Monde* (10 mai 1989): 17.

4 "We may say that, of all these three kinds of liking (the agreeable, the beautiful, and the good), only the liking involved in taste for the beautiful is disinterested and *free*,

since we are not compelled to give our approval by any interest, whether of sense or of reason". Immanuel Kant, *Critique de la faculté de juger* (Vrin, 1986), pp. 54–55. [*The Critique of Judgement*, trans. Werner S.Pluhar (Indianapolis: Hackett Publishing, 1987), p. 52.]

5 "Le problème du contenu, du matériau et de la forme dans l'oeuvre littéraire", in *Esthétique et théorie du roman* (Gallimard, 1978). ["The Problem of Content, Material, and Form in Verbal Art", trans. Kenneth Brostrom, in *Art and Answerability: Early Philosophical Essays* by M.M.Bakhtin, Michael Holquist and Vadim Liapunov, eds. (Austin: University of Texas Press, 1990).]

6 Bakhtin, p. 308–9.

7 On the question of the "return" in hypnotism and suggestion, see *Le Coeur et la raison. L'hypnose en question de Lavoisier à Lacan*, Léon Chertok and Isabelle Stengers (Paris: Payot, 1989).

8 Guattari, *L'Inconscient machinique* (Paris: Editions Recherches, 1979).

9 See the role of dreams in the mythic cartographies of Australian aboriginals, Barbara Glowczewski, *Les Rêveurs du désert* (Paris: Plon, 1989).

10 The reference is to the Polish playwright, painter and philosopher Stanislaw Ignacy Witkiewicz (1885–1939), or "Witkacy" as he referred to himself. Witkacy developed a theory and practice of a non-naturalistic, arealistic theatre which he called "Pure Form", whose goal was to arouse "metaphysical feeling through a grasp of formal constructions", even if the latter were necessarily impure given that works are created by individuals and thus constitute "individualized Form". See "Pure Form in the Theatre" [1921], in *The Witkiewicz Reader*, ed. and trans. Daniel Gerould (Evanston: Northwestern University Press, 1992), pp. 147–52.

11 Sartre theorizes what he calls serial being in Book I, Chapter 4, on "Collectivities" in *The Critique of Dialectical Reason*, Vol I, trans. Alan Sheridan-Smith (London: New Left Books, 1976), p. 256ff. Briefly, the members of a series are united in being turned towards an exterior object, in which they have a common interest, without having a project in common and without necessarily being aware of one another. The unity of the series is not active, rather, it is passive and contingent because it is prefabricated.

Translated by Sophie Thomas

18

A Liberation of Desire

An Interview by George Stambolian

GEORGE STAMBOLIAN – In 1970 the authorities forbade the sale to minors of Pierre Guyotat's novel *Eden, Eden, Eden*. More recently they outlawed and seized the special issue of the review *Recherches* ("Encyclopédie des homosexualités") to which you had made important contributions. You were even taken to court on the matter. How would you explain these reactions by the French government.

FÉLIX GUATTARI – They were rather old-fashioned reactions. I do not think that the present government would behave the same way because there is, on the surface at least, a certain nonchalance regarding the literary and cinematographic expression of sexuality. But I don't have to tell you that this is an even more subtle, cunning, and repressive policy. During the trial the judges were completely ill at ease with what they were being asked to do.

GS – Wasn't it because this issue of *Recherches* treated homosexuality, and not just sexuality?

FG – I'm not sure, because among the things that most shocked the judges was one of the most original parts of this work – a discussion of masturbation. I think that a work devoted to homosexuality in a more or less traditional manner would have had no difficulty. What shocked perhaps was the expression of sexuality going in all directions. And then there were the illustrations – they were what set it off.

GS – In your opinion, what is the best way to arrive at a true sexual liberation, and what dangers confront this liberation?

FG – The problem as I see it is not a sexual liberation but a liberation of desire. Once desire is specified as sexuality, it enters into forms of particularized power, into the stratification of castes, of styles, of sexual classes. The sexual liberation – for example, of homosexuals, or transvestites, or sadomasochists – belongs to a series of other liberation problems among which there is an a priori and evident solidarity, the need to participate in a necessary fight. But I don't consider that to be a liberation as such of desire, since in each of these groups and movements one finds repressive systems.

GS – What do you mean by "desire"?

FG – For Gilles Deleuze and me desire is everything that exists *before* the opposition between subject and object, *before* representation and production. It's everything whereby the world and affects constitute us outside of ourselves, in spite of ourselves. It's everything that overflows from us. That's why we define it as flow [*flux*]. Within this context we were led to forge a new notion in order to specify in what way this kind of desire is not some sort of undifferentiated magma, and thereby dangerous, suspicious, or incestuous. So we speak of machines, of "desiring machines", in order to indicate that there is as yet no question here of "structure", that is, of any subjective position, objective redundancy, or coordinates of reference. Machines arrange and connect flows. They do not recognize distinctions between persons, organs, material flows, and semiotic flows.

GS – Your remarks on sexuality reveal a similar rejection of established distinctions. You have said, for example, that all forms of sexuality are minority forms and reveal themselves as being irreducible to homo–hetero oppositions. You have also said that these forms are nevertheless closer to homosexuality and to what you call a "feminine becoming" [*un devenir féminin*]. Would you develop this idea, in particular by defining what you mean by "feminine"?

FG – Yes, that was a very ambiguous formulation. What I mean is that the relation to the body, what I call the semiotics of the body, is something specifically repressed by the capitalist- socialist-bureaucratic system. So I would say that each time the body is emphasized in a situation – by dancers, by homosexuals, etc. – something breaks with the dominant semiotics that crush these semiotics of the body. In heterosexual relations as well, when a man becomes body, he becomes feminine. In a certain way, a successful heterosexual relation becomes homosexual and feminine. This does not at all mean that I am speaking of women as such; that's where the ambiguity lies, because the feminine relation itself can lose the semiotics of the body and become phallocentric. So it is only by provocation that I say feminine, because I would say first that there is only one sexuality, it is homosexual; there is only one sexuality, it is feminine. But I would add finally: there is only one sexuality, it is neither masculine, nor feminine, nor infantile; it is something that is ultimately flow, body. It seems to me that in true love there is always a moment when the man is no longer a man. This does not mean that he becomes a woman. But because of her alienation woman is relatively closer to the situation of desire. And in a sense, perhaps from the point of view of representation, to accede to desire implies for a man first a position of homosexuality as such, and second a feminine becoming. But I would add as well a becoming as animal, or a becoming as plant, a becoming as cosmos, etc. That's why this formulation is very tentative and ambiguous.

GS – Isn't your formulation based in part on the fact that our civilization has associated body and woman?

FG – No, it's because woman has preserved the surfaces of the body, a bodily *jouissance* and pleasure much greater than that of man. He has concentrated his libido on – one can't even say his penis – on domination, on the rupture of ejaculation: "I possessed you", "I had you". Look at all the expressions like these used by men: "I screwed you", "I made her". It's no longer the totality of the body's surface that counts, it's just this sign of power: "I dominated you", "I marked you". This obsession with power is such that man ultimately denies himself all sexuality. On the other hand, in order to exist as body he is obliged to beg his sexual partners to transform him a bit into a woman or a homosexual. I don't know if homosexuals can easily accept what I'm saying, because I don't mean to say that homosexuals are women. That would be a misunderstanding. But I think that in a certain way there is a kind of interaction between the situation of male homosexuals, of transvestites, and of women. There is a kind of common struggle in their relation to the body.

GS – "Interaction", "transformation", "becoming", "flow" – these words suggest a recognition of our sexual or psychic multiplicity and fluidity which, as I understand it, is an essential aspect of what you call schizoanalysis. What then is the basic difference between schizoanalysis and psychoanalysis which, I believe, you have completely abandoned.

FG – I was Lacan's student, I was analyzed by Lacan, and I practiced psychoanalysis for twelve years; and now I've broken with that practice. Psychoanalysis transforms and deforms the unconscious by forcing it to pass through the grid of its system of inscription and representation. For psychoanalysis the unconscious is always *already there*, genetically programmed, structured, and finalized on objectives of conformity to social norms. For schizoanalysis it's a question of constructing an unconscious, not only with phrases but with all possible semiotic means, and not only with individuals or relations between individuals, but also with groups, with physiological and perceptual systems, with machines, struggles, and arrangements of every nature. There's no question here of transference, interpretation, or delegation of power to a specialist.

GS – Do you believe that psychoanalysis has deformed not only the unconscious but the interpretation of life in general and perhaps of literature as well?

FG – Yes, but even beyond what one imagines, in the sense that it's not simply a question of psychoanalysts or even of psychoanalytical ideas as they are propagated in the commercial press or in the universities, but of interpretative and representational attitudes toward desire that one finds in persons who don't know psychoanalysis, but who put themselves in the position of interpreters, of gurus, and who generalize the technique of transference.

GS – With Deleuze, you have just finished a schizoanalysis of Kafka's work. Why *this* method to analyze and to comprehend literature?

FG – It's not a question of method or of doctrine. It's simply that I've been living with Kafka for a very long time. I therefore tried, together with Deleuze, to put into our work the part of me that was, in a way, a becoming of Kafka. In a sense the book is a schizoanalysis of our relation to Kafka's work, but also of the period of Vienna in 1920 and of a certain bureaucratic eros which crystallized in that period, and which fascinated Kafka.

GS – In a long note you speak of Kafka's joy, and you suggest that psychoanalysis has found only Kafka's sadness or his tragic aspect.

FG – In his *Diaries* Kafka gives us a glimpse of the diabolic pleasure he found in his writing. He says that it was a kind of demonic world he entered at night to work. I think that everything that produces the violence, richness, and incredible humor of Kafka's work belongs to this world of his.

GS – Aren't you really proposing that creation is something joyful, and that this joy can't be reduced to a psychosis?

FG – Absolutely – or to a lack.

GS – In the same book on Kafka you say that a "minor literature", which is produced by a minority in a major language, always "deterritorializes" that language, connects the individual to politics, and gives everything a collective value. These are for you, in fact, the revolutionary qualities of any literature within the established one. Does homosexuality necessarily produce a literature having these three qualities?

FG – Unfortunately, no. There are certainly homosexual writers who conduct their writing in the form of an oedipal homosexuality. Even very great writers – I think of Gide. Apart from a few works, Gide always transcribed his homosexuality and in a sense betrayed it.

GS – Despite the fact that he tried to prove the value of homosexuality in works such as *Corydon*?

FG – Yes, but I wonder if he did it in just one part of his work, and if the rest of his writing isn't different.

GS – In the *Anti-Oedipe* you and Deleuze note that Proust described two types of homosexuality – one that is Oedipal and therefore exclusive, global, and neurotic, and one that is a-Oedipal or inclusive, partial, and localized. In fact, the latter is for you an expression of what you call "transsexuality". So if there are two Gides, aren't there also two Prousts, or at least the possibility of two different readings of his work?

FG – I can't answer for Proust the man, but it seems to me that his work does present the two aspects, and one can justify the two readings because both things in effect exist.

GS – You spoke of the demonic in Kafka. Well, Gide, Proust, and Genet have been accused of being fascinated by the demonic aspect of homosexuality. Would you agree?

FG – To a point. I wonder sometimes, not specifically concerning the three names you mention, if it isn't a matter of persons who were more fascinated by the demonic than by homosexuality. Isn't homosexuality a means of access to the demonic? That is, they are the heirs of Goethe in a certain way, and what Goethe called the demonic was in itself a dimension of mystery.

GS – But the fact remains that in our civilization homosexuality is often associated with the demonic.

FG – Yes, but so is crime. There's a whole genre of crime literature that contains a similar demonic aspect. The demonic or the mysterious is really a residue of desire in the social world. There are so few places for mystery that one looks for it everywhere, in anything that escapes or becomes marginal. For example, there's something demonic in the life of a movie star. That's why it's used by the sensational press.

GS – Doesn't that tell us that we are hungry for the demonic; that we are hungry for things that aren't "natural"; that we have exploited movie stars and homosexuals to satisfy our need for the demonic?

FG – I'm not against that because I'm not at all for nature. Therefore artifice, the artificially demonic, is something that rather charms me. Only it is one thing to live it in a relationship of immediate desire, and another thing to transform it into a repressive machine.

GS – Let's go back to the homosexual writers. I'd like to quote here a remark of yours that struck me. It's the last paragraph of you interview published in the August 1975 issue of *La Quinzaine littéraire*. You say: "Everything that breaks something, everything that breaks with the established order, has something to do with homosexuality, or with a becoming as animal, a becoming as woman, etc. Any break in semioticization implies a break in sexuality. It is therefore not necessary, in my opinion, to raise the question of homosexual writers, but rather to look for what is homosexual, in any case, in a great writer, even if he is in other respects heterosexual". Doesn't this idea contain a new way to approach or perhaps to go beyond a question that has obsessed certain Freudian critics and psychoanalysts – namely, the connection between homosexuality, or all sexuality, and creativity?

FG – Yes, of course. For me, a literary machine starts itself, or can start itself, when writing connects with other machines of desire. I'd like to talk about Virginia Woolf in her relation to a becoming as man which is itself a becoming as woman, because the paradox is complete. I'm thinking about a book I like very much, *Orlando*. You have this character who follows the course of the story as a man, and in the second part of the novel he becomes a woman. Well, Virginia Woolf herself was a woman, but one sees that in order to become a woman writer, she had to follow a certain trajectory of a becoming as woman, and for that she had to begin by being a man. One could certainly find in George Sand things perhaps more remarkable than this. So my question is whether writing as such, the signifier as such, relates to nothing, only to itself, or to power. Writing begins to function in something else, as for example for the Beat Generation in the relation with drugs; for Kerouac in the relation with travel, or with mountains, with yoga. Then something begins to vibrate, begins to function. Rhythms appear, a need, a desire to speak. Where is it possible for a writer to start this literary machine if it isn't precisely outside of writing and of the field of literature. A break in sexuality – therefore homosexuality, a becoming as woman, as addict, as missionary, who knows? It's a factory, the means of transmitting energy to a writing machine.

GS – Can a break in semiotization precede a break in sexuality?

FG – It's not a break in semiotization, but a semiotic connection. I'll give you a more familiar example. Take what are called mad people from a poor background from the point of view of intellectual formation – peasants who have never read anything, who have gone only to grade school. Well, when they have an attack of dissociation, a psychotic attack, it happens sometimes that they begin to write, to paint, to express extraordinary things, extraordinarily beautiful and poetic! And when they are "cured", they return to the fields, to the sugar-beets and asparagus, and they don't write any more at all. You have something of a psychotic attack like that in Rimbaud. When he became normal, he went into commerce; all that stopped. It's always a question of a connection. Something that was a little scholastic writing machine, really without any quality, connects with fabulously perceptive semiotics that start in psychosis, or in drugs, or in war, and that can animate this little writing machine and produce extraordinary things. You have a group of disconnected machines, and at a given moment there is a transmission among them, and everything begins not only to function but to produce an acceleration of operations. So you see, I'm not talking about sexuality. Sexuality is already specified as sex, caste, forms of sexual practice, sexual ritual. But creativity and desire are for me the same thing, the same formula.

GS – I'd still like to ask you the following question. Could you begin the search for what is homosexual in a heterosexual writer with a great writer like, for example, Beckett, whose work offers us a "homosexuality" which seems at times to be the product of extraordinary semiotic connections, and which, in any case, confounds all previous representations and goes beyond them?

FG – I think of those characters who travel by twos and who have no sexual practice because they live completely outside of sexuality, but who nevertheless represent a kind of collective set-up of enunciation, a collective way of perceiving everything that happens. And so many things are happening that it's necessary to select, to narrow down, in order to receive and distill each element, as if one were using a microscope to capture each of the intensities. Indeed, there is perhaps in Beckett a movement outside of the sexes, but then there is the absolutely fabulous relation to objects, a sexual relation to objects. I'm thinking of the sucking stones in *Molloy*.

GS – Then how does one explain the elements of homosexuality, of sadomasochism, in his work?

FG – But that's theater, because if there's a constant in Beckett's work, it's that even when he writes novels, he creates theater, in the sense of a *mise en scène*, a *mise en acte*, of giving something to be seen. So then inevitably, he gathers up representations, but he articulates them to create literature. What's more, Beckett is someone, I think, who was very interested in the insane, in psychopathology, and therefore he picked up a lot of representations. The use he makes of them is essentially literary, of course, but what he uses them for is not a translation, it's a college, it's like a dance. He plays with these representations, or rather, he makes them play.

GS – You said in your article on the cinema[1] that any representation expresses a certain position with respect to power. But I wonder if Beckett hasn't succeeded in writing a politically "innocent" text.

FG – I no more believe in innocence than I do in nature. One thing should be made clear – if one finds innocence, there's reason to worry, there's reason to look not for guilt, of course, because that's the same thing as innocence, it's symmetry, but for what is politically in germination, for a politics *en pointillé*. Take Kafka again. Although his text isn't innocent, the supremely innocent character is K., and yet he is neither innocent nor guilty. He's waiting to enter a political scene. That's not fiction; it's not Borges, because he did enter a political scene in Prague, where one of the biggest political dramas was played around Kafka's work. So, innocence is always the anticipation of a political problem.

GS – Everything that's written is therefore linked in one way or another to a political position?

FG – Yes, with two fundamental axes: everything that's written in refusing the connection with the referent, with reality, implies a politics of individuation of the subject and of the object, of a turning of writing on itself, and by that puts itself in the service of all hierarchies, of all centralized systems of power, and of what Deleuze and I call "arborescences", the regime of unifiable multiplicities. The second axis, in opposition to arborescence, is that of the "rhizome", the regime of pure multiplicities. It's what even innocent texts, even gratuitous games like those of the Dadaists, even collages, cut-ups, perhaps especially these things, will make possible one day to reveal – the pattern of similar breaks in reality, in the social field, and in the field of economic, cosmic, and other flows.

GS – So sexual liberation is not going to rid us of political connections.

FG – Sexual liberation is a mystification. I believe in, and will fight for, the taking of power by other castes and sexual systems, but I believe that liberation will occur when sexuality becomes desire, and that desire is the freedom to be sexual, that is, to be something else at the same time.

GS – How does one escape from this dilemma in which one caste replaces another?

FG – What these liberation movements will reveal by their failures and difficulties is that there really aren't any castes. There's the possibility that society will reform itself through other types of subjective arrangements that are not based on individuals in constellation or on relations of power that communication institutes between speaker and listener. There will be arrangements, I don't know what, based neither on families, nor on communes, nor on groups, where the goals of life, politics, and work will always be conjugated with the analysis of unconscious relations, of relations of micro-power, of micro-fascism. On the day when these movements fix as their goals not only the liberation of homosexuals, women, and children, but also the struggle against themselves in their constant power relations, in their relation of alienation, of repression against their bodies, their thoughts, their ways of speaking, then indeed, we will see another kind of struggle appear, another kind of possibility. The micro-fascist elements in all our relations with others must be found, because when we fight on the molecular level, we'll have a much better chance of preventing a truly fascist, a macro-fascist formation on the molar level.

GS – You and Deleuze often speak of Artaud, who wanted to rid us of masterpieces and perhaps even of written texts. Can one say that the written text already contains a form of micro-fascism?

FG – No, because a written text can be lengthened. Graffiti in the street can be erased or added to. A written text can be contradictory, can be made into a palimpsest. It can be something extremely alive. What is much less alive is a work, *une oeuvre* (and Artaud himself did not write a work) or a book. But then one never writes a book. One picks up on books that have been written; one places oneself in a phylum. To write a book that wants to be an eternal and universal manual, yes, you're right; but to write after one thing and before another, that means participating in a chain, in a chain of love as well.

GS – I'd like to return for a moment to what you said about desire and the problem of liberation. I think of people who might profit from that kind of formulation in order to circumvent the question of homosexuality and the specificity of this struggle, by saying that all that is just sexuality and that sexuality alone matters.

FG – I'm very sympathetic to what you say. It's a bit like what they say to us regarding the struggle of the working class. I understand that, but I'd still like to give the same answer: it's up to the homosexuals. I'm not a worker or a homosexual. I'm a homosexual in my own way, but I'm not a homosexual in the world of reality or of the group.

GS – Yes, but the theories one proposes on homosexuality are always important, and they are never innocent. Before writing *Corydon*, Gide read theories. Before writing *La recherche*, Proust was totally aware of the psychological thought of his time. Even Genet was influenced after the fact by the theories of Sartre. Obviously, it's often writers themselves who are the first to see things that others transform into theories. I'm thinking of Dostoevsky, Proust, and of course, Kafka. You've already begun to use your own theories to study the literature of the past, and they are related perhaps to what may someday be called a 'literature of desire'. Writers, critics, and homosexuals have the choice of accepting or rejecting these theories, or of playing with them. But they can neither forget them nor ignore the words of moralists, psychoanalysts, and philosophers, certainly not today and certainly not in France.

FG – Right, I completely agree. It's truly a pollution. But in any case, what do you think of the few theoretical propositions I've advanced here? It's my turn to question you.

GS – Judging your position by what you've said here and by what you've written, I think that you and Deleuze have seriously questioned Freud's system. You have turned our attention away from the individual and toward the group, and you have shown to what extent the whole Oedipal structure reflects our society's paranoia and has become an instrument for interiorizing social and political oppression. Also, I'd like to quote the following passage from the *Anti-Oedipe*: "We are heterosexuals statistically or in molar terms, but homosexuals personally, whether we know it or not, and finally transsexuals elementarily, molecularly". I can't claim to understand fully this or other aspects of your theory, but you do show that the time has come to address ourselves to the question of sexuality in another way, and that's a kind of liberation.

FG – Well, I want to say to those people who say 'all that is sexuality' that they must go farther and try to see what in fact is the sexuality not only of the homosexual, but also of the sadomasochist, the transvestite, the prostitute, even the murderer, anyone for that matter, in order not to go in the direction of reassurance. They must see what a terrible world of repression they will enter.

GS – Despite the passage from your work I just quoted, when you speak you often cite groups that are always outside the dominant field of heterosexuality.

FG – For me desire is always 'outside'; it always belongs to a minority. For me there is no heterosexual sexuality. Once there's heterosexuality, in fact, once there's marriage, there's no more desire, no more sexuality. In all my twenty-five years of work in the field I've never seen a hetero-sexual married couple that functioned along the line of desire. Never. They don't exist. So don't say that I'm marginalizing sexuality with homosexuals, etc., because for me there is no heterosexuality possible.

GS – Following the same logic there is no homosexuality possible.

FG – In a sense yes, because in a sense homosexuality is counterdepend-ent on heterosexuality. Part of the problem is the reduction of the body. It's the impossibility of becoming a totally sexed body. The sexed body is something that includes all perceptions, everything that occurs in the mind. The problem is how to sexualize the body, how to make bodies desire, vibrate – all aspects of the body.

GS – There are still the fantasies each of us brings. That's often what's interesting in some homosexual writing – this expression of fantasies that are very specialized, very specific.

FG – I don't think it's in terms of fantasies that things are played but in terms of representations. There are fantasies of representations. In desire what functions are semiotic flows of a totally different nature, including verbal flows. It's not fantasies; it's something that functions, words that function, speech, rhythms, poetry. A phantasmal representation in poetry is never the essential thing, no more than is the content. Phantasy is always related to content. What counts is expression, the way express-ion connects with the body. For example, poetry is a rhythm that trans-mits itself to the body, to perception. A phantasy when it operates does not do so as a phantasy that represents a content, but as something that puts into play, that brings out something that carries us away, that draws us, that locks us onto something.

GS – Aren't there phantasies of form as well?

FG – Phantasies of form, phantasies of expression, become in effect micro-fascistic crystallizations. This implies, for example, in scenes of power of a sadomasochistic character: 'Put yourself in exactly this posi-tion. Follow this scenario so that it will produce in me such an effect'. That becomes a kind of phantasy of form, but what counts there is not the application of the phantasy, it's the relation to the other person, it's complicity! Desire escapes from formal redundancies, escapes from power formations. Desire is not informed, informing; it's not information or content. Desire is not something that deforms, but that disconnects, changes, modifies, organizes other forms, and then abandons them.

GS – So, a literary text escapes all categorization as well as any sexuality that can be called one thing or another?

FG – Take any literary work you love very much. Well, you will see that you love it because it is for you a particular form of sexuality or desire, I leave the term to you. The first time I made love with Joyce while reading *Ulysses* was absolutely unforgettable! It was extraordinary! I made love with Kafka, and I think one can say that, truly.

GS – Proust said it: 'To love Balzac; to love Baudelaire'. And he was speaking of a love that could not be reduced to any one definition.

FG – Absolutely. And one doesn't make love in the same way with Joyce as with Kafka. If one began to make love in the same way, there would be reason to worry – one might be becoming a professor of literature!

GS – Perhaps! Then literature can be a liberation of desire, and the text is a way of multiplying the sexes.

FG – Certain texts, texts that function. Nothing can be done about those that don't function. But those that do function multiply our functioning. They turn us into madmen; they make us vibrate.

Notes

This interview appeared in G. Stambolian and Elaine Marks (eds.), *Homosexualities and French Literature: Cultural Contexts/Critical Texts*, Ithaca: Cornell University Press, 1979, pp. 56–69. An earlier discussion of queer issues may be found in Guattari, 'Une sexualisation en rupture' [Interview by C. Deschamps], *La Quinzaine littéraire* 215 (août 1975): 14–15.

1 See Guattari, 'Le divan du pauvre', *Communications* 23 (1975): 96–103.

Translated by George Stambolian

19

Toward a New Perspective on
Identity

An Interview by Jean-Charles Jambon and Nathalie Magnan

J.-C. JAMBON and N. MAGNAN – You invoke subjectivity, an important term in your thought, and one you say gets a bad press. Why?
FÉLIX GUATTARI – Nowadays we try through various means, such as the mass media and standardized behaviour, to neuroleptize subjectivity. Subjectivity is both being in a relation to the other, to inventiveness, to creativity, and at the same time being on the shooting, terrifying threshold of meaninglessness. We do not stand before a subjectivity already given, fitted and packed; rather, we are called to produce it. Confronted with the conditions we meet constantly in daily life something must be done, and the key to this action is the question of assuming extremes. This is just the opposite of turning toward a being already there, already formed, because being is above all becoming, event, production.

All dominant subjectivity is constructed to prevent this alternative which I refer to as *chaosmic*, in the interplay between complexity and chaos. Everything is done to erase what, from the side of creation, of an opening onto the world, can disturb it. These are the things, however, that the pubescent world, the emerging homosexual world, homosexual becoming, knows well . . . .
J & M – How do you define this problematic of becoming? How can it be related to the problematic of homosexuality?
FG – There is in the question of becoming a paradox related to time. It is a matter not of a progressivist view of history, but of seeing how problematizings occur. From a psychogenetic, psychoanalytic point of view, homosexuality is the consequence of a pre-Oedipal, pre-genital fixation – it is always pre-something. We are waiting for the proper genitality, the proper acceptance of castration. You know the song! As for me, I think that, in order to accede to the ontological dimensions thrown into question by homosexuality, we must abandon this progressivist view of time. In effect, it is possible to escape the world of discursivity structured by the poles masculine – feminine, object – subject . . ., that set of dualist categories forever haunted by a transcendent object.

Escapes are possible which allow access to what I call an intensive, existential relation, a relation of immanence that no longer posits a before, an after, a black, a white, a male, a female . . . We are dealing here with a point of crystallization, existence's point of convergence, which is not a pure abstraction, a pure idea, but is rather embodied in a relation to music, to the flesh, in what I call precisely a becoming. This emergence of becoming is linked to a praxis. Put another way, even if we come to be homosexual, before being homosexual we have to become homosexual, to make ourselves homosexual. Here we have the idea of an existential praxis of homosexuality, even if it refers ultimately to the most banal homosexual conjugality, one which rejoins the world of dominant significations. We can hardly dispense with the constitution of micro-territories into which we retreat in order to experience being, to feel recognised. It is a matter of a perspective on identity which has no meaning unless identities explode. We have to return to an ontological pluralism which allows you to become homosexual, but not only within a relation of sexuality, since it also carries this sexuality into the relation to the other, into the cosmos, into multiple dimensions. Otherwise, we fall into the reductionist view of the dominant society, which is of no interest to me whatsoever.

There is always a double movement, on the one hand of closure, and on the other of opening, of a bursting of coordinates that risks unbinding, madness, disorder. This is part of the micro-politics proper to any oppositional group whose territories also depend on what exists outside, on what we call macro-politics – together both call into question the subjectivity I spoke of.

J & M – Reference was often made in the 1960s and 1970s to the notion of identity. How do you understand the latter?

FG – We must start from a multivalent logic, and accept the notion of identity which I call *existential territory*, because we cannot live outside our bodies, our friends, some sort of human cluster, and at the same time, we are bursting out of this situation. The question which poses itself then is one of the conditions which allow the acceptance of the other, the acceptance of a subjective pluralism. It is a matter not only of tolerating another group, another ethnicity, another sex, but also of a desire for dissensus, otherness, difference. Accepting otherness is a question not so much of right as of desire. This acceptance is possible precisely on the condition of assuming the multiplicity within oneself.

J & M – Félix Guattari, "who would like, in his way, to stem the pervading dullness and passivity", never stops, from one book to the next, envisaging a world of new social practices, new aesthetic practices, new practices of the self in its relation to the other, the stranger, and the strange.

Notes

This short interview was originally published in the Parisian gay weekly magazine *Gai Pied Hebdo* 532 (August 1992). *Gai Pied Hebdo* folded in August 1992. This translation appeared in *Angelaki* 1/1 (1993): 96–98. The translator Josep-Anton Fernández published a companion piece in the same issue of *Angelaki* entitled "Félix Guattari: Toward a Queer Chaosmosis" (pp. 99–112) in which he – while drawing on his own experiences of queer cultural activism in Catalonia – uses Guattari's transversalist theory of subjectivity to question, on the one hand, a lingering psychoanalytic sense of failure attached to the invention of queer identity and to suggest, on the other, what a practice of queer reading based on chaosmic principles might look like.

Translated by Joseph–Anton Fernández

20

Genet Regained

Jean Genet died four years after the massacres at Sabra and Shatila, while correcting the proofs of *Un captif amoureux*. He writes that the book grew out of the massacres like a cancer deriving from a single cell whose subsequent course no one could have predicted.[1] It is immense, far exceeding ordinary literary dimensions. Although that may explain why so many critics have overlooked its true significance, it does not excuse them.

The book comes in waves. The same scenes, the same characters ride in with the surf, ten times, twenty times, bringing the flotsam of new memories. *Memories* is Genet's modest subtitle for the book: memories, he says, that should be read as reporting (503). Images, he adds. It is a book of images, a book of margins providing a field for a singular polyphony in which the poet's most secret dimensions interlace with the metaphysical struggles (198 and 448) of the Feyadeen and the Black Panthers, in counterpoint to Genet's own endless wanderings (427).

He writes that the Palestinian revolution was written on nothingness, as an artifact in the void, and asks if the white space between the words is not more real than the black signs themselves (11). Does that mean that for Genet the revolution was only a pretext to make literature? Then in what way is he different from the poets of the revolution he so cruelly mocks? (420) But it is obvious that the routing of his Palestinian experience through writing is in no way comparable to a vulgar enterprise in literary recuperation. It never even occurred to him that he could be open to that accusation.

Of course Genet's visceral rejection of the writer's position, which would have placed him on the bourgeois side of the barricade, did not escape Jean-Paul Sartre's notice.[2] But that did not prevent Sartre from approaching Genet from an exclusively literary angle and considering it his inescapable destiny to "end" in literature. In hindsight, this appears to be the reason why the colossal and sumptuous monument – not to mention mausoleum – that Sartre built to Genet in the form of a 700 page preface has proven unequal to the breadth of character later displayed by Genet. Sartre missed the wellspring of the process that was his life and work. According to Sartre, Genet underwent three metamorphoses: thief, aesthete, and writer. These metamorphoses took him successively from act to gesture, from gesture to word, and then from word to the work (423). By his account, we are dealing with the transformation of a perverted psychopath into a "rhétoriqueur" who is a captive of the imagination and whose soul has been duly pacified. "Genet, the sole hero of his books, has fallen entirely into the imaginary, he becomes the imaginary *in person*" (Sartre, 422). Although Sartre's existential psychoanalysis largely dissociated itself from Freudian conceptions, it is evident that it retained a certain reductionist schematicism. Or perhaps I should say reductionist tics. He compares Genet's works to religions on the road to humanization that replace human sacrifice with symbolic sacrifice (485); the writing of each of his books functions as a "cathartic attack of possession" or psychodrama (544); *Our Lady of the Flowers* is equated with a detoxication of narcissism (449); and after ten years of literature that Sartre says are the equivalent of psychoanalytic treatment (544), it is triumphantly announced that the patient has been cured and has finally resolved to start a small family. "Somewhere between Saint-Raphaël and Nice a house is awaiting him. I have seen him there, surrounded with children, playing with the older ones and dressing up the younger ones, passionately discussing their upbringing" (581). A miracle of literature! And above all, pure Sartre! Naive, touching, and secretly conformist. All that is fine and well, but it is obviously not the way the future was to be. Genet would never start a family; he would never "fixate" on a territory or choose a house, except, to paraphrase Sartre, in the nihilation mode. This brings to mind the daydream Genet relates in *Un captif amoureux* of a home set in a "nonspatial" place (430). The bewitchment is immediately threatened by the superimposition of another, older image from Jordan. A high Palestinian official points to a beautiful house and offers to have the PLO rent it for him. The house suddenly turns dirty and gray in Genet's mind (433).

Thus Genet did not fall into either aestheticism or literary professionalism. Being recognized as one of the century's greatest writers did not prompt him to end his aesthetic wandering, or even to renounce theft. Figuratively, he continued to equate theft with poetic apperception;[3] in reality, he carefully maintained contact with former or potential convicts,[4] and on occasion would swindle his editors and partners, some of whom, it is said, obligingly accommodated the maneuver. Freudian psychogenetic stages, even as revised by Sartre, cannot explain why, if the condition of the writer suited him so well, he was led to end all literary and dramatic production for twenty years. And what of the dazzling comeback a few years before his death? In my opinion, the only way to begin to understand it is to say that "before" the life and "before" the work there has always been a subterranean process operating in this exceptional being, an essential dynamic, a creative madness that literally subjugated him. This is what he was getting at in a 1983 interview when he said that what had enabled him to write an article on Sabra and Shatila was not the books he had written earlier, but the disposition that had led to those books.[5] In relation to this primary disposition, the life and work were always mere by-products. As are the usual dichotomies between the real and the imaginary. In the same interview, he says that his association with the Black Panthers and later the Palestinians was more a function of the real world than the world of dreams or grammar. But he adds: "Of course, if you take the analysis far enough, it becomes evident that dreaming also belongs to the real world. Dreams are realities". It is clear that Genet never progressed through the famous stages of development and adaptation to the real that according to some authors take shape around weaning, toilet training, the Oedipus complex and castration, and pre-and post-pubescent latency periods. For Genet, everything worked together. He never let go of his dreams and infantile "perversions". But that did not prevent him from being involved in contemporary historical realities in the most lucid, "adult" fashion. I might add that it would be futile to try to save the psychogenetic schema by recourse to the structuralistic triad that adds the Symbolic to the Real-Imaginary dyad. For it is obvious that the triumphant accession to the "symbolic order" through literature and theater had no redemptive effect in his case. Sublimation decidedly did not work for him! His writing resulted not in a dialectical uplifting, but in an exacerbation of his contradictions and upheavals.

We must look elsewhere, to something that orders the real, the imaginary, and creation in a different way. Something that makes them not separate agencies but rather mutually engendering. An imaginary-symbolic productive of new realities; a subjective disposition capable of receiving imaginary charges conveyed by the real. We could legitimately combine statements in which Genet recoils his subjectivity into the most "limited" reality with others in which, conversely, the real irrupts outside of itself in an "objective" process of subjectification. This would provide us with a smooth transition from the thesis that *Un captif amoureux* is merely reporting, to passages (so surprising from an apologist for betrayal in all its forms; 367) in which he worries about betraying the informative mission he was initially assigned because he has ordered the episodes he lived through in the Palestinian resistance according to the apparent disorder of dream images (416), to passages in which, finally, he states that the real is more inventive than his nightmares and memories (460).

The function of oscillation, eclipse, evanescence, or effacement in the work of Genet deserves theoretical elaboration. It is a recurring theme.

One of his prototypical images of it is steam on a windowpane. When it dissipates, the landscape becomes visible again, and it seems that the room could extend forever (440). Adjacent to this image – for one image calls forth another – is that of the hand crisscrossing the blackboard erasing chalk writing (440). Deterritorialization of space, time, and words. The fedayee is also essentially a disappearing being; in one passage, a fedayee turns a bend, leaving only his back and his shadow in view (32). His struggle as such also has to do with eclipse. Genet says that he watched the resistance as though it would disappear tomorrow (33). In the final analysis, it is Genet who obliterates himself, infinitely shrinking as he moves toward the horizon (160). But we must be careful not to present these merely as phenomena of annihilation. These efface-ments leave trails like stroboscopic afterimages of other universes; their shadow play heralds the coming to light of other existential dimensions (407). When he was working on *The Screens*, he asked that Roger Blin's production "illuminate the world of the dead";[6] there is no doubt that even what he had in mind was a subjugation of the living. On the eve of his own death, he sometimes felt that his skin glowed like a lampshade around a lit bulb (425). It should not be thought, however, that these transformations herald mystical revelations. On the contrary, they par-ticipate in an entire life's labor on perception, imagination, and their various modes of semiotization.

It was wrong for Sartre to project onto Genet his conception of the imaging unconscious as a derealizing function (Sartre, 146). In doing so he condemned him to encirclement by an imaginary wholly invested by malevolent phantasmagorias; and he denied him any effective escape from accursed solitude. It is true that Genet's creative process always made a strong appeal to fabulation[7] (masturbatory or otherwise) but his fundamental aim nevertheless remained a poetics with social impact. The writing of his first texts is inseparable from his experience of the prison condition. His "theatre of cruelty" revolved around themes of prostitu-tion, negritude, colonial wars. We must not forget that *Un captif amoure-ux* began as a militant work written on the personal request of Yasser Arafat, coupled with more general reflections on the movements of the 1960s and after (the Zengakuren, the Red Guards, the Berkeley revolt, the Black Panthers, May '68 in Paris, the Palestinians; 442). Of course, he was careful not to give his blanket approval to these revolutionary undertakings. He rejected their wooden language and dogmatism; he had a fair estimation of their theatricality for the benefit of the media (390); and he was remarkably lucid in his denunciation of certain bureaucratic and corrupt aspects of the Palestinian movement.[8] What fascinated him was everything in those movements that transcended particular interests, their fundamental precariousness as well as their metaphysical concerns.

He was especially captivated by one of their essential mechanisms: what could be called their image function. An example is the ways of being and dressing adopted by militant Black Panthers, which practically overnight changed the ways blacks as a whole perceived the color of their skin and the texture of their hair. Genet saw in these dimensions of the body, sex, dance, intonations, and gestures, a whole enunciative texture – we could say a whole eventuation [*évènementiation*] infinitely more profound than today's fashion mentality. He speaks of fabulous images whose potency is based on being at once exemplary and singularizing, and on conspicuousness rather than power (354). I believe that it is valid to enlarge the scope of this kind of expression to include all imaginary formations, which then acquire a special capacity to bridge times of life and existential levels as well as social segments, and, why not?, even cosmic stratifications: a capacity of transversality. We must look for Genet in all of these places simultaneously. This indeed makes him a man of our century, one who, perhaps more than any other, brought forth new ways of seeing. I repeat: Genet is a man of the real. By which I mean, a man of the future real. He is not a saint, as Sartre pretends to think; and he is certainly not a saint condemned to perpetually metamorphose into a vermin, and whose calling it is to convey history into mythic categories (Sartre, 13). In fact, myths and their images are only important to him to the extent that collective operators succeed in endowing them with historical consistency. Under these conditions, becoming a fabulous and solitary hero who is exemplary and therefore singular (354) is no longer the opposite of collective fusion (206). Becoming the hero of forms of sensibility yet to come is in perfect accord with his will to effacement, and even his desire for invisibility.[9] Bringing his dreamer function (206) to the Panthers and later the Palestinians is not a derealization of these movements. It is perhaps even a way of endowing them with a more intense subjective consistency.

I will apply the term "processive praxis" to this creative agency that is set in place "before" the manifestation of the life and work and that enables Genet to move from derealizing fabulation to fabulous images productive of the real. This praxis is composed not of three stages but of three levels – the modular, the polyphonic, and synaptic.

1 The Level of Modular Crystallizations

A multitude of meaning fragments sweep helter-skelter across the world and the psyche. Anyone who is highborn, in other words whose reflexes and mind have been duly normalized, knows how to discipline or silence these essentially heretical, dissident, and perverse voices. But Genet was lowborn, and never contemplated a rebirth into the common world. ("I was always haunted by the idea of a murder that would irremediably separate me from your world".) Rather than experiencing these whirlwinds as so many calamities or abysses of anxiety and guilt, Genet opted to accommodate himself to them, to tame and transmute them. ("Repudiating the virtues of our world, criminals hopelessly agree to organize a forbidden universe".)[10] He gains partial control over this primary processiveness of meaning through rhythms, refrains, passwords, and magico-mnemonic formulas. Sartre had a supberb formula for *Our Lady of the Flowers*: he said it was a collection of Genet's erotic talismans (Sartre, 448). But it is crucial to understand that this entire labor of primary recrystallization of meaning involves one's perception of the world as much as it does language. I needed to drill into a language mass, he writes in *The Thief's Journal*; echoing this in *Un captif amoureux* he describes prison as a world full of ready-made holes and alveoli, in each of which a man invents a time and rhythm of his own (442). In the first case, the signifier leads the dance; in the second, the signified. Actually, the traditional opposition between expression and content proves relative and inadequate. What matters to Genet is not the communication of a message, but the constitution of an expression that overspills its linguistic components in every direction (97). The figures of the signifier and those of the signified must converge in such a way that a matter of expression fertilizes a context, and, reciprocally, a context imprints its impulses, its paradigmatic perversions, upon discursive chains of linguistic or nonlinguistic nature.

Let us consider these various access routes from the angle of a particularly important module that crystallizes around the names "Fatah" and "Palestinian". Genet begins by scrutinizing the scriptive manner of "Fatah". He notes that the word was artificially forged from the Arab acronym for Palestinian Liberation Movement, FTH (31). Since this does not help him, he looks to other possibilities for the clandestine germination of the semantic content. We should note that at this stage he confines himself to the significations that surface in Arabic; he does not indulge in "free association". The first significations Fatah yield are crack, fissure, and God-given victory. Then it yields "mefta", or key, the fact that "Fatah" conceals three fundamental letters. Then comes "Fatiha", the

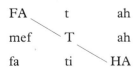

opening sura of the Koran. This triple transformation diagonally reconstitutes the original structure of the acronym, FA.TH.HA. So here is the signifier in the position of structural key to the signifier! A child's game, a philologist's game, exclaims Genet. However, that is not what is essential. The essential thing is that this association of ideas has enabled him to join three universes of reference in a single constellation: the sexual, the divine, and the revolutionary (31). We are not far from Freud; but it is Freud in his prime, in the mad years of *The Interpretation of Dreams* and *Jokes and Their Relation to the Unconscious*.

The word "Palestinian" transports us from the terrain of letters and etymologies (Palestinian = Philistine) to that of phonemes and vocal timbre. The mere sound of "Palestini . . .", Genet explains, triggers a shudder in him, an affect of sadness linked to a key image: a tomb in the form of a watchful shadow at the foot of a Palestinian fighter (444). This rectangular shadow is like the label of his singularity, the guarantee of his total lucidity in the face of death, in contrast to the white world, which moves without shadows (468). Here we have the same type of modular schema; light is treated by shadow in numerous variations on the theme of white and black in relation to writing: Blacks in white America are like ink on a white page, they are the signs that give history its meaning.[11] Beyond Manicheism, the function of the Fatah-Palestinian module seems to be to connect opposites at the most extreme point of their antagonism. Even the rivalry between "Palestine will prevail" and "Israel will live" seems to harbor traces of a hyperparadoxical complicity between landless peoples of the past and present. It has been said that the primary quality of the Palestinians is their resolute assumption of finitude, whereas the Israelis persist in nurturing pernicious dreams of eternal life.[12]

I could have taken more deterritorialized modules to illustrate this first, modular level of processive praxis. I have already mentioned the problematic of drilling holes in the real and language. There is also the flattening technique applied to Hamza's mother, who is described as being like a cardboard figure (477); this prior modular treatment is necessary in order for her to play her key role in the "family romance" Genet forges. And there is the extraordinary cardless card game that stretches like a red thread through the entire work, an abstract machine for chipping at and kneading the real and preparing it for new possibilities. Of course, modular concatenations similar to these are used to underpin the creations of many writers. The first example we would have to cite is Proust, with his procession of leitmoifs, fertile moments, and refrains.[13] But Genet puts traits of intensity to a different usage. He does not lock himself into the universe of memory. On the contrary, the process is always exposing itself to encounters with heterogeneous realities apt to shift its course, to make it deviate significantly from preexisting equilibriums, or even to overturn it. I am not saying that Proust goes in circles. An entire world is brought to expression in his work. But it is a world mastered in the manner of the "well-tempered clavier"; it is a world that is definitely closed. There is something (and perhaps in another sense, something less) in Genet: an opening onto the expanses of the sea, and the insistent presence of death, finitude, and the danger of total and permanent incomprehension.

2 The Polyphonic Level of Fabulous Images

On this level, it is no longer a question of extracting from each primary module all the voices that can be expressed through it, but rather of conjugating heterogeneous voices, widening fields of virtuality, enabling the emergence of new universes of reference and of singular modalities of enunciation. In a word: producing another real in correlation with another subjectivity.

It can happen that a module engenders significations that are so loose and so opposite one another that the module loses control. An example of this occurs in *Funeral Rites* when Genet writes the word "Hitlerian" and sees the Church of the Trinity swoop down on him like the eagle of the Third Reich.[14] Things are very different when two modules entertain what Bakhtin calls dialogical relations. Not only are the most outlandish exchanges sustainable, but they can even engender a surplus-value of meaning, a supplement of singularity, an existential taking on of consistency. Proust superimposed the love play of a bumblebee and an orchid onto the voyeuristic revelation of guilty relations between Charlus and Jupien.[15] In Genet, the flower mates with the convict: "Convict garb is striped pink and white. Though it was at my heart's bidding that I chose the universe wherein I delight, I at least have the power of finding therein the many meanings I wish to find: there is a close relationship between flowers and convicts".[16] Two, three universes crystallize together: the penal colony, flowers, and poetry. Anything else? Excitation. Genet specifies in a note that it results from the oscillation between flowers and convicts.

We have already noted in the example of the cardless card game that a transmitter module can override the terms it conjoins and set to work on its own account. The card game is the Obon festival in Japan during which the dead are supposed to visit the living (40); it is what Genet calls dry masturbation (44); it is Lieutenant Mubarak's air guitar (290). It is many things. And in the final analysis, it is nothing in particular, it is a style, a principle of deterritorialization. "Fabulous images" take this

autonomy further. We will now take a more detailed look at their modalities of expression. The best example is Mubarak, a Sudanese lieutenant and high-ranking PLO official. It is impossible to evaluate how much
of Genet's portrait of this composite figure is his own imagination.[17]
Described as a black man with tribal markings, a lover of glitter, a
fabulous animal, a former warrior and graduate of Sandhurst Academy,
a reader of Spinoza, a dancer to African rock, a pervert, a voyeur, a pimp,
a whore, this "black bitch" is one of the rare protagonists of *Un captif
amoureux* who succeeds in bringing Genet out of the sexual reserve he
maintained – at least psychically – during his Palestinian travels (265).
But what is it exactly about this extravagant character that really affects
him? It seems to be certain traits with various avatars: the quality of his
voice (197), his way of speaking French like Maurice Chevalier . . . and
his limp, something both he and Genet had in common. And also his
silhouette. That is very important. We must mention in this connection
a curious transferral of existential cut-outs between the narrator and the
Sudanese that took place one day when the latter was doing a playful
imitation of the way Genet walked, in response to an imitation of him
Genet had just done. He represented Genet climbing and descending a
stairway; Genet saw himself before his own eyes, a gigantic figure out-
lined against a dark sky. He understood that he was seeing himself for the
first time, and that it was not in a mirror called the psyche but through
an eye or eyes that had discovered him (288–89). The point is that the
fabulous image has nothing to do with the image one confronts in
the mirror of the psyche or in that of pure alterity. No more mirage of the
reflection-reflecting and the reflection-reflected; no more imaginary
burdened with identifications, phantasies or anything of the kind. What
Genet owes to Mubarak is the ability to apprehend himself from an angle
and in a light all the truer and more real for having been reworked,
rewritten, repainted, and restaged. In return, Genet recalls Mubarak in a
polychromy with violet and Prussian blue as the dominant colors (394).
A black of all colors[18] who expands Genet's understanding of the constellation of universes of sex, violence, and theological virtue around which
he has revolved for so long. A black chameleon at the crossroads of his
dream of Africa, his prison loves, black America, and the region of
shadow in the Palestinian struggles. Gone are the days of Archibald's
imprecations in *The Blacks*: "Let Negroes negrify themselves. Let them
persist to the point of madness in what they're condemned to, in their
ebony, in their odor, in their yellow eyes, in their cannibal tastes".[19]
Black is no longer the reverse of white, or its limit. It has become a probe
capable of exploring values that have been repressed in the West and
logics that suspend "discontinuity and number, those two names of
death" (Sartre, 464). We will have to make way for yet another enuncia-

tive procedure, for the fabulous image in turn displays limits. Mubarak wavers, cracks, and shatters in a fragmentation of body and world; there is a threat that the solution that will impose itself will be for the process to become continual. Genet is surprised one day to witness the world bisected. It was sunset and Mubarak was walking in front of him. Mubarak was the knife, or rather the handle of the knife that was cutting the world in two, separating the shadows from the light (448).

3 The Synaptic Level of Existential Operators

Both the modular concatenation of signalling and cosmic fluctuations and the "fabulous" harmonics produced by voices not generally destined to meet remove the subject from the creative process, placing it in a position of passive contemplation or active orchestration. Now it is enunciation as such on which the subject sets its sights, in something like a return to the idea of primordial swallowing. Is this a mad attempt at self-mastery ("selfness", in Sartre's terminology) or a methodical project of producing a mutant subjectivity? It will all depend on the ability of the process in question to escape being locked into phantasy.

One day in October 1971 Genet met two Palestinians in a Jordanian refugee camp: Hamza and his mother. This meeting which profoundly troubled him for reasons he could never comprehend, led him to reevaluate his relation to the Palestinian revolution and created an axis for the book that was to be *Un captif amoureux*. It provided the basis for what I call an existential operator of synapse, in other words an assemblage that is simultaneously psychic, material, and social, and is capable of instituting a new type of enunciation and consequently a new subjective production.

Hamza was a seventeen-year-old fighter to whose care Genet was entrusted by his Palestinian friends. They spent only a few hours together, before and after the young man went into action against the Jordanian army. Genet had no further news of him for fourteen years. That first night, Hamza's mother lodged Genet in her son's room. He recalls with emotion how she entered the room in semi-darkness to bring him a Turkish coffee and a glass of water on a platter. He remained silent, his eyes closed. He understood that the woman had served him as she would her son. Genet was smitten by these people he hardly knew; they became a fixed point or pole star in relation to which he would regulate his existence. This fixed point, he writes, is perhaps named love. But what kind of love was this that imbued him for fourteen years after having known two people a total of twenty-two hours? (460)

We find the same elements of fabulous conversation that we described earlier. We find the same semiotic distortions, in particular Hamza's silhouette against thick shadow. When Genet evokes the mother, for example, he sees the son still at her side, immense, guarding over her with rifle in hand. It got to the point that he never imagines a figure alone. There would always be two, one of normal appearance and another of giant, mythic proportions, one human another fabulous (241). Coupled with this labor of fabulous image creation is another labor I will term sanctification. The mother–Hamza couple is literally bound to the Pieta–Christ couple in a kind of family romance akin to those used by certain children to attribute themselves noble origins; but, Genet, not content to cease being an orphan, voluptuously occupies all possible positions: man, woman, crucifixion, victim, what have you (348, and especially 241–43). He had already undertaken a similar religious transformation long ago, in his magnification of the penal colony: "I call the Virgin Mother and Guiana the Comforters of the Afflicted".[20] But the Holy Land obviously lends itself better to this kind of operation. We will remark in passing that both cases involve a deterritorialized land; we note that the strength of Genet's nostalgia for the penal colony depends on its having been abolished, on the fact that it is a dream prison; and that Genet's sympathy for the Palestinians' desire to recover their land is proportionate to the unlikelihood of its realization. But this is not what is essential. The essential thing is the supplement of processing potential conferred upon the fabulous image by this religiously derived narrative grafting. The image is no longer simply a crossroads of heterogeneous paths; it sets to work on its own account. In a sense, it becomes self-sufficient, self-referential, self-processing. This does not preclude it widening its field of action on memory and events. Like the fabulous image, it functions to produce a singular temporality, a specific way of making subjectivity discursive. But it operates in an even more open manner; it stops circling the contours of an icon, and instead continuously deploys new lines of possibility. It was in his prison days that Genet first tested his self-divination procedure: "It was within me that I established this divinity – origin and disposition of myself. I swallowed it. I dedicated to it songs of my own invention. At night I would whistle. The melody was a religious one. It was slow. Its rhythm was somewhat heavy. I thought I was thereby entering into communication with God: which is what happened, God being only the hope and fervor contained in my song".[21] One has to admit, however, that this God seems a little stale! In fact, this coupling of the Virgin and prison represented a veritable tour de force in the attempt to surmount a crack in the universe that might have seemed irrevocable and incurable. We are not far from Sartre's equation, imaginary = derealization = evil = solitude (Sartre, 183–84). With Lieutenant

Mubarak, however, good and evil, white and black begin to entertain different, complex relations. Reality not only opens, but it also assumes an infinity of virtualities. His figure, however, remains too massively mythological; it has limited ability to enter into finespun procedures of subjectification, and as we have seen, in the end itself becomes the agent of a new cleavage of the world. Everything is different in the case of synaptic double articulation:

$$\text{Genet} \begin{cases} \text{Hamza/mother} \\ \\ \text{Christ/Virgin} \end{cases}$$

The term synaptic is used to indicate that we may justifiably expect this operator to yield something entirely different than mere afterimages or harmonics of meaning; we may expect a pragmatic effect, an existential surplus-value, the extraction of new constellations of universes of reference. The relations are now less dependent on identification, less personological – however tempted we may be to reduce them to Oedipus and incest. Henceforth, the numen will no longer stick to the image pan, but will instead be distilled in praxes that are much more molecular and better able to transform everyday perception of the world as well as its eschatological horizons.[22] Moreover, Hamza is not even a believer, in Islam or in Christianity. It would change nothing if he were. When Genet hears word of him fourteen years later, the fact that he is married and living in Germany, and is probably the father of a gaggle of children, does not desacralize him; it does not deactivate the existential operator. For the good reason that its efficacy does not reside in its visible gears but in a machine of abstract intensities that conjugates universes of pleasure, poetry, freedom, and impending death in innovative ways. That machine resolved something for Genet. It gave birth to another Genet. The rift, the rending is gone. He explains that this couple placed him in a continuum of time, space, and parental, family, and national belonging (242). Even the present, past, and future seem to want to superimpose themselves in one of those retroactive smoothings of time so dear to René Thom: the Palestinian revolution seems to be integral to Genet's oldest memories (288). What if now even death were in truth no more than a resurrection of the moment, a wellspring of absence, of potential . . . . To have been dangerous a fraction of a second, beautiful a fraction of a second, to have been anything, and then to rest. What more is there? (318)

Notes

"Genet retrouvé" was published in the *Revue d'études Palestiniennes* 21 (1986): 27–42. It subsequently appeared in Guattari's *Cartographies schizoanalytiques* (Paris: Galilée, 1989), pp. 269–90. This translation was published by the now defunct arm of the Museum of Modern Art in Los Angeles, the Los Angeles Institute of Contemporary Art, in their similarly defunct magazine called *Journal: A Contemporary Art Magazine* 47/5 (Spring 1987): 34–40.

1 Jean Genet, *Un captif amoureaux* (Paris: Gallimard, 1986), p. 502. (*Trans.* At this time [1986], permission to translate quotes from this book is not available from the owners of the English language rights. It has therefore been necessary to paraphrase or delete passages cited by Guattari. Subsequent page references to the French edition are placed in parenthesis.)

2 Jean-Paul Sartre, *Saint Jean Genet: Actor and Martyr*, trans. Bernard Frechtman (New York: George Brazilier, 1963). Especially "On the Fine Arts Considered as Murder", pp. 483–542.

3 Genet, *The Thief's Journal*, trans. B. Frechtman (New York: Grove Press, 1964), p. 243.

4 Ibid., p. 250.

5 Rudiger Wischenbart, "Conversation avec Jean Genet et Lelia Chahid", *Revue d'études Palestiniennes*.

6 Genet, *Letters to Roger Blin*, trans. Richard Seaver (New York: Grove Press, 1969), p. 5.

7 *The Thief's Journal*, p. 86 ff.

8 The references are very numerous on this point. See in particular pages 125, 128, 172, 282, 309, 391, 459, 462.

9 Interview with R. Wischenbart.

10 *The Thief's Journal*, p. 9.

11 Page 290. See also pp. 11, 297.

12 Pages 91, 455. At times Genet cannot refrain from making appalling tips of the hat in the direction of the cruelest adversaries of the Palestinian refugees. Examples are a very beautiful passage on the dance of the Bedouin soldiers (p. 95 ff); the incredible homage to Israeli brutality on p. 449, and the tender description of fake gay (or real?) Israeli agents sent to Beirut to assassinate Palestinian leaders (pp. 218–222).

13 See F. Guattari, *L'Inconscient machinique* (Paris: Recherches, 1979), "Les ritournelles du Temps perdu", pp. 239–336.

14 Genet, *Funeral Rites*, trans. B. Frechtman (New York: Grove Press, 1969), p. 10.

15 Marcel Proust, *Remembrance of Things Past*, vol. 2, *Cities of the Plain*, trans. C.K.Scott Moncrieff and Terence Kilmartin (New York: Random House, 1981), pp. 624–29.

16 *The Thief's Journal*, p. 9.

17 Pages 194, 196, 208, 211, 265, 272, 278, 288–89, 296, 421, 406, 423, 448.

18 The illustration that automatically comes to mind is the series by Gérard Fromanger entitled "Un balayeur noir à la porte de sa benne" (1974).

19 Genet, *The Blacks*, trans. B. Frechtman (New York: Grove Press, 1960), p. 52.

20 *The Thief's Journal*, p. 254.

21 Ibid., p. 86.

22 This theme recurs several times, with an inversion in the age relations between mother and son (231, 240), and with a slip of the pen that makes Mary Jesus's wife (307).

Translated by Brian Massumi

PART VI

Red and Green Micropolitical Ecologies

21

Capitalistic Systems, Structures and Processes

With Eric Alliez

The question of capitalism can be envisaged from a number of angles, but those of economy and the social constitute a necessary starting point.

First, capitalism can be defined as a general function of semiotization of a certain mode of production, circulation and distribution. Capitalism, the "method" of Capital, will be considered as a specific procedure of valorization of commodities, such as goods, activities and services, founded on index and symbolization systems drawn from a particular syntax and allowing the over-coding and control of the management running it.

This "formalist" definition can be sustained because, despite being indissociable from those of the technical and socio-economic arrangements [*agencements*] to which it is related, such a function of semiotization has no less an intrinsic coherence. From this point of view the styles [*modes*] of capitalistic "writing" (cf. Derrida) could be compared to the mathematical corpus whose axiomatic consistency is not called in question by the application which might be made in extra-mathematical fields. We propose to call this first level the *semiotic system* of capitalism, or the *semiotic of capitalistic valorization*.

Second, capitalism appears more as the generator of a particular type of social relations; here regulation, laws, usages and practices come to the fore. The procedures of economic writing may vary; what counts is the maintenance of a certain type of social order founded on the division of roles between those who monopolize power and those who are subject to it, and that just as much in the areas of work and economic life, as in those of life-styles, knowledge and culture. All these divisions, with those of sex, age-groups and race, end up by constituting "at the arrival point" the concrete segments of the socius. This second level will be defined as the *structure of segmentarity*, a level which seems also to maintain a certain degree of internal coherence whatever the transformations or the upheavals imposed upon it by history.

It is clear, however, that the "codage" of capitalism does not proceed from a "table of law" defining once and for all inter-human relations.

The order which it imposes evolves just as does its own economic syntax. In this domain, as in many others, the influences are not unilateral, we are never confronted with a one-way causality. Neither is it a question of being satisfied with a simple opposition between semiotic system and structure of segmentarity. These two aspects always go together, and their distinction will become pertinent only to the extent that it allows us to clarify the interactions which each has with a third equally important, level: that of the *process of production*. Let us be clear straight-away that, in the present perspective, this lesser level should not be identified with what Marxists designate by the expression "relations of production" or "economic relations of the infrastructure". Doubtless our category of "process of production" subsumes the Marxist one, but it goes largely beyond it in the infinitely extensible domain of concrete and abstract machines. These processual components have therefore to include material forces, human labor, social relations as well as in-vestments of desire. In the cases where the *ordering* of these compo-nents leads to an enrichment of their potentialities – where the whole exceeds the sum of the parts – these processual interactions shall be called diagrammatic – and we shall speak of machinic surplus-value.

Is it still legitimate, under these conditions, to continue to envisage capitalism as a general entity? Will not these formal definitions which are proposed for it be condemned to obliterate its diversity in time and space? What is the place of history in capitalism? The only element of historical continuity which seems capable of characterizing its various experiences seems to be precisely the processual character of its sphere of production, in the very wide sense we have just proposed. One can "find" capitalism in all places and at all times, as soon as one considers it either from the point of view of the exploitation of proletarian classes, or from that of the setting-to-work of means of economic semiotization facilitat-ing the rise of the great markets (paper money, money in circulation, credit, etc.). Nevertheless it remains true that the capitalisms of the last three centuries have really "taken off" only from the moment when the sciences, the industrial and commercial techniques and society have tied their futures together within a single process of generalized transforma-tion (a process combined with deterritorialization). And everything leads us to believe that in the absence of such a "machinic knot", of such a proliferation of the "mecanosphere", the societies in which capitalist forms have developed would have been incapable of overcoming the major shocks which are brought about by world crises and wars and would certainly have ended up in the same sorts of blind alleys that were experienced by certain other great civilizations: an interminable agony or a sudden "inexplicable" death.

Capitalism would therefore represent a paroxystic form of integration of different types of machinisms: technical machines, economic machines, but also conceptual machines, religious machines, aesthetic machines, perceptual machines, desiring machines. Its work of semiotization – the method of *Capital* – would form at the same time both a sort of collective computer[1] of society and production, and a "homing head" of innovations adapted to its internal drives. In these conditions, its raw material, its basic diet, would not be, directly, human labor or machine labor but the whole gamut of the *means of semiotic pilotage* relative to the instrumentation, to the insertion in society, to the reproduction, to the circulation of many component parts concerned by the process of machinic integration. What capitalizes capital is semiotic power. But not just any power – because in that case there would be no way of demarcating the earlier forms of exploitation – a semiotically deterritorialized power. Capitalism confers on certain social sub-aggregates a capacity for the selective control of society and production by means of a system of collective semiotization. What specifies it historically is that it only tries to control the different components which come together to maintain its processual character. Capitalism does not seek to exercise despotic power over all the wheels of society. It is even crucial to its survival that it manages to arrange marginal freedoms, relative spaces for creativity. What is of primary importance to it is the mastery of the semiotic wheels which are essential for the key productive arrangements and especially of those which are involved in changing machine processes (the adjustments of machine power). Doubtless it is obliged by the force of history to interest itself in all domains of the social – public order, education, religion, the arts, etc. But, originally, this is not its problem; it is first of all and continuously a *mode of evaluation and technical means of control* of the power arrangements and their corresponding formulations.

All its "mystery" comes from the way it manages to articulate, within one and the same general system of inscription and equivalence, entities which at first sight would seem radically heterogeneous: of material and economic *goods*, of individual and collective human *activities*, and of technical, industrial and scientific *processes*. And the key to this mystery lies in the fact that it does not content itself with standardizing, comparing, ordering, informatizing these multiple domains but, with the opportunity offered by these diverse operations, it extracts from each of them one and the same *machinic surplus-value* or *value of machinic exploitation*. It is its capacity to re-order through a single system of semiotization the most heterogeneous machinic values which gives capitalism its hold, not only over material machines of the economic sphere (artisanal, manufacturing, industrial, etc.) but equally over the non-material machines working in the heart of human activities (productive–unproductive, public–private, real–imaginary, etc.).

Each "manifest" economic market thus displays in parallel different "latent" areas of machinic values, values of desire, aesthetic values, etc., which we could call values of content. The conscious and "flat" economic valorization is thus doubled by modes of "deep" valorization, relatively unconscious if compared to explicit systems of exchange valorizations. But the fact that these values of content are made, in the framework of the given relations of production, to give an account of themselves to the formal economic values is not without incidence on their internal organization. They find themselves somehow in spite of themselves, brought within a logic of equivalence, brought into a generalized market of values of reference – and the whole problematic which turns around the division use value/exchange value is thus shown to be completely invalid by the fact that the setting-up of this logic of capitalist equivalence has as its effect to evacuate these forms of their social content. Use value is somehow drawn into the orbit of exchange value, thus eliminating from the surface of the capitalist process all that remained of naturalness, all spontaneity of "needs". Exit the unidimensional perspectives of revolutionary reappropriation of use value.

(Does this mean that the reign of exchange value is inevitable? Unless it means that we must rather imagine arrangements of desire which are so complex that they can express a subversive de-naturizing of human relations to exchange values? It being agreed that we shall speak here of value, or of *arrangements* of desire to mark ourselves off from any mythology of Otherness and of Absence which only takes up again, at another level, the project of "re-naturalization" of worldly relationships destroyed by capitalism.)

At the end of this process of integration, capitalistic valorization takes over based upon a double articulation with:
– the general market of formal economic values;

– the general market of machinic values.
It is in this system of the dual market that the essentially inegalitarian and manipulative character of exchange operations in a capitalistic context has its origin. It is in the nature of the mode of semiotization of capitalistic arrangements that, in the last instance, it always proceeds from a contradictory operation:

1   of putting into communication and formal equivalence, asymmetric forces and powers from heterogeneous domains;

2   of delimiting closed territories (rule of the laws of property) and of instituting social segmentarity based upon the programming of

distribution of goods and rights, and similarly based on the definition of modes of feeling, of taste, of "unconscious" choices appropriate to different social groups.

(We are thus faced with another type of difficulty: threatened now with no longer being able to get out of a simple opposition between economic form and machinic content, we run the risk of hypostatizing a historical necessity in the generation of valorization processes, while the arrangements of pre-capitalist valorization waiting to be overcoded by a deterritorializing capitalist valorization, by their qualitative specificities, their heterogeneity, the unequal character of their relationships would appear as territorialized residues of an essentially quantifying movement of valorization, one that homogenizes and "equalizes".) If it is true, as Fernand Braudel has shown,[2] that the basically unequal character of capitalist markets was much more visible, much less "genteel", at the time of world economies centered around cities such as Venice, Antwerp, Genoa, Amsterdam, than all that of contemporary world markets, these latter have not as a result become transparent and neutral surfaces of inscription. On the contrary it is clear that the exploitation of the Third World does not belong to equal relationships, but rather to that of pillage "compensated" by the export of technological trinkets and a few luxury gadgets destined for consumption by a handful of privileged natives. All of which does not stop the "new economists" and "neo-liberals" from preaching the saving graces of the capitalist market, in all places and all situations.

According to them, only this is capable of guaranteeing an optimum arbitration of cost and constraint.[3] The most reactionary economists seem thus to have interiorized an inverted dialectical vision of the progress of history. Since the worst aberrations are just part of historical necessity, one might just as well jump straight in without reservations. The market is thus alleged to be the only system which will ensure an optimal *mobilization* of all the information necessary to the regulation of complex societies. The market, explains Hayek,[4] is not only an anonymous machinery allowing the exchange of goods and services or a "static mechanism for the sharing of poverty", but, above all, a dynamic instrument for the production or diffusion of knowledge distributed to the social body. In short, it is the very idea of "freedom" which will be linked to the notion of information, and which finds itself taken in a "cybernetic" approach. Following Vera Lutz, it is "the imperfection of information which gives to capitalism its fundamental *raison d'être* as a system of social organization. If information were perfect, there would be no need for capitalists; we could all be, without any trouble, socialists."[5] Inequality of exchanges, according to the people who hold this theory, in the end depends only upon "imperfections" of the structures of *information cost* in these societies.[6] One more effort on the costs and everything will work out! However, it is clear that the Third World does not really "exchange" its labor and its riches for crates of Coca-Cola or even barrels of oil. It is aggressed and bled to death by the intrusion of dominant economies. And it is the same, though in different proportions, with the third and fourth worlds in the rich countries.

The unequal nature of capitalist markets does not represent a streak of archaism, a historical residue. The pseudo-egalitarian presentation of "exchanges" on the world market no more results from a lack of information than from an ideological disguise of the processes of social subjection. It is the essential complement of the techniques of integration of the collective subjectivity in order to obtain from it an optimal libidinal consent, even an active submission to the relations of exploitation and segregation. Compared with the machinic values and the values of desire, the relevance of the distinction between goods and activities would seem likely to blur. In a particular type of arrangement, human activities, properly controlled and guided by the capitalistic society, generate active machinic goods, while the evolution of other arrangements makes certain goods economically dated, and they thus find their "machinic virulence" devalued. In the first case, a power of activity (a power asset) is transformed into a highly valorizable *machinic power*; in the second case a machinic power (an Authority) tends to the side of the *formal powers*.

(We have seen that if we satisfy ourselves with an opposition – economic semiotic system (for example, that of the market) and the structure of social segmentarity – we are lacking the machinic integrating factors. On the other hand, if we stop at an opposition semiotic system – for example, economic information – and machinic process, we risk losing the territorialized collective investments, the effective structures of the economic and social ethology. In the former case, we get bogged down in formalistic sociological reductions, and in the latter we fly off into dialectical extrapolations which lead us away from historical realities. We therefore have to "hold" together the three components, systematic, structural and processual, of capitalism without granting anything but contingent priority to any one of them.)

The different evaluative formula which economists generally present as mutually exclusive[7] have, in fact, always been closely linked – either in competition or in complementarity – in real economic history.[8] Is there not a case for seeking to qualify each of them more clearly? Their different forms of existence (commercial, industrial, financial, monopolistic, statist or bureaucratic valorization) are the result of placing in the foreground one or other of their fundamental components, "selected" from within the same range of basic components, which has thus been reduced here to three terms:

- the *processes* of machinic production,

- the *structures* of social segmentarity,

- the dominant economic semiotic *systems*.

From this minimum model – necessary, but hardly sufficient, because it is never a question of simple components themselves structured according to their own systems of priority – we now proceed to examine a sort of generative chemistry of arrangements of economic valorization resulting from the combination of contingent priorities between basic components.

In the following table of structures of capitalistic valorization:

1 the structures of social segmentarity shall only be considered from the point of view of the economic problematic of the *State* (the analysis of the consequences of centralist direction of an important part of economic movements – which can be observed in the national accounting – on the stratification of segmentary relations);

2 the systems of economic semiotization will be considered only from the angle of the problematic of the *market* (in the widest sense, as referred to earlier, of markets of men, ideas, phantasms, etc.);

3 the productive processes will not be further specified.

The six formulae of structures of capitalistic valorization

Order of priorities	Examples
a) State ➤ production ➤ market	Asiatic mode of production* Nazi-type war economy
b) Market ➤ production ➤ state	Commercial proto-captitalism World economies centred on a network of cities**
c) Market ➤ state ➤ production	Liberal capitalism
d) Production ➤ state ➤ market	Colonial monopoly capitalism
e) Production ➤ market ➤ state	Integrated world capitalism
f) State ➤ market ➤ production	State capitalism

(The priorities between components are indicated by arrows)
* For instance, China in the second and third centuries BC. Cf. *Sur le mode de production asiatique*. Sociales, 1969.
** For instance, Venice, Antwerp, Genoa, Amsterdam, between the thirteenth and seventeenth centuries.

The object of this table, it should be emphasized, is not at all to present a general typology of historical forms of capitalism, but solely to show that capitalism cannot be identified with a single formulation (for example, market economy). One could make it more complex and refine it by introducing supplementary components or by differentiating the internal components of each cluster; the barriers are by no means watertight (there is "machinic production" in the semiotic wheels of the market and at the level of the State – for example, in public buildings and in the media; there is "State power" at the heart of the most liberal economic syntaxes; moreover these last-named always play a determinant role within the productive spheres). It is proposed here only to try to throw into relief, starting from certain correlations emerging from the second system of articulation which is found in each formula, certain correlations between systems which appear to be very distant the one from the other, but which go in the same historical direction.

In a general way:

1   The capacity of certain arrangements to take on major historical upheavals or, to paraphrase a formula which is very dear to Ilya Prigogine, their capacity to direct "processes far from historical equilibria" will depend on the primacy of productive components.

2   The degree of resistance to change of the axioms of clan, ethnic, religious, urbanistic stratification, of castes, of classes, etc., depends on the primacy of the components of social segmentarity.

3   On the more or less innovatory character of their semiotic valorization (the fact that these should be capable, or not, of adaptation, of growing richer by new procedures: their degree of "diagrammacity") will depend on their integrative power, their capacity to "colonize" not only economic life, but also social life, libidinal life, in other words, their possibility to transform society, to subjugate it to the machinic phylum.

The fact that the "direction of history" should be related here to the evolutive phylum of production does not necessarily imply, it is worth noting, a finalization of history in transcendent objectives. The existence of a "machinic direction" of history does not at all stop this from "going in all directions". The *machinic phylum* inhabits and directs the *historical rhizome* of capitalism but without ever mastering its destiny which continues to be played out in an equal match between social segmentarity and the evolution of modes of economic valorization.

Let us look again at these different formulae of priorities:

1 Priorities of the market Priority (b), relegating the question of the State to the third line, that, for example, of the *commercial proto-capitalism* of the thirteenth and fourteenth centuries (questions of State came so far behind commercial interests for the merchants of the Dutch United Provinces of the seventeenth century that no one was really shocked by the fact that they provided arms for their Portuguese or French enemies).[9] It sets up a specific problem with the extension and consolidation of capitalism to the whole of society through a sort of baroque flowering of all the productive cultural and institutional spheres.

The phenomenon of credit – via the trade in letters of exchange which thrusts its roots into international commerce – constituted the "clutch" of such a flowering. It should be noted that medieval law sought in vain to obstruct the free circulation of the effects of commerce; this practice ran into the hostility of public powers who wanted to stabilize exchanges and control monetary circulation. Hence the story of the "endorsement war", declared by these merchant bankers who, *de facto*, extended to the letter of exchange (bank-deposited money) what had already been admitted for the schedules (currency in circulation): the *right of transfer* (the schedules circulated by simple discount, while the letters of exchange were not – in law – freely transferable). The answer, though long awaited, was no less clear, without being decisive: in Venice, for example, the accountants of the Banco del Giro were forbidden, by the decree of 6 July 1652, to allow book transfers in order to pay endorsed letters of exchange. This fact would have remained marginal if it had not been symptomatic of the slowness and the incapacity of the (para-)statist structures to control the capitalistic monetary movements. In 1766 Accarias de Serionne was still able to write: "If ten or twelve first-class Amsterdam merchants got together for a banking operation, they could in a moment set into circulation throughout Europe more than two hundred millions of paper-money florins which were preferred to spot cash. There is no Sovereign who could do such a thing. . . . Such credit is a power which these ten or twelve merchants wield in all the States of Europe with absolute independence of all authority".[10]

Priority (c), relegating the question of production to the third line, that, for example, of the *crude liberalism of nineteenth-century capitalism*. It sets a specific historical problem with the constitution of modern territorialized States. Paradoxically, liberalism is always more preoccupied with the setting-up of a State apparatus than with a generalized growth of production. If one accepts Habermas's analysis that perhaps "no ideology, properly speaking, existed at that time,"[11] then one understands more easily that, far from crowning the free- trading edifice, Say's Law – the theory of general equilibrium – represents its *juridical* formulation; it "throws the knife in the sea" and makes the body disappear in its fictional work. *Jurisdictio* of a linear, exclusive, algebraic representation; bring together therefore over-exploitation of the productive potential, general mobilization of the labor force, acceleration of the speed of circulation of goods, men and capital – and you will get an automatic equilibrium of supply and demand, thus verifying the self-regulation of the whole system . . . *"But on the condition that there be no interference, other than economic in the exchanges"*.[12]

It can be seen what a unique historical conjunction was needed so that the liberal dream of a society free from any intervention from whatever authority could be set forth. Because the equilibrium of free competition is more or less that: *power without authority*. Without the affirmation (of the reality) of this distinction, Hobbes's formula would never have resulted in that terrible inversion – *veritas non auctoritas facit legem*. The truth of a power, England, which, through its industrial potential, is sufficiently in control of the market channels to play the game of putting the political aspects of material wealth in the background and still win more than that . . . (the repeal of the English Corn Laws dates, after all, only from the middle of the nineteenth century). In fact, the essence of liberalism is in the reverse movement, inseparable from that equivalence of content which translates the utopia of the absence of authority in terms of the affirmation of supreme power: *veritas* will only become *ratio* (the postulate of homogeneity, general equilibrium, henceforth drawing its legitimacy from the "national" order which they display) if it enters into the essential relationship with a constant *rationalization* of domination. Which, in plain terms, means that the State "has always been at least as strong as the social and political situation demanded".[13] Scarcely modified translation of the celebrated phrase of Hobbes: *Wealth is power and power is wealth* . . .

The existence of a large market implies central control – albeit a subtle one – which is absolutely necessary. The "teleguiding" of production based on an expanding market complements the interventions and arbitrages of territorialized States, without which the system would come up against its own limits. It would reveal itself, in particular, incapable of producing basic equipment (of the infrastructure, public services, collective facilities, military equipment, etc.).

2 *Priorities of the State*   Priority (a), which relegates the market to third place is, for example, the *Asiatic mode of production*, or the *Nazi type of war economy* (forced labor, relatively minor role of monetary economy, incarnation of the all-powerful nature of the State in the Pharaoh or the Führer, etc.). This sets us specific historical problems:

1   With the control of the accumulation of capital. Surplus-value has to be accumulated as a matter of priority off the power of the State

and its military machine; the growth of the economic and social power of diverse aristocratic strata has to be limited, otherwise it would eventually threaten the ruling caste; it would eventually lead to the development of social classes. In the case of "Asiatic" empires, this regulation can be brought about by the stopping of production,[14] by massive sacrificial consumption, by sumptuous constructions, luxury consumption, etc. In the case of Nazi regimes, by internal extermination and total war.

2   With machinic intrusions from outside, especially innovations in military techniques which they fail to develop in time, because of their conservatism, and the difficulty they have in letting creative initiative develop. (Certain Asiatic empires have been liquidated in the space of a few years by nomadic war machines carrying some military innovation.)

Priority (f), which relegates the question of production to the third place is, for example, *State capitalism of the Soviet type* (Stalinist forms of planning, etc.), of which the affinities with the Asiatic mode of production have been many times underlined. (The Chinese model, at least that of the Maoist period, by its methods of massive enslavement of the collective labor force, belongs perhaps more to formula (a) than to formula (f).) This sets up a specific historical problem with the question of the instruments of economic semiotization, particularly with the setting-up of markets not only of economic values but also of prestige values, values of innovation, and of desire. In this sort of system, the disturbance of the market systems combined with a hyper-stratification of social segmentarity, is the correlate of an authoritarian control which can subsist only to the extent that its sphere of influence is not too exposed to outside influences, to competition from other branches of the machinic productive phylum. Thus, in the end, the Gulag system is tenable only in so far as the Soviet economy freezes, at least partially, innovative arrangements in the advanced technological, scientific and cultural domains. This problematic is now prolonged by that of the demands for a democratization of the apparatus of social-semiotic control of the system (example: the Polish workers' struggle for "workers' control").

3 *Priorities of production*   Priority (d), which relegates the question of the market to third place, for example, *classical imperialist exploitation*, constitutes a supplementary form of accumulation for the great capitalist entities without significant machinic involvement[15] and without thought of the effects of disorganization on the colonized society. The commercial monopolism of the periphery tended to favor the tendencies of monopoly capital in the metropolis and the strengthening of the

authority of the State. It sets up a specific historical question with the reconstitution of the devastated colonial society, including the setting-up of a highly artificial State.

Priority (e), which relegates the question of the State to third place, for example, *Integrated World Capitalism*, sets itself up "above" and "below" the pre-capitalist and capitalist segmentary relations (that is to say, at one and the same time, at the world level and at the molecular level), and based upon semiotic means of evaluation and valorization of capital which are completely new and have an increased capacity for the machinic integration of all human activities and faculties.

In principle, "the entire society becomes productive; the rhythm of production is the rhythm of life".[16] Considerably simplifying, we can say that this high point of the ascendancy of capital over society is established only on the conjunction between machinic integration and social reproduction – this latter incidentally the result of a complex conservative machinic reterritorialization if not of the exact terms of social segregation, at least of its essential axioms (hierarchical, racist, sexist, etc.). We shall speak here of *social-machinic capital* and it is this which will lead us to take the rise of neo-liberal thought quite seriously, starting from the intrusion of information theory in the economic sphere. When information claims first place in the social machine, it would seem, in effect, that it ceases to be linked to the simple organization of the sphere of circulation to become, in its way, a factor of production. *Information as a factor of production* . . . here is the latest formula for decoding society through the formation of cybernetic capital. This is no longer the age of transcendental schematism à la Keynes (finding a new space and a new rhythm of production based on an investment of statist mediation, as a function of the quest for equilibrium), and circulation will no longer be just a vector of the social validation of the profits of power; it becomes immediately production – reterritorializtion – capitalization of machinic profits, taking the form of manipulation and control of the segmentarized reproduction of society. Henceforth capital seems to operate on "a totality without origins, without contradictions, without criticism. Analytic of the totality where the totality is taken for granted"[17] and is itself indissociable from a totalitarian discourse which finds its form of expression in the cynicism of the "new economics". It should also be said that neo-liberal theory has no content outside this cynicism, which is all part of the will to affirm *production for production's sake, finally and in its most classic form* (it is in this context that we should place the unbelievable increase of American spending on military research). Hence the restructuration of productive space which will no longer be considered as it arises, in function of the need to integrate new planetary "data": *permanent restructuration* has become the rule of the capitalist process itself, and crisis, the form itself of circulation. "Restructuration is not a rule for this phase, but an operation to develop in any phase, at all periods of the social process".[18] Only the crisis permits such a degree of integrative fusion between production and circulation, production and information, production and resegmentalization of society, and to realize the expansive 'intension' of freed capital gaining a maximalized synergetic fluidity.

This fluidity can be verified at two levels:

—that of the mobile factory: it is indirectly through circulation that these "pseudo-commodities", which are now only indirectly products of labor, will be made (the social conditions of production having fallen under the control of organization and information, the work process is now no more than a simple element in the process of valorization). For J.-P. de Gaudemar "any productive unit thus tends to appear as a nodal point in a fluid network, a point of connections or of temporary breakdowns of fluidity, but which can only be analysed relative to the place it occupies in the network".[19] The management of productive space now becomes the adjustment of its optimal fluidity (temporary labor being, of course, an important part of this).

— from the territorial state to the "mobile" State (better known, in liberal terminology, under the name of "minimum" State); no longer conceiver and protector of an original national space of the valorization of capital, but promoter of increased participation in the trans-national space of valorization.[20] From contractual mechanics to thermodynamic balance – a long way from equilibrium.

The specific historical question which therefore arises with Integrated World Capitalism concerns the potential limits of its integrative power. It is by no means clear that it will indefinitely manage to innovate and to take over techniques and subjectivities. It is useful, once again, to underline here that Integrated World Capitalism is not a self-sufficient entity. Although it presents itself today as "the highest stage of capitalism", it is, after all, only one capitalist formula among others. It accommodates itself to the survival of large zones of archaic economy; it lives in symbiosis with liberal and colonial economies of the classic type; it co-exists with Stalinist-type economies. Relatively progressive in the field of technico-scientific change, it is basically conservative in the social domain (not for ideological reasons, but for functional reasons). In addition one has the right to ask if we are not here dealing with one of its insurmountable contradictions. The capacity for adapting and reconversion shown by the economic structures of Integrated World Capitalism will perhaps find its limit with the renewal of the capacities of resistance of all social groups who refuse its "unidimensionalizing" ends. Certainly the internal contradictions of Integrated World Capitalism are not such that it must necessarily die of them. But its sickness is perhaps no less mortal: it results from the accumulation of all the *lateral* crises it throws up. The power of the productive process of Integrated World Capitalism seems inexorable, and its social effects incapable of being turned back; but it overturns so many things, comes into conflict with so many ways of life and social valorizations, that it does not seem at all absurd to anticipate that the development of new collective responses – new structures of declaration, evaluation and action – coming from the greatest variety of horizons, might finally succeed in bringing it down. (The appearance of new peoples' war machines as in El Salvador; the struggles for workers' control in the countries of Eastern Europe; self-valorization of work in the Italian style; a multitude of vectors of molecular revolution in all spheres of society.) As we see it, it is only through this sort of hypothesis that the redefinition of the objectives of the revolutionary transformation of society can be appreciated.

Notes

This article was originally published as "Systèmes, structures et processus capitalistiques", *Change International* 2 (1984). It was collected in Guattari's *Les Années D'Hiver: 1980–1985* (Paris: Bernard Barrault, 1986), pp. 167–92. This translation appeared in *Molecular Revolution* (Harmondsworth: Penguin, 1984), pp. 273–87.

1 Oskar Lange compares the capitalist market to a "proto-computer". Quoted by Fernand Braudel, *Civilisation matérielle, économie et capitalisme*, Vol. II (Editions Armand Colins, 1979), p. 192.

2 According to Fernand Braudel, the capitalist proto-markets were deployed in concentric zones starting from the metropolises which held economic keys allowing them to draw in most of the surplus value, while towards the peripheries they tended to a sort of zero point, because of the lethargy of exchanges and the low level of prices found there. Braudel considers that each economy-world was necessarily based on a single city-world. But perhaps he is a bit too systematic on this point. Could one not imagine urban and capitalist processes which are not developed according to a mono-centered model, but according to a multi-polar stock of "archipelagos of towns"?

3 Cf. Henri Lepage, *Demain le capitalisme* (Livre de Poche), p. 419.

4 *Individualism and Economic Order* (London: Routledge and Kegan Paul, 1949).

5 Vera Lutz, *Central Planning for the Market Economy* (London: Longmans, 1969).

6 In contrast with what the theoreticians of "public choice" proclaim, the growth of information in this domain – in particular of mass media information controlled by the system – can only accentuate the unequalizing effects of these techniques of integration. The project which consisted of wanting to complete the theory of production and exchange of market goods or services with an equivalent theory which would be, as far as possible, compatible with the workings of the political markets (James Buchanan) perhaps started out with good intentions, but the least one can say is that it was incomplete and that it turned sour (cf. the devastating exploits in Pinochet's Chile, of the "Chicago Boys" of Milton Friedman). Economic, political and institutional markets are one thing, machinic and libidinal markets are another. And it is only on the side of these latter that one can manage to seize the essential springs of social valorization and machinic creativity.

7 On these modes of evaluation, cf. Alain Cotta, *Théorie générale du capital, de la croissance et des fluctuations* (Paris, 1967) and *Encyclopedia Universalis*, entry "Capital".

8 Examples of complementarity: the fact that the proto-capitalism of the fifteenth and sixteenth centuries, although predominantly market and finance, should have become industrial in certain circumstances (cf. the recovery of Antwerp by industrialization, discussed by Braudel, op. cit., Vol. III, p. 127); and the fact that a market economy, whatever its apparent "liberalism", should always carry a certain dose of State intervention or of "centralist" planning (Stalinist plans, for example), should have always preserved a minimum of market economy, either within its sphere of influence or in its relationship to the world market.

9 Braudel, op. cit., Vol. III, pp. 172–3.

10 Ibid, III, p. 207. And Braudel adds, magnanimously: "multi-national companies of today have, as we see, ancestors".

11 J. Habermas, *L'Espace publique, archéologie de la publicité comme dimension constitutive de la société bourgeoise* (Paris: Payot, 1978), p. 98.

12 Ibid., p. 89. M. Aglietta correctly relates classical (and neo-classical) economic theory to a theological construction "purely internal to the world of ideas, and the stricter it is the more cut off it is from any reality". Such would be the fate of the theory of general equilibrium, if "the end of theory is to express the essence in stripping it of all contingency; institutions, social interactions, conflicts . . . are the dross we must get rid of in order to find economic behaviour in its pure state" (M. Aglietta, *Régulation et crises du capitalisme* (Calman-Lévy, 1976), p. 12).

13 F. Neumann, *Der Funktionswandel des Gesetzes im Recht der Jürgerlichen Gesellschaft*, quoted by Habermas.

14 Etienne Balazs, *La Bureaucratie céleste* (Paris: Gallimard, 1968).

15 And, doubtless, slowing up the development of machicic production in the metropolis: cf. F. Sternberg, *Kapitalismus une Socialismus vor dem Weltgericht* (1951): "The alliance between European imperialism and colonial feudalism . . . slowed down, in an extraordinary way, industrial development and in general the progressive development of the economy of the colonial empires" (quoted by Maximilien Rubel in *Marx* (Pléiade edn.), Vol I).

16 Antonio Negri, *Macchina Tempo* (Feltrinelli, 1982), p. 271.

17 Ibid., p. 278.

18 Ibid., p. 275.

19 Jean Paul de Gaudemar, "Naissance de l'usine mobile, in *Usine et ouvrier, figure du nouvel ordre productif* (Paris: Maspero, 1980), p. 24.

20 This formulation, which we borrow in part from Pascal Arnaud, escapes, in our view, the limits and restrictions which might be inherent in his frame of analysis (*Le Monétarisme appliqué aux économies chilienne et argentine*, cf. *Critiques de l'économie politique*, no. 18).

Translated by Brian Darling

22

Communist Propositions

With Antonio Negri

New Lines of Alliance

At the end of a period of defensive retrenchment – the result of the current repressive wave under the aegis of capitalist and/or socialist organization – a special form of alliance can and must be realized between the constitutive categories of the new proletariat and the most dynamic sectors of productive society. Distinguishing this alliance is, first, that it can break the corporatist obstacles to restructuring, which have shown themselves to be particularly effective amongst the industrial working classes as well as in the tertiary service and scientific sectors of social production. The basic revolutionary sequence presently confronting us concerns the possibilities of making the working classes, the tertiary production sectors, and those innumerable components of the universe of the "non-guaranteed" connect and interact.[1] The movement will have to take up this problematic of conjunction with all of its intelligence and energy. Not because the working class would remain the determining element of the revolutionary process. Neither that the tertiary, intellectual, marginal, etc., sectors would be the bearers of essential economic changes. There's nothing to gain from entertaining such historic misunderstandings. It is clear that the discourses on workers' centrality and hegemony are thoroughly defunct and that they cannot serve as a basis for the organization of new political and productive alliances, or even simply as a point of reference. Breaking with this sort of trap, the true question concerns the invention of a system, not of unification, but of multivalent engagement of all social forces which are not only in the process of articulating new subjective forces, but also of breaking the blocks of capitalist power – in particular their powers of mass-media suggestion on a considerable portion of the oppressed.

It would be fictive and artificial to expect to find these new affiliations only at ruptures in the structure, in areas of friction in the labor market and the corporatist reorganization of different segments of the working class. Such an attitude would still be part of the spirit of IWC, which is always more ready to apply repression than to consider attempts to liberate production. Now, we have seen that the question of recomposing the movement's conjunctive unity goes hand in hand with that of the self-production of emancipation – at once intrinsically singular and externally offensive in their tendency – by each of its components. Now self-production implies effective and unreserved recognition of everything that really participates in new types of cooperation and subjectivity, unalloyed with the dominant power formations. The new anti-capitalist alliance will destroy the corporatist chains of repression and help replace their viewpoint with those of a collective self-transformation.

Instead of new political alliances, we could say just as well: new productive cooperation.

One always returns to the same point, that of production – production of useful goods, production of communication and of social solidarity, production of aesthetic universes, production of freedom . . .

The fact is that the center of gravity of these productive processes has been displaced toward the molecular web of marginal and minority concerns. Nevertheless, it's not a matter of founding a new religion and creating point by point oppositions between the whole group of guaranteed workers and the non-guaranteed workers. On the contrary, it has to do with finishing with the latter representing themselves as a heterogeneous ensemble, excluded in essence from the "true realities" of production, as all the representational coordinates of capitalism and/or socialism beguile them into thinking . . . . Yet such a transformation implies as well that numerous sectors of the working class and the privileged categories of the productive proletariats give themselves other "representations" than those which they possess today and which, for the most part, are part of the corporatist regime. The molecular revolutions, the new subjective arrangements, autonomies and processes of singularization are capable of restoring a revolutionary meaning to the struggles of the working class and indeed many sectors of the collective force of labor, which are now reduced to vegetating in their sociological statifications. We believe that the "proletarian recomposition" can head off the IWC strategy of "precarization" of the labor market, and of pitting against each other those social segments which find themselves confronting the same market. On a small or a large scale, the potentials for molecular revolution appear every time that processes of detotalization and of deterritorialization encroach on the stratification of corporatism.

Now, if it's true that the fundamental question is the inversion of the corporatist tendency, it seems equally true that the motor of that diminution of "social entropy" resides in consistently making a decompartmentalization of productive society the revolutionary project. And not only as an ideal horizon, as a communist ethics, but above all as a strategic struggle capable of taking the movement out of its current "failure neurosis". The most demoralizing situations and the most negative comparisons of apparent strength can rapidly change as soon as the precariousness of the current forms of IWC domination appears in an even more pronounced way. Even the most "conservative" segments of the working class are beginning to manifest their unrest, their impatience, and their disgust in regard to those who are supposed to represent them. The idea, for so long accepted in good faith, by virtue of which there existed only one political economy as a reference point – that of IWC – has had its day. The dismantling of companies, of branches of industries, of entire regions, the social and ecological costs of the crisis can no longer be written off as a necessary reconversion of the system. In fact, it has been clear for some time that this is not an ordinary crisis, but a radical attempt to destroy more than half a century's worth of "acquired advantages" and social victories of the reformism which corresponded to the previous forms of capitalism.

Obviously, this does not mean that capitalism is in the process of collapsing on its own and that we have come, almost despite ourselves, to the eve of the "Great Night". What is certain is that capitalism and/or socialism intend to install a regime of frenzied "disciplinarization" over the entire planet, in which each segment of the collective labor force, each people, each ethnic group will be forced to submit to permanent control. In this regard, the guaranteed workers will be placed under the same regime as the non-guaranteed, and everything will be nuances, minute non-empirical transitions. No longer will anyone be able to assume a true statutory guarantee.

The traditional working classes should resign themselves to this. But what could the meaning of their revolt be if they do not understand that they no longer represent a social majority – neither numerically, nor as an ideal value, not even as a produced economic value? They are obliged, if they want to legitimate their rebellion, to socially recompose themselves, in alliance with the immense mass of exploited people, of marginalized people, which includes the large majority of young, women, immigrants, the sub-proletarians of the Third World and minorities of every kind. The principle task has become the reunification of the traditional components of the class struggle against exploitation with the new liberation movements and communist projects.

It is on this terrain that the new lines of alliance will be drawn. We draw a line through the tradition of the Third International, a black line over its totalitarian and/or corporatist results. A new revolutionary movement is in search of itself. It is born both inside and outside the traditional workers' movement; it proliferates and potentially converges along a front intrinsically unified by exploitation. It will destroy the repressive norms of the workday and of the capitalist appropriation of the totality of lifetime. New domains of struggle become possible everywhere. But the privileged point, the hot point in the production of new machines of revolutionary struggle resides within the zones of marginalized subjectivity. And there as well, it goes without saying, not in and of themselves – but because they are inscribed in the meaning of creative production processes considered in their evolutionary position, that is, not arbitrarily isolated within the capitalist economic sphere.

The social imaginary can recompose itself only through radical changes. In this regard, one should take into account that marginal phenomena are part of a context which does not define them as being at the margin, but which, on the contrary, confers on them a central place in the capitalist strategy. The marginal subjectivities, in as much as they are the product and the best "analyzers" of command tendencies, are also those which resist it the best. The physical, bodily, plastic and external aspects of the liberation experiences of marginal subjects become equally the material of a new form of expression and creation. Language and image here are never ideological but always incarnated. Here, more than anywhere else, one can find the symptoms of the appearance of a new right to transformation and communitarian life, under the impetus of subjects in revolt.

New alliances: as a project of the production of singularities and as the possibility of conferring on this project a subversive social meaning. The self-analytical methods of the forms of social subjectivity becomes revolutionary substance in the sense that it permits the semiotic understanding and political amplification of the implosion points of corporatism and the upheaval of its own lines of alliance. The common consciousness has already perceived this process of conjunction; the revolutionary imagination has begun to apprehend it; what remains is to make it the basis of the constitution of the future movement.

Think and Live in Another Way

Resentment, empty repetition and sectarianism are the modalities by which we live the betrayed hopes of the traditional workers' movement. For all that we do not renounce the history of struggles; on the contrary we celebrate it because it is an integral part of our mental coordinates and sensibility. If we are dwarves on the shoulders of giants, we assume the benefits as much as the deplorable aspects of their heritage. At any rate, we want to move forward. Reuniting with the human roots of communism, we want to return to the sources of hope, that is, to a "being-for", to a collective intentionality, turned toward doing rather than toward a "being against", secured to impotent catchphrases of resentment. It is in real history that we intend to explore and experience the many realms of possibility which we call forth from everywhere. Let a thousand flowers bloom on the terrains which attempt to undermine capitalist destruction. Let a thousand machines of life, art, solidarity, and action sweep away the stupid and sclerotic arrogance of the old organizations! What does it matter if the movement trips over its own immaturity, over its "spontaneism" – its power of expression will ultimately only be reinforced. Without even being aware of it, despite the cacophony of the molecular movements which sustain it, an organizational crystallization is opening, oriented in the direction of new collective subjectivities. "Let a thousand flowers blossom, a thousand machines of struggle and of life", is not an organizational slogan and even less an enlightened prediction, but an analytic key to the new revolutionary subjectivity, a given on the basis of which can be grasped the social characteristics and dimensions of the singularities of productive labor. It is through an analysis of the real that they will be recomposed and will multiply as a subversive and innovative presence. The enemy has been incarnated in current forms of social command, through the elimination of differences and the imposition of a reductive logic of domination. Bringing to light the hegemony of singularization processes on the horizon of social production constitutes today the specific hallmark of communist political struggle.

The development, defense and expression of changing productive subjectivities, of dissident singularities, and of new proletarian temperaments has become, in some respects, the primary content and task of the movement. That can take the form of the struggle on the welfare front, for the establishment of a guaranteed egalitarian income, against poverty in all its forms, for the defense and enlargement of alternative rights, and against the mechanisms of corporatist division . . . . If one wants, one will find there as well the tradition of struggles against rent, and this such that it is not only fundamental, real, and financial, but that it is essentially undergirded by the articulations of capitalist command; i.e. a political rent, a rent reflecting position in the hierarchy of corporatist strata. New subjective components of production and revolution will find their first intervention opportunity at this level, redefining it in a positive mode as a liberation struggle against corporatist slavery and reactionary structures of production and as affirming the processes of singularity as an essential spring of social production.

This recomposition of the revolutionary movement implies, of course, immense efforts of courage, patience, and above all, intelligence. But what progress has already been made compared to preceding periods of struggle – which were indefatigable and often despairing – by the first groups conscious of this problematic, who only rarely succeeded in opening breaches in the union ghetto or in the political monopoly of the supposed labor parties! Here as well, lifetime must be imposed on production time. At this crossroads the second task of the revolutionary communist movement will be posed: consciously organizing the collective labor force independently of the capitalist and/or socialist structures, that is, of everything which touches on the production and reproduction of the mode of life. One thing, an effect, is to reveal new social productive forces and another is to organize them outside and against capitalist and/or socialist structures. The development of science and technology and their massive incorporation in this transformation program are necessary, but not sufficient, conditions. No transformation is conceivable unless the entire field of productive labor is confronted with large movements of collective experimentation which break those conceptions which relate to profit-centered capitalist accumulation.

It is in this direction that the expansion power of the collective labor force should be grasped. Thus a double movement will be established, like that of the human heart, between the diastole of the expansive force of social production and the systole of radical innovation and rearrangement of the work day. The movement of the social proletariat and new collective subjectivities must lay siege to the corporations, viz. the stakes regarding legislation governing the length of the work day, and impose its redefinitions and its permanent experimentation. It must impose not only a productive renewal, but also new ways of imagining and of studying production.

Think, live, experiment, and struggle in another way: such will be the motto of a working class which can no longer perceive itself as "self-sufficient" and which has everything to win by renouncing its arrogant myths of social centrality. As soon as one has finished with this sort of mystification, which ultimately has only profited the capitalist and/or socialist power formations, one will discover the great significance of the new lines of alliance which tie together the multiform and multivalent social stages at the heart of our era's productive forces. It is time that communism's imagination raise itself to the height of the changing waves which are in the process of submerging the old dominant 'realities'.

Now it is necessary to introduce certain considerations regarding a first "diagrammatic proposition" integrating the definitions of the perspectives just introduced. It's only too evident that every effort at taking control of the length of the workday, by the movement of the new subjectivities, will be illusory if it does not attack frontally the network of command put in place by IWC. To tackle this network means putting in question the East–West relation, to derail the mechanism integrating the two superpowers, which has overcoded, from the 70s until today, all international relations. Breaking the relation of domination laboriously established between capitalism and socialism, and radically reversing the alliances – especially the European ones – in the direction of the North–South axis, against the East–West axis, constitutes an essential foundation for recomposing the intellectual and working class proletariat in the advanced capitalist countries. A basis of social production which will win its independence against hierarchical oppression and the command of the great powers; a basis which only has meaning if it begins with a collective will to create alternative flows and structures to those of the East–West relation. We are not fallbacks to "Third Worldism"; we do not pretend to transform it by way of a traditional "insurrectionism"; neither for all that do we believe in its independent capacity for development and "redemption" at least in the current capitalist context. None of the successful revolutions in the developed countries has succeeded in transforming in a lasting way the structures of the State. It is not likely that those of the Third World will do any better. No, it is rather toward revolutionary cooperation and aggregation of forces among the intellectual and working proletariat of the North with the great mass of the proletariat of the South that it is necessary to turn to fulfill this historic task. All of this may seem utopian, even extravagant, because today we, the workers and intellectuals of the countries of the North, are slaves of corporatist politics, of segmentary divisions, of the logic of profit, of blocking and extermination operations, of the fear of nuclear war, as they are imposed on us and with which we make ourselves accomplices. Our liberation requires creating a project and a practice which unifies, in the same revolutionary will, the intellectual forces and the proletariats of the North and of the South.

As the union of processes of singularity advances toward the project of reinventing communism, the problem of power will be posed with increasing acuity; it remains at the heart of the antagonism between proletarian components and the capitalist and/or socialist State. The traditional workers' movement wanted to respond to this question in a simple and radical way through the conquest of State power, then through the progressive disappearance of the State. Everything was supposed to follow from itself. One would oppose destruction with destruction and terror with terror. It would be useless today to provide an epilogue regarding the fictive and mystifying character of this dialectic or to underline the scandalous reference by holders of this doctrine to the heroic experience of the Paris Commune.

The first basic task of the revolutionary communist movement consists in having done with this sort of conception and in affirming the movement's radical separation not only from the State which it directly confronts but also, more fundamentally, from the very model of the capitalist State and all its successors, replacements, derived forms, and assorted functions in all the wheels of the socius, at all levels of subjectivity. Thus, to the struggles around welfare, against the organization of productive labor and of labor's social time, and to communitarian initiatives in this domain, should be added questioning the State as the determinant of different forms of oppression, the machine for overdetermining social relations, in order to reduce, block and radically subjugate them, under the threat of its forces of death and destruction.

This question leads us to formulate a second diagrammatic proposition of communism and liberation: it concerns the urgency of reterritorializing political practice. Confronting the State today means fighting against this particular formation of the State, which is entirely integrated into IWC.

After Yalta, political relations were further emptied of their territorial legitimacy and drifted towards levels impossible to attain. Communism represents the tendential destruction of those mechanisms which make of money and other abstract equivalents the only territories of man. This does not imply nostalgia for "native lands", the dream of a return to primitive civilizations or to the supposed communism of the "good savage". It is not a question of denying the levels of abstraction which the deterritorialized processes of production made man conquer.

What is contested by communism are all types of conservative, degrading, oppressive reterritorialization imposed by the capitalist and/or socialist State, with its administrative functions, institutional organs, its collective means of normalization and blockage, its media, etc . . . . The reterritorialization induced by communist practice is of an entirely different nature; it does not pretend to return to a natural or universal origin; it is not a circular revolution; rather it allows an "ungluing" of the dominant realities and significations, by creating conditions which permit people to "make their territory", to conquer their individual and collective destiny within the most deterritorialized flows.

(In this regard, one is led to distinguish very concretely: the movements of nationalist reterritorialization – Basque, Palestinian, Kurdish . . . . – which assume, to a certain extent, the great deterritorialized flows of Third World struggles and immigrant proletariats, and the movements of reactionary nationalist reterritorialization).

Our problem is to reconquer the communitarian spaces of liberty, dialogue and desire. A certain number of them are starting to proliferate in different countries of Europe. But it is necessary to construct, against the pseudo-reterritorializations of IWC (example: the "decentralization" of France, or of the Common Market), a great movement of reterritorializing bodies and minds: Europe must be reinvented as a reterritorialization of politics and as a foundation for reversing the alliances of the North–South axis.

The third task of the revolutionary communist movement is thus also to "disarticulate" and dismantle the repressive functions of the State and its specialized apparatuses. This is the sole terrain on which new collective subjects confront the initiatives of the State, and only in the sense that the latter dispatches its "teutonic cavaliers" over those areas liberated by the revolutionary arrangements. Forces of love and humor should be put to work here so that they are not abolished, as is usually the case, in the mortally abstract and symbolic lunar image of their capitalist adversary! Repression is first and foremost the eradication and perversion of the singular. It's necessary to combat it within real life relations of force; it's also necessary to get rid of it in the registers of intelligence, imagination, and of collective sensitivity and happiness. Everywhere it's necessary to extract, including from oneself, the powers of implosion and despair which empty reality and history of their substance.

The State, for its part, can live out its days in the isolation and encirclement reserved for it by a reconstructed civil society! But if it appears about to come out of its "retreat" and to reconquer our spaces of freedom, then we will respond by submerging it within a new kind of general mobilization, of multiform subversive alliances. Until it dies smothered in its own fury.

The fourth task: Here we are inevitably returning to the anti-nuclear struggle and the struggle for peace. Only, now it is in relation to a paradigm which brings to light the catastrophic implications of science's position in relation to the State, a position which presupposes a dissociation between the "legitimacy" of power and the goal of power. It is truly a sinister mockery that States accumulate thousands of nuclear warheads in the name of their responsibility to guarantee peace and international order, although it is evident that such an accumulation can only guarantee destruction and death. But this ultimate "ethical" legitimation of the State, to which reaction attaches itself as to a rampart, is also in the process of collapsing, and not only on a theoretical level, but also in the consciousness of those who know or suspect that collective production, freedom, and peace are in their proper place fundamentally irreducible to power.

Prevent the catastrophe of which the State is the bearer while revealing the extent to which that catastrophe is essential to the State. It remains true that "capitalism carries war as clouds carry storms". But, in a manner different than in the past, through other means and on a horizon of horror which at this point escapes all possible imagination, this perspective of the final holocaust has, in effect, become the basis of a veritable world civil war conducted by capitalist power and constituted by a thousand permanently erupting, pulverizing wars against social emancipation struggles and molecular revolutions. Nevertheless, in this domain, as in no other, nothing is fated. Not all the victories and defeats of the movement's new lines of alliance are inscribed in a mechanistic causality or a supposed dialectic of history. Everything is to be redone, everything is constantly to be reconsidered. And it's good that it is so. The State is only a cold monster, a vampire in interminable agony which derives vitality only from those who abandon themselves to its simulacra.

In '68, no one could imagine that war would so quickly become such a close and encroaching horizon. Today, war is no longer a prospect: it has become the permanent frame of our lives.

The third great imperialist war has already begun. A war no doubt grows old after thirty years, like the Thirty Years War, and no one recognizes it any longer; even though it has become the daily bread of "certain" among the press. Yet such has resulted from capitalism's reorganization and its furious assaults against the world proletariats. The third diagrammatic proposition of communism and liberation consists in becoming aware of this situation and assuming the problematic of peace as fundamental to the process of reversing alliances along the North–South axis. Less than ever, peace is not an empty slogan; a formula of "good conscience"; a vague aspiration.

Peace is the alpha and omega of the revolutionary program. The anguish of war sticks to our skin, pollutes our days and nights. Many people take refuge in a neutralist politics. But even this unconsciousness generates anguish. Communism will tear men and women away from the stupidity programmed by IWC and make them face the reality of this violence and death, which the human species can conquer if it succeeds in conjugating its singular potentials of love and reason.

And finally, to these alliances of productive organization and liberated collective subjectivities should be added a fifth dimension – of which we have already spoken – that of organization itself. The time has come to move from sparse resistance to constituting determinate fronts and machines of struggles which, in order to be effective, will lose nothing of their richness, their complexity, of the multivalent desires that they bear. It belongs to us to work for this transition.

To sum up: five tasks await the movements of the future: the concrete redefinition of the work force; taking control over and liberating the time of the work day; a permanent struggle against the repressive functions of the State; constructing peace and organizing machines of struggle capable of assuming these tasks.

These five tasks are made "diagrammatic" by three propositions: contribute to reorienting the lines of proletarian alliance along a North–South axis; conquer and invent new territories of desire and of political action, radically separated from the State and from IWC; fight against

war and work at constructing the proletariat's revolutionary movement
for peace.

We are still far from emerging from the storm; everything suggests that
the end of the "leaden years" will still be marked by difficult tests; but it
is with lucidity, and without any messianism, that we envisage the reconstruction of a movement of revolution and liberation, more effective,
more intelligent, more human, more happy than it has ever been.

Notes

This selection is taken from *Communists Like Us* (New York: Semiotext(e), 1990), pp.
121–47 (Sections V and VI). The selection was originally published in *Les nouveaux espaces
de liberté* (Paris: Dominique Bedou, 1985).
1   Guaranteed workers are subsidized with unemployment insurance by the state. Non-
       guaranteed workers are more marginal and are not insured.

Translated by Michael Ryan

23

The Left as Processual Passion

In the wake of the European elections of June 17 [1984], Fascism has established a real mass base in France for the first time in half a century.[1] It is urgent to evaluate the significance of this event. There are of course arrangements to be made, ranks to close, alliances to forge. But none of that implies there will have been a thorough debate within the ranks of the Left concerning what could have lead it to such a bitter failure, and of the particular responsibility of its intellectual elements in this affair.

From amongst them, during the preceding period, we heard proclamations *ad nauseam* about the inanity of the left–right split: "because socialism is the Gulag; because French missiles and the 'American umbrella' are a necessary evil; because the crisis forces a renunciation of all social transformation, of any liberatory utopia . . .". A new "Libé style", affecting renunciation, torpor, and, frequently, cynicism, has not ceased to gain ground. A stew of so-called "new philosophy", "post-modernism", "the implosion of the social", I would suggest, all to the end of poisoning the intellectual atmosphere and contributing to the discouragement of any embryonic political engagement within the womb of the intellectual milieux. Without having caused much alarm, a Restoration of traditional values has been accomplished, preparing the ground for the rightist revolution which is being unleashed. And this whole business – not lacking in pungency – has been cooked up within the cloying, saccharine context of a yuppie socialism in power, so anxious to maintain its corporate image with the financiers and the traditional oligarchies. And what results is this: a significantly low voter turn-out on June 17; Fascism constituting itself as a force; the frittering away of the collective capacity to resist conservatism; the rise of racism and a stony inertia.

It was all played out by 1981, or at least replayed, because there has been, it seems, a recursion of the conditions that followed the events of '68. In that period, the Coluche[2] episode revealed the continually widening chasm that lies between the professional politicians and a considerable part of public opinion. After their quasi-accidental electoral victory, the socialist cadres established themselves in the corridors of power, without the slightest questioning of existing institutions, and with no hint of a proposition for rebuilding a humane society out of the current disaster. Mitterand, more and more identified with De Gaulle, first allowed the various dogmatic tendencies of his government to pull hither and thither, then resigned himself to the installation, step by step, of a management team whose differences in language with Reagan's "Chicago boys" are not likely to mask how it leads us to the same kind of aberrations.

We are forced to conclude that the French socialists have lost the memory of the people. Most of them see nothing more in the left–right polarity than what may distinguish them momentarily under specific circumstances. Who among them still thinks that the oppressed, in France as in the rest of the world, are bearers of future creative potentials? Who still bets on democracy as a means of transformation (inasmuch as it is a means whereby current conditions may be grasped)? Having failed to work in time towards the crystallization of new modes of sociality, articulated through "molecular revolutions" that cut across science, technology, communications, and the collective consciousness, the left has passed up the historic opportunity it was offered. It is engaged in an absurd bidding war with the right on the terrain of security, austerity and conservatism. And so, it could have obtained all the inevitable sacrifices for facing the crisis, and redeployments on an economic plane, if it had actually helped to organize *new collective modes of expression*: it has in fact allowed hope to shatter, corporatism to be reaffirmed, and the old fascist perversions to regain ground.

What is it that separates the left from the right? Upon what does this essential ethico–political polarity rest? Fundamentally, it is nothing but a processual calling, a *processual passion*. There is no Manicheism in this division, because it does not involve the niceties of cut and dried sociological distinctions. (There does exist a deep-rooted conservatism in the soil of the left, and sometimes a progressivism in that of the right.)

At issue here is the collective recapturing of those dynamics that can destratify the moribund structures and reorganize life and society in accordance with other forms of equilibrium, other worlds.

Everything follows from that: how to put an end to a certain type of state function and to the old racist, herd-mentality reflexes; how to reinvent a trans-national culture, a new type of social fabric, involving other cities, other alliances with the Third World; how to counterbalance the two-headed imperialism of the USA–USSR? It's all there within reach, everything that could reverse the situation in a flash, and dispel the shadows and the nightmare.

Notes

This article was published in *La Quinzaine littéraire* 422 (du 1ᵉʳ au 31 août 1984): 4.

1 Guattari is referring to the success of the Front National in the European elections of 1984. The Front National is an extreme right-wing party led by J.-M. Le Pen, a former Poujadist in Pierre Poujade's protest movement of small shopkeepers in the mid-1950s. Le Pen is commonly referred to on the left as a torturer and murderer (his war record in Algeria is shady), a racist (his party is anti-immigration and promotes violence against minorities) and a liar, to boot.

2 Coluche (Michel Colluchi) is a comic actor known for his parodies of racist attitudes and everyday stupidities. He announced in late 1980 that he would stand for the Presidency of the Republic in the 1981 elections. His candidature was a gesture of contempt for politics and politicians, and was endorsed by many French intellectuals. After receiving threats from the extreme right, Coluche withdrew from the race, leaving Giscard d'Estaing, who was seeking re-election, and François Mitterand to contest the election, with the latter emerging as the victor. Mitterand's 14-year tenure ended with the victory of Jacques Chirac in May, 1995.

Translated by Ben Freedman

24

Remaking Social Practices[1]

The routines of daily life, and the banality of the world represented to us by the media, surround us with a reassuring atmosphere in which nothing is any longer of real consequence. We cover our eyes; we forbid ourselves to think about the turbulent passage of our times, which swiftly thrusts far behind us our familiar past, which effaces ways of being and living that are still fresh in our minds, and which slaps our future onto an opaque horizon, heavy with thick clouds and miasmas. We depend all the more on the reassurance that nothing is assured. The two "superpowers" of yesterday, for so long buttressed against each other, have been destabilized by the disintegration of one among them. The countries of the former USSR and Eastern Europe have been drawn into a drama with no apparent outcome. The United States, for its part, has not been spared the violent upheavals of civilization, as we saw in Los Angeles. Third World countries have not been able to shake off paralysis; Africa, in particular, finds itself at an atrocious impasse. Ecological disasters, famine, unemployment, the escalation of racism and xenophobia, haunt, like so many threats, the end of this millenium. At the same time, science and technology have evolved with extreme rapidity, supplying man with virtually all the necessary means to solve his material problems. But humanity has not seized upon these; it remains stupified, powerless before the challenges that confront it. It passively contributes to the pollution of water and the air, to the destruction of forests, to the disturbance of climates, to the disappearance of a multitude of living species, to the impoverishment of the genetic capital of the biosphere, to the destruction of natural landscapes, to the suffocation of its cities, and to the progressive abandonment of cultural values and moral references in the areas of human solidarity and fraternity . . . . Humanity seems to have lost its head, or, more precisely, its head is no longer functioning with its body. How can it find a compass by which to reorient itself within a modernity whose complexity overwhelms it?

To think through this complexity, to renounce, in particular, the reductive approach of scientism when a questioning of its prejudices and short-term interests is required: such is the necessary perspective for entry into an era that I have qualified as "post-media", as all great contemporary upheavals, positive or negative, are currently judged on the basis of information filtered through the mass media industry, which retains only a description of events [*le petit côté événementiel*] and never problematizes what is at stake, in its full amplitude.

It is true that it is difficult to bring individuals out of themselves, to disengage themselves from their immediate preoccupations, in order to reflect on the present and the future of the world. They lack collective incitements to do so. Most older methods of communication, reflection and dialogue have dissolved in favor of an individualism and a solitude that are often synonymous with anxiety and neurosis. It is for this reason that I advocate – under the aegis of a new conjunction of environmental ecology, social ecology and mental ecology – the invention of new collective assemblages of enunciation concerning the couple, the family, the school, the neighbourhood, etc.

The functioning of current *mass media*, and television in particular, runs counter to such a perspective. The tele-spectator remains passive in front of a screen, prisoner of a quasi-hypnotic relation, cut off from the other, stripped of any awareness of responsibility.

Nevertheless, this situation is not made to last indefinitely. Technological evolution will introduce new possibilities for interaction between the medium and its user, and between users themselves. The junction of the audiovisual screen, the telematic screen and the computer screen could lead to a real reactivation of a collective sensibility and intelligence. The current equation (media=passivity) will perhaps disappear more quickly than one would think. Obviously, we cannot expect a miracle from these technologies: it will all depend, ultimately, on the capacity of groups of people to take hold of them, and apply them to appropriate ends.

The constitution of large economic markets and homogeneous political spaces, as Europe and the West are tending to become, will likewise have an impact on our vision of the world. But these factors tend in opposite directions, such that their outcome will depend on the evolution of the power relations between social groups, which, we must recognize, remain undefined. As industrial and economic antagonism between the United States, Japan, and Europe is accentuated, the decrease in production costs, the development of productivity and the conquering of "market shares" will become increasingly high stakes, increasing structural unemployment and leading to an always more pronounced social "dualization" within capitalist citadels. This is not to mention their break with the Third World, which will take a more and more conflictual and dramatic turn, as a result of population growth.

On the other hand, the reinforcement of these large axes of power will undoubtedly contribute to the institution of a regulation – if not of a "planetary order" – then of a geopolitical and ecological nature. By favoring large concentrations of resources on research objectives or on ecological and humanitarian programs, the presence of these axes could play a determining role in the future of humanity. But it would be, at the same time, immoral and unrealistic to accept that the current, quasi-Manichean duality between rich and poor, weak and strong, would increase indefinitely. It was unfortunately from this perspective that, undoubtedly in spite of themselves, the signatories to the so-called Heidelberg Appeal presented at the Rio conference were committed to the suggestion that the fundamental choices of humanity in the area of ecology be left to the initiatives of scientific elites (see, in *Le Monde Diplomatique*, the editorial by Ignacio Ramonet, July of 1992, and the article by Jean-Marc Lévy-Leblond, August 1992). This proceeds from an unbelievable scientistic myopia. How, in effect, can one not see that an essential part of the ecological stakes of the planet arises from this break in collective subjectivity between rich and poor? The scientists are to find their place within a new international democracy that they themselves must promote. And this is not to foster the myth of their omnipotence that advances them along this path!

How could we reconnect the head to the body, how could we join science and technology with human values? How could we agree upon common projects while respecting the singularity of individual positions? By what means, in the current climate of passivity, could we unleash a mass awakening, a new renaissance? Will fear of catastrophe be sufficient provocation? Ecological accidents, such as Chernobyl, have certainly led to a rousing of opinion. But it is not just a matter of brandishing threats; it is necessary to move toward practical achievements. It is also necessary to recall that danger can itself exert a power of fascination. The presentiment of catastrophe can release an unconscious desire for catastrophe, a longing for nothingness, a drive to abolish. It was thus that the German masses in the Nazi epoch lived in the grip of a fantasy of the end of the world associated with a mythic redemption of humanity. Emphasis must be placed, above all, on the reconstruction of a collective dialogue capable of producing innovative practices. Without a change in mentalities, without entry into a post-media era, there can be no enduring hold over the environment. Yet, without modifications to the social and material environment, there can be no change in mentalities. Here, we are in the presence of a circle that leads me to postulate the necessity of founding an "ecosophy" that would link environmental ecology to social ecology and to mental ecology.

From this ecosophic perspective, there would be no question of reconstituting a hegemonic ideology, as were the major religions or Marxism. It is absurd, for example, for the International Monetary Fund (IMF) and the World Bank to advocate the generalization of a unique model of growth in the Third World. Africa, Latin America, and Asia must be able to embark on specific social and cultural paths of development.

The world market does not have to lead the production of each group of people in the name of a notion of universal growth. Capitalist growth remains purely quantitative, while a complex development would essentially concern the qualitative. It is neither the preeminence of the State (in the manner of bureaucratic socialism), nor that of the world market (under the aegis of neo-liberal ideologies), that must dictate the future of human activites and their essential objectives. It is thus necessary to establish a planetary dialogue and to promote a new ethic of difference that substitutes for current capitalist powers a politics based on the desires of peoples. But wouldn't such an approach lead to chaos? To that I would respond that the transcendence of power leads, in any case, to chaos, as the current crisis demonstrates. On the whole, democratic chaos is better than the chaos that results from authoritarianism!

The individual and the group cannot avoid a certain existential plunge into chaos. This is already what we do each night when we abandon ourselves to the world of dreams. The main question is to know what we gain from this plunge: a sense of disaster, or the revelation of new outlines of the possible? Who is controlling the capitalist chaos today? The stock market, multinationals, and, to a lesser extent, the powers of the state! For the most part, decerebrated organizations! The existence of a world market is certainly indispensable for the structuring of international economic relations. But we cannot expect this market to miraculously regulate human exchange on this planet. The real estate market contributes to the disorder of our cities. The art market perverts aesthetic creation. It is thus of primordial importance that, alongside the capitalist market, there appear territorialized markets that rely on the support of substantial formations, that affirm their modes of valorization. Out of the capitalist chaos must come what I call "attractors" of values: values that are diverse, heterogeneous, dissensual [*dissensuelle*].

Marxists based historical movement on a necessary dialectical progression of the class struggle. Liberal economists blindly place their trust in the free play of the market to resolve tensions and disparities, and to bring about the best of worlds. And yet events confirm, if that were necessary, that progress is neither mechanically nor dialectically related to the class struggle, to the development of science and technology, to economic growth, or to the free play of the market . . . . Growth is not synonymous with progress, as the barbaric resurgence of social and urban confrontations, inter-ethnic conflicts and world-wide economic tensions cruelly reveals.

Social and moral progress is inseparable from the collective and individual practices that advance it. Nazism and fascism were not transitory maladies, the accidents of history, thereafter overcome. They constitute potentialities that are always present; they continue to inhabit our universe of virtuality; the Stalinism of the Gulag, Maoist despotism, can reappear tomorrow in new contexts. In various forms, a microfascism proliferates in our societies, manifested in racism, xenophobia, the rise of religious fundamentalisms, militarism, and the oppression of women. History does not guarantee the irreversible crossing of "progressive thresholds". Only human practices, a collective voluntarism, can guard us against falling into worse barbarities. In this respect, it would be altogether illusory to leave it up to formal imperatives for the defense of the "rights of man" or "rights of peoples". Rights are not guaranteed by a divine authority; they depend on the vitality of the institutions and power formations that sustain their existence.

An essential condition for succeeding in the promotion of a new planetary consciousness would thus reside in our collective capacity for the recreation of value systems that would escape the moral, psychological and social lamination of capitalist valorization, which is only centered on economic profit. The joy of living, solidarity, and compassion with regard to others, are sentiments that are about to disappear and that must be protected, enlivened, and propelled in new directions. Ethical and aesthetic values do not arise from imperatives and transcendent codes. They call for an existential participation based on an immanence that must be endlessly reconquered. How do we create or expand upon such a universe of values? Certainly by not dispensing with moral lessons.

The suggestive power of the theory of information has contributed to masking the importance of the enunciative dimensions of communication. It leads us to forget that a message must be received, and not just transmitted, in order to have meaning. Information cannot be reduced to its objective manifestations; it is, essentially, the production of subjectivity, the becoming-consistent [*prise de consistance*] of incorporeal universes. These last aspects cannot be reduced to an analysis in terms of improbability and calculated on the basis of binary choices. The truth of information refers to an existential event occuring in those who receive it. Its register is not that of the exactitude of facts, but that of the significance of a problem, of the consistency of a universe of values. The current crisis of the media and the opening up of a post-media era are the symptoms of a much more profound crisis.

What I want to emphasize is the fundamentally pluralist, multi-centered, and heterogeneous character of contemporary subjectivity, in spite of the homogenization it is subjected to by the mass media. In this respect, an individual is already a "collective" of heterogeneous components. A subjective phenomenon refers to personal territories – the body, the self – but also, at the same time, to collective territories – the family, the community, the ethnic group. And to that must be added all the procedures for subjectivation embodied in speech, writing, computing, and technological machines.

In pre-capitalist societies, initiation into the things of life and the mysteries of the world were transmitted through relations of family, peer-group, of clan, guild, ritual, etc. This type of direct exchange between individuals has tended to become rare. Subjectivity is forged through multiple mediations, whereas individual relations between generations, sexes, and proximal groups have weakened. For example, the role of grandparents as an intergenerational memory support for children has very often disappeared. The child develops in a context shadowed by television, computer games, telecommunications, comic strips. . . . A new machinic solitude is being born, which is certainly not without merit, but which deserves to be continually reworked such that it can accord with renewed forms of sociality. Rather than relations of opposition, it is a matter of forging polyphonic interlacings between the individual and the social. Thus, a subjective music remains to be thereby composed.

The new planetary consciousness will have to rethink machinism. We frequently continue to oppose the machine to the human spirit. Certain philosophies hold that modern technology has blocked access to our ontological foundations, to primordial being. And what if, on the contrary, a revival of spirit and human values could be attendant upon a new alliance with machines?

Biologists now associate life with a new approach to machinism concerning the cell, and the organs of the living body; linguists, mathematicians, and sociologists explore other modalities of machinism. In thus enlarging the concept of the machine, we are led to emphasize certain of its aspects that have been insufficiently explored to date. Machines are not totalities enclosed upon themselves. They maintain determined relations with a spatio-temporal exteriority, as well as with universes of signs and fields of virtuality. The relation between the inside and the outside of a machinic system is not only the result of a consummation of energy, of the production of an object: it is equally manifested through genetic phylums.[2] A machine rises to the surface of the present like the completion of a past lineage, and it is the point of restarting, or of rupture, from which an evolutionary lineage will spread in the future. The emergence of these genealogies and fields of alterity is complex. It is continually worked over by all the creative forces of the sciences, the arts, social innovations, which become entangled and constitute a mecanosphere surrounding our biosphere – not as a constraining yoke of an exterior armor, but as an abstract, machinic efflorescence, exploring the future of humanity.

Human life is taken up, for example, in a race with the AIDS retrovirus. Biological sciences and medical technology will win the battle with this illness or, in the end, the human species will be eliminated. Similarly, intelligence and sensibility have undergone a total mutation as a result of new computer technology, which has increasingly insinuated itself into the motivating forces of sensibility, acts, and intelligence. We are currently witnessing a mutation of subjectivity that perhaps surpasses the invention of writing, or the printing press, in importance.

Humanity must undertake a marriage of reason and sentiment with the multiple off-shoots of machinism, or else it risks sinking into chaos. A renewal of democracy could have, as an objective, a pluralist management of its machinic components. In this way, the judiciary and the legislature will be brought to forge new ties with the world of technology and of research (this is already the case with commissions on ethics investigating problems in biology and contemporary medicine; but we must also rapidly create commissions for the ethics of the media, of urbanism, of education). It is necessary, in sum, to delineate again the real existential entities of our epoch, which no longer correspond to those of still only a few decades ago. The individual, the social, and the machinic all overlap – as do the juridical, the ethical, the aesthetic, and the political. A major shift in objectives is in progress: values such as the resingularization of existence, ecological responsibility, and machinic creativity are called upon to install themselves as the centre of a new progressive polarity in place of the old left–right dichotomy.

The production machines at the basis of the world economy are aligned uniquely with so-called leading industries. They do not take account of other sectors which fall by the wayside because they do not generate capitalist profits. Machinic democracy will have to undertake a re-balancing of current systems of valorization. To produce a city that is clean, livable, lively, rich in social interactions; to develop a humane and effective medicine, and an enriching education, are objectives that are equally worthwhile as a production-line of automobiles, or high-performance electronic equipment.

Current machines – technological, scientific, social – are potentially capable of feeding, clothing, transporting and educating all humans: the means are there, within reach, to support life for ten billion inhabitants on this planet. It is the motivating systems for producing the goods and distributing them fairly that are inadequate. To be engaged in developing material and moral well-being, in social and mental ecology, should be every bit as valued as working in leading sectors or in financial speculation.

It is the nature of work itself that has changed, as a result of the ever increasing prevalence of immaterial aspects in its composition: knowledge, desire, aesthetic taste, ecological preoccupations. The physical and mental activity of man finds itself in increasing adjacence to technical, computer and communication devices. In this, the old Fordist or Taylorist conceptions of the organization of industrial sites and of ergonomics have been superseded. In the future, it will be more and more necessary to appeal to individual and collective initiative, at all stages of production and distribution (and even of consumption). The constitution of a new landscape of collective assemblages of work – particularly resulting from the predominant role played by telematics, computers and robotics – will call into question old hierarchical structures and, as a consequence, call for a revision of current salarial norms.

Consider the agricultural crisis in developed countries. It is legitimate that agricultural markets open themselves up to the Third World, where climatic conditions and productivity are often much more favorable for production than countries situated more to the north. But does this mean that American, European and Japanese farmers must abandon the countryside and migrate to the cities? On the contrary, it is necessary to redefine agriculture and animal farming in these countries, in order to adequately valorize their ecological aspects and to preserve the environment. Forests, mountains, rivers, coast-lines – all constitute a non-capitalist capital, a qualitative investment, that should be made to yield a return, and must be continually re-valorized, which implies, in particular, a radical rethinking of the position of the farmer and the fisherman.

The same goes for domestic labor: it will be necessary for the women and men who are responsible for the raising of children – a task which continues to become more complex – to be appropriately remunerated. In a general way, a number of "private" activities would thereby be called upon to take their place in a new system of economic valorization that would take into account the diversity and heterogeneity of human activities that are socially, aesthetically, or ethically useful.

To permit an enlargement of the wage-earning class to include the multitude of social activities that deserve to be valorized, economists will perhaps have to imagine a renewal of current monetary systems and wage systems. The coexistence, for example, of strong currencies, open to the high seas of global economic competition, with protected currencies that are unconvertible and territorialized over a given social space, would allow for the alleviation of extreme misery, by distributing the goods that arise exclusively from an internal market and allowing a wide range of social activities to proliferate – activities which would thereby lose their apparently marginal character.

Such a revision of the division and valorization of labor does not necessarily imply an indefinite diminution of the work-week, or an advancing of the retirement age. Certainly, machinism tends to liberate more and more "freetime". But free for what? To devote onself to prefabricated leisure activities? To stay glued to the television? How many retirees would sink, after some months of their new situation, into despair and depression, from their inactivity? Paradoxically, an ecosophic redefinition of labor could go together with an increase in the duration of wage-earning. This would imply a skillful separation of working time allotted for the economic market and such time relating to an economy of social and mental values. One could imagine, for example, modulated retirements that would allow the workers, employees and managers who desire it to not be cut off from the activities of their companies, especially those with social and cultural implications. Is it not absurd that they are abruptly rejected at precisely the moment when they have the best knowledge of their field, and when they could be of most service in the areas of training and research? The perspective of such a social and cultural recomposition of labor would lead naturally to the promotion of a new transversality between productive assemblages and the rest of the community.

Certain union experiments are already moving in this direction. In Chile, for example, there exist new union practices that are joined organically with their social environment. The militants of "territorial unionization" are not only preoccupied with the defense of unionized workers, but also with the difficulties encountered by the unemployed, by women, and by the children of the neighbourhood where the company is located. They participate in the organization of educational and cultural programs, and involve themselves in the problems of health, hygiene, ecology, and urbanism. (Such an enlargement of the field of worker competence and action is far from favorably regarded by the hierarchical forces of the union apparatus.) In this country, groups for the "ecology of retirement" devote themselves to the cultural and relational organization of the elderly.

It is difficult, and yet essential, to turn the page on old reference systems based on an oppositional split of left–right, socialist–capitalist, market economy–state planned economy. . . . It is not a question of creating a "centrist" pole of reference, equidistant from the other two, but of disengaging from this type of system that is founded on a total adhesion, on a supposedly scientific foundation, or on transcendent juridical and ethical givens. Public opinion, before the political classes, has become allergic to programmatic speeches, to dogmas that are intolerant of diverse points of view. But while the public debate and the means of discussion have not acquired renewed forms of expression, there is a great risk that they will turn more and more away from the exercise of democracy, and toward either the passivity of abstention, or to the activism of reactionary factions. This means that in a political campaign, it is less a case of conquering massive public support for an idea, than of seeing public opinion structure itself into multiple and vital social segments. The reality is no longer one and indivisible. It is multiple, and marked by lines of possibility that human praxis can catch in flight. Alongside energy, information and new materials, the will to choose and to assume risk place themselves at the heart of new machinic undertakings, whether they be technological, social, theoretical or aesthetic.

The "ecosophic cartographies" that must be instituted will have, as their own particularity, that they will not only assume the dimensions of the present, but also those of the future. They will be as preoccupied by what human life on Earth will be in thirty years, as by what public transit will be in three years. They imply an assumption of responsibility for future generations, what philosopher Hans Jonas calls "an ethic of responsibility".[3] It is inevitable that choices for the long term will conflict with the choices of short-term interests. The social groups affected by such problems must be brought to reflect on them, to modify their habits and mental coordinates, to adopt new values and to postulate a human meaning for future technological transformations. In a word, to negotiate the present in the name of the future.

It is not, for all that, a question of falling back into totalitarian and authoritarian visions of history, messianisms which, in the name of "paradise" or of ecological equilibrium, would claim to rule over the life of each and everyone. Each "cartography" represents a particular vision of the world which, even when adopted by a large number of individuals, would always harbor an element of uncertainty at its heart. That is, in truth, its most precious capital; on its basis, an authentic hearing of the other could be established. A hearing of disparity, singularity, marginality, even of madness, does not arise only from the imperatives of tolerance and fraternity. It constitutes an essential preparation, a permanent appeal to this order of uncertainty, a stripping of forces of chaos that always haunt structures that are dominant, self-sufficient, and that believe in their own superiority. Such a hearing could overturn or restore direction to these structures, by recharging them with potentiality, by deploying, through them, new lines of creative flow.

In the midst of this state of affairs, a shaft of meaning must be discovered, that cuts through my impatience for the other to adopt my point of view, and through the lack of good will in the attempt to bend the other to my desires. Not only must I accept this adversity, I must love it for its own sake: I must seek it out, communicate with it, delve into it, increase it. It will get me out of my narcissism, my bureaucratic blindness, and will restore for me a sense of finitude that all the infantilizing subjectivity of the mass media attempts to conceal. Ecosophic democracy would not give itself up to the facility for consensual agreement: it will invest itself in a dissensual metamodelization. With it, responsibility emerges from the self in order to pass to the other.

Without the promotion of such a subjectivity of difference, of the atypical, of utopia, our epoch could topple into atrocious conflicts of identity, like those the people of the former Yugoslavia are suffering. It would be vain to appeal to morality and respect for rights. Subjectivity disappears into the empty stakes of profit and power. Refusing the status of the current media, combined with a search for new social interactivities, for an institutional creativity and an enrichment of values, would already constitute an important step on the way to a remaking of social practices.

Notes

This article appeared under the title of "Pour une refondation des pratiques sociales" in *Le Monde Diplomatique* (Oct. 1992): 26–7.

1 A few weeks before his sudden death on August 29, 1992, Félix Guattari sent us [*Le Monde Diplomatique*] the following text. With the additional weight conferred upon it by its author's tragic disappearance, this ambitious and all-encompassing series of reflections takes on, in some sense, the character of a philosophical will or testament.

2 The editors of *Le Monde Dip.* insert a note here on the definition of a phylum: it is the primitive stock from which a genealogical series issues.

3 Hans Jonas, *Le Principe responsabilité. Une éthique pour la civilisation technologique*, trad. de l'allemand par Jean Greisch (Paris: Editions du Cerf, 1990). *The Imperative of Responsibility: In Search of an Ethics for the Technological Age*, trans. by H. Jonas and D. Herr (Chicago: University of Chicago Press, 1984).

Translated by Sophie Thomas

A Select Bibliography of Works by Pierre-Félix Guattari

This is by no means an exhaustive bibliography of Guattari's writings. The reader may wish to consult other partial bibliographic sources such as Charles Stivale (1984) "Bibliography: Gilles Deleuze and Félix Guattari", *Sub stance* 44–45: 96–105; see also Ronald Bogue (1989) *Deleuze and Guattari* (New York: Routledge), pp. 180–87 and Brian Massumi in Deleuze and Guattari, *A Thousand Plateaus* (Minneapolis: University of Minnesota Press, 1987), pp. 579–85.

1970 "La contestation psychiatrique" [Review of Franco Basaglia, *L'institution en négation*], *La Quinzaine littéraire* 94: 24–5.

1972 *Psychanalyse et transversalité*. Paris: François Maspero.

—— "Laing divisé" [Review of R.D. Laing, *Soi et les autres*, *Noeuds* and Laing and Esterson, *L'équilibre mental, la folie et la famille*], *La Quinzaine littéraire* 132 (du 1er au 15 jan.): 22–3.

—— With Gilles Deleuze. *L'Anti-Oedipe: Capitalisme et schizophrénie*, Paris: Minuit.

1973 "Le 'voyage' de Mary Barnes", *Le Nouvel observateur* (28 mai): 82–4, 87–93, 96, 101, 104, 109–10.

1974 "Interview/Félix Guattari" [by Mark Seem], *diacritics* IV/3 (Fall): 38–41.

—— With Deleuze. "Bilan-Programme pour machines désirantes", appendix to *L'Anti-Oedipe*, 2nd ed. Paris: Minuit.

1975 "Une sexualisation en rupture" [Interview by Christian Deschamps], *La Quinzaine littéraire* 215: 14–15.

—— "Le programmiste institutionnel comme analyseur de la libido sociale" [2 juillet 1974], *Recherches* 17: 430–37.

—— "Le divan du pauvre", *Communications* 23: 96–103.

—— "Sémiologies signifiantes et sémiologies asignifiantes", in *Psychanalyse et sémiotique* [Colloque tenu à Milan en mai 1974 sous la direction de Armando Verdiglione], Paris: Union Générale d'Editions, pp. 151–63.

1977 "Psycho-Analysis and Schizo-Analysis" [Int. by Arno Munster, trans. J. Forman], *Semiotext(e)* II/3: 77–85.

—— "Freudo-Marxism", trans. J. Forman, *Semiotext(e)* II/3: 73–5.

—— "La Borde un lieu psychiatrique pas comme les autres" [Discussion. C. Deschamps, Roger Gentis, Jean Oury, J-C Pollack, and F. Guattari], *La Quinzaine littéraire* 250: 20–1.

—— With Deleuze. "Balance-Sheet: Program for Desiring Machines", trans. R. Hurley, *Semiotext(e)* II/3: 117–35.

—— *La Révolution moléculaire*, Fontenay-sous-Bois: Encres/Recherches.

—— With Deleuze. *Anti-Oedipus: Capitalism and Schizophrenia*, trans. Robert Hurley, Mark Seem, Helen R. Lane, New York: The Viking Press.

—— "Mary Barnes' Trip", trans. Ruth Ohayon, *Semiotext(e)* II/3: 63–71.

1978 "Les radios libres populaires", *La Nouvelle Critique* 115(296): 77–9.

1979 "A Liberation of Desire" [Int. by George Stambolian], in *Homosexualities and French Literature: Cultural Contexts/Critical Texts*, eds. G. Stambolian and Elaine Marks, Ithaca: Cornell University Press, pp. 56–69.

—— *L'Inconscient machinique: essais de schizo-analyse*, Fontenay-sous-Bois: Encres/Recherches.

1980 "Why Italy?" trans. John Johnston, *Semiotext(e)* [Autonomia] III/3: 234–37.

—— "The Proliferation of Margins", trans. R. Gardner and S. Walker, *Semiotext(e)* III/3: 108–111.

—— *La Révolution moléculaire*, Paris: Union générale d'éditions.

—— With Deleuze. *Mille Plateaux: Capitalisme et schizophrénie*, Paris: Minuit.

1981 "Becoming-woman", trans. R. McComas and S. Metzidakis, *Semiotext(e)* IV/1: 86–8.

—— With Deleuze. "A Bloated Oedipus", trans. R. McComas, *Semiotext(e)* IV/1: 97–101.

—— "Interpretance and Significance", trans. R. De Vere, *Semiotica* [Special Supplement on É. Benveniste]: 119–25.

—— "I Have Even Met Happy Travelos", trans. R. McComas, *Semiotext(e)* IV/1: 80–1.

—— "Mitterrand et le tiers état", *Le Nouvel observateur* 876 (Août): 12–13.

1982 "The New Alliance" [Int. by S. Lotringer], *Impulse* 10/2: 41–4.

—— "Like the Echo of a Collective Melancholia", trans. Mark Polizzotti, *Semiotext(e)* [The German Issue] IV/2: 102–10.

1983 "Plaidoyer pour un 'dictateur' ", *Le Nouvel observateur* 961 (Avril): 27–8.

1984 *Molecular Revolution: Psychiatry and Politics*, trans. Rosemary Sheed, Harmondsworth, Middlesex: Penguin.

—— "La Gauche comme passion processuelle", *La Quinzaine littéraire* 422 (du 1er au 31 août): 4.

1985 With A. Negri. *Les Nouveaux espaces de liberté* [suivi de "Des Libertés en Europe" and "Lettre Archéologique"], Paris: Dominique Bedou.

—— And Oury, Jean and Tosquelles, François. *Pratique de l'institutionnel et politique*, ed. Jacques Pain, Vigneux: Matrice.

1986 "Questionnaire 17" [On the City], trans. B. Benderson, *Zone* I/2: 460.

—— *Les Années D'Hiver* 1980–1985. Paris: Bernard Barrault.

—— With Deleuze. *Kafka: Toward a minor literature*, trans. Dana Polan, Minneapolis: University of Minnesota Press.

—— "L'impasse post-moderne", *La Quinzaine littéraire* 456 (du 1er au 15 Fév.): 21.

—— "The Postmodern Dead End", trans. Nancy Blake, *Flash Art* 128: 40–1.

1987 "Cracks in the Street", trans. A. Gibault and J. Johnson, *Flash Art* 135 (Summer): 82–5.

—— "Genet Regained", trans. B. Massumi, *Journal: A Contemporary Art Magazine* 47/5 (Spring): 34–40.

—— With Deleuze. *A Thousand Plateaus: Capitalism and Schizophrenia*, trans. Brian Massumi, Minneapolis: University of Minnesota Press.

1988 With Gisèle Donnard, "Nationalité et citoyenneté", *Le Monde* (9 fév.): 2.

—— "*Urgences*: la folie est dans le champ", *Le Monde* (9 mars): 22.

—— "Un scrabble avec Lacan" [hommage à Françoise Dolto], *Le Monde* (28–29 août): 6.

1989 "La famille selon Elkaïm" [review of Mony Elkaïm, *Si tu m'aimes, ne m'aime pas*], *Le Monde* (10 mai): 17.

—— "Un entretien avec Félix Guattari" [Int. by Jean-Yves Nau], *Le Monde* (6 sept.): 19, 21.

—— "The Three Ecologies", trans. Chris Turner, *New formations* 8: 131–47.

—— *Les Trois écologies*, Paris: Galilée.

—— *Cartographies schizoanalytiques*, Paris: Galilée.

1990 "Entretien sur *L'Anti-oedipus*", in Deleuze, *Pourparlers*. Paris: Minuit, pp. 24–38.

—— "La machine à images", *Cahiers du cinéma* 437: 70–2.

—— "Réinventer la politique", *Le Monde* (8 mars): 2.

—— "La Terre-patrie en danger" [Review of *La Planète mise à sac, Le Monde Diplomatique*, mai 1990], *Le Monde* (6 juin): 2.

—— "La révolution moléculaire", *Le Monde* (7 déc.): 2.

—— With Antonio Negri. *Communists Like Us*, trans. Michael Ryan, New York: semiotext(e).

—— "Ritornellos and Existential Affects", trans. Juliana Schiesari and Georges Van Den Abbeele, *Discourse* 12/2: 66–81.

—— "Des subjectivités, pour le meilleur et pour le pire", *Chimères* 8: 23–37.

1991 "Pour une éthique des médias", *Le Monde* (6 nov.): 2.

—— With Deleuze. *Qu'est-ce que la philosophie?* Paris: Minuit

—— "Les folies de l'humanité" [Review of Xavier Emmanuel, *Les Prédateurs de l'action humanitaire*], *Le Monde* (18 déc.): 12.

1992 "Une autre vision du futur", *Le Monde* (15 fév.): 8.

—— "Un nouvel axe progressiste", *Le Monde* (4 juin): 2.

—— with Edgar Morin and Edgard Pisani, "Un appel" [pour Yougoslavie], *Le Monde* (19 juin): 2.

—— "Machinic Heterogenesis", trans. James Creech, in *Rethinking Technologies*, ed. Verena Andermatt Conley on behalf of the Miami Theory Collective, Minneapolis: University of Minnesota Press, 1992, pp. 13–27.

—— "Regimes, Pathways, Subjects", trans. Brian Massumi, in *Incorporations*, eds. J. Crary and S. Kwinter, New York: Urzone, pp. 16–37.

—— "Pour une refondation des pratiques sociales", *Le Monde Diplomatique* (oct.): 26–7.

—— *Chaosmose* Paris: Galilée.

1992–93 "Félix Guattari" [Int. by A-M Richard and R. Martel], *Inter* 55–56 (Automne-hiver): 11–13.
1993 "Postmodernism and Ethical Abdication" [Int. by N. Zurbrugg], *photofile* 39 (July): 11–13.
—— "Toward a New Perspective on Identity" [Int. by Jean-Charles Jambon and Nathalie Magnan], trans. Josep-Anton Fernández, *Angelaki* I/: 96–9.
1994 With Deleuze. *What Is Philosophy?* trans. Hugh Tomlinson and Graham Burchell, New York: Columbia University Press.
—— "Les machines architecturales de Shin Takamatsu", *Chimères* 21: 127–41.

Index